History and Polemics
in the
French Reformation

Portrait of Florimond de Raemond by C. de Mallery. This appeared on the first (1605) edition of his *Histoire de la Naissance, Progrez et Décadence de l'hérésie de ce siècle*. It is a copy of Thomas de Leu's original portrait, engraved on ivory, for the 1601 (Latin) edition of the *Erreur Populaire de la Papesse Jane*.

History and Polemics in the French Reformation

Florimond de Raemond:
Defender of the Church

Barbara Sher Tinsley

Selinsgrove: Susquehanna University Press
London and Toronto: Associated University Presses

© 1992 by Associated University Presses, Inc.

All rights reserved. Authorization to photocopy items for internal or personal use, or the internal or personal use of specific clients, is granted by the copyright owner, provided that a base fee of $10.00, plus eight cents per page, per copy is paid directly to the Copyright Clearance Center, 27 Congress Street, Salem, Massachusetts 01970. [0-945636-29-6/92 $10.00 + 8¢ pp, pc.]

Associated University Presses
440 Forsgate Drive
Cranbury, NJ 08512

Associated University Presses
25 Sicilian Avenue
London WC1A 2QH, England

Associated University Presses
P.O. Box 39, Clarkson Pstl. Stn.
Mississauga, Ontario,
L5J 3X9 Canada

The paper used in this publication meets the requirements of the American National Standard for Permanence of Paper for Printed Library Materials Z39.48-1984.

Library of Congress Cataloging-in-Publication Data

Tinsley, Barbara Sher, 1938–
    History and polemics in the French Reformation: Florimond de Raemond, defender of the Church/Barbara Sher Tinsley.
    p.   cm.
    Includes bibliographical references (p.) and index.
    ISBN 0-945636-29-6 (alk. paper)
    1. Rémond, Florimond de, ca. 1540–1601. I. Title.
BX4705.R4377T56 1992
282'.092—dc20
[B]   91-50102
                                                                 CIP

PRINTED IN THE UNITED STATES OF AMERICA

For Ruth, Bill, Claire and Yve

Tower of La Combe-Suquet, Raemond's family seat. Located near Agen (Lot-et-Garonne), this is now styled simply Suquet.

Contents

Preface	9
Acknowledgments	15
1. Raemond's Life in Brief	19
2. Exchange of Views: Catholics, Protestants, and Politiques	33
3. Pen and *Parlement*	48
4. Pope Joan	66
5. The Antichrist	79
6. Luther and Lutheranism	93
7. Calvin and Calvinism	106
8. History and Politics	124
9. Postscript	140
Notes	153
Bibliography	216
Index	233

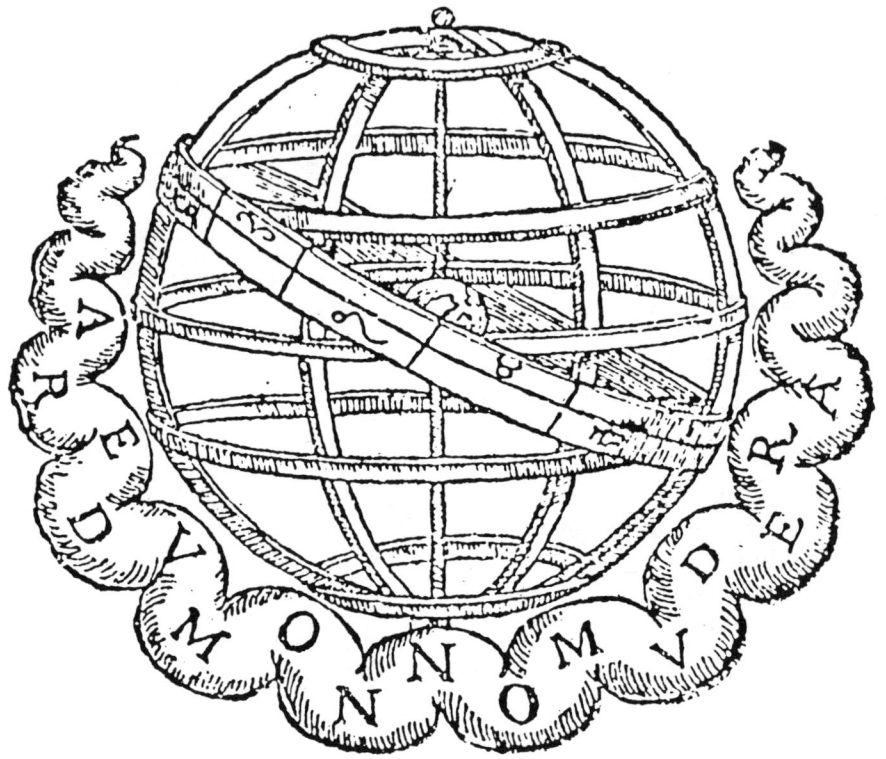

Armillary sphere bearing Raemond's motto in the regional patois. This first appeared on the title page of the 1594 (third) edition of the *Erreur Populaire de la Papesse Jane*.

Preface

Florimond de Raemond (1540–1601), a polemical historian and sixteenth-century *conseiller* in the Bordeaux *parlement*, was one of the most widely read historians of the late sixteenth and seventeenth century in France. The main reason for his enormous popularity was that his three books on religious history — on Pope Joan, on the Antichrist, and on the rise and growth of Protestantism — gave expression to what were, or what through his efforts came to be, the views of the majority of Frenchmen. Raemond's works were best-sellers during his own lifetime, and were reprinted in numerous editions during the greater part of the seventeenth century. They were read and copied by many people, Protestants as well as Catholics. Raemond's books treated many problems that were addressed by all manner of theologians, moralists, and historical researchers.

Although monographs on intellectual figures have not been so prominent in recent decades as they formerly were, their importance to our understanding of the new history of socially defined groups and subgroups or *mentalités* cannot be ignored. Raemond's historical impact derived from his having participated in the use of the historical polemic of Catholic orthodoxy, and from his having understood how the writing of history affected the piety, psychology, and patriotism of marginal social types or classes. Had he owned a computer he would have been able to quantify his research, for those marginal sectarians intrigued him in a way that political entities and individuals did not. Lacking modern inventions Raemond was obliged to gather his information about the sectarians as he could and to relate anecdotally their experiences and beliefs. His methods and his subject matter coalesced in a product that can be viewed today as an early attempt at social history. His popularity was due in part to the lack of information about popular belief and religious rites among the radical sectarians. Consequently, his writing made an impact on the common reader which no other convenient source afforded. Raemond's history of Protestantism broke new ground. Moreover, he claims our attention because he was one of the first to write in a vernacular language (French) with the express intention of reaching out to ordinary readers, providing them with the means for educating themselves about historical and theological topics formerly reserved by an arcane language (Latin) for an elite class.

Certainly no religious or historical polemic is formed out of thin air, but rather by men rooted in the political, social, and religious history of their times. Therefore, the first three chapters of this book are biographical. They are designed not merely to tell the story of Raemond's life, but to illustrate the way he functioned vis-à-vis his peers and critics — a variety of learned and publicly involved men of affairs whose views ranged from Protestant to *politique* Catholic and who were, despite their confessional and intellectual differences, men of Raemond's own class.

This approach differs from that taken by Raemond's first and only other biographer, Philip Tamizey de Larroque. His *Essai sur la vie et les ouvrages de Florimond de Raymond* (1867) contained the facts of Raemond's life without any attempt at analysis. Whereas Larroque was satisfied to describe Raemond's social contacts, the present study reveals how they affected his growth, or where no symbiosis is discernible, how their views differed. Here it is shown not simply what Raemond did, but whenever possible, what in his background made him do it. This procedure has been followed either by examining such of his correspondence as has survived (chap. 2), by viewing him in his role as a magistrate (chap. 3), or, and this is the means that has proved most productive given the importance of his books and the scarcity of biographical information, by a careful examination of those books (chap. 4–7).

To the scholar who has avoided reading historical polemic, fearing that it will prove more tedious than informative and objecting that the subject matter is absurd (chap. 4 concerns a female pope who never lived) or absurdly hysterical (chap. 5 is about Antichrist), a word of encouragement is offered. The chapter on Joan, the fictitious lady pope, is, among other things, an essay concerning textual criticism and analysis. The Antichrist chapter obliged Raemond to review the reformers' own accounts of the history of the early and medieval church with the object of proving that the Roman church had remained faithful to the tradition. These are not trivial topics. In fact, there were no topics more significant for the Reformation than the issue of papal supremacy and inviolability. The chapter on Joan canvasses the contentions of both parties, Catholic and Protestant, concerning the purity of the apostolic succession (which Joan was said to have interrupted). That on Antichrist reveals the positions both parties took with respect to papal primacy.

Readers will recognize the importance of such topics and will expect to learn whether Raemond can lay claim to any original ideas other than those connected to the use of vernacular language and an examination of nonelite group behavior. He can. In chapter 6, concerning Luther and his followers, Raemond goes beyond the portrayal of the reformer as the sum total of heretical beliefs — a position that he also asserts when it serves his purpose — and anticipates the modern view that Luther was the major source of the spiritualism that came to bloom so exotically in a number of radical fringe sects. In other words, the recent school of twentieth-century historians who are concerned with the religious and anthropological subtleties of Luther's reform program will discern in Raemond's history of Protestantism an insight that, however intuitive, was no less the product of his considerable research into lesser-known expressions of popular piety. At the same time, no scholar will fail to recognize the clarity with which Raemond anticipated the twentieth-century Catholic rediscovery of Luther's own considerable catholicity. Raemond's verbal pyrotechnics should not blind the reader to his intellectual subtlety and sophistication.

Having reached the section on Calvinism and its early growth on French soil (chap. 7), we shall see how profound an interest Raemond took in the rites and rituals of religious life (and death), an interest that again anticipated a recent trend in current scholarship into the social institutions that most intimately affected ordinary people. Baptism, communion, marriage, and funerals, and the emotions they aroused, fascinated Raemond. His persistent interviewing of people who had personally participated in the first rituals of Calvinism when it was a clandestine movement in Poitou recalls recent work in oral history. In his treatment of the origins of French reform, Raemond recognized the importance of the reformers at Meaux, while insisting that without the input of Lutheranism these native reform efforts would not have gotten out of hand. On the whole, Raemond stressed the Lutheran influence through Strasbourg on the reform movement in France, while attributing Calvin's conversion to the latter's German tutor, Wolmar. Nevertheless, he took the trouble to investigate the French milieu that gave to early Calvinism its first theological expression as well as its earliest ritual and institutional forms. Had Raemond not recorded the activities of Calvin at Angoulême and in Poitou, our knowledge of his movement would be much reduced, for Raemond's history is the main source for knowledge of this early period of Calvinism's development. It may seem incongruous, but Raemond's professional jealousy as a magistrate caused him to react against Calvinist consistories, or church courts, leading him to defend the individual's right to privacy. He especially disliked their prying into marital disputes.

Chapter 8 conveys some notion of the historian's politics and of the politician's approach to history. As far as the former subject is concerned, it is difficult to treat of Raemond's politics because he was far less interested in the subject than he was in church doctrine and ritual. Not surprisingly, his specialty in research was not secular history, as was that of Jean Bodin, François Hotman, or Etienne Pasquier, but church history. What he shared with secular, constitutional historians was an admiration for philology and preferences for strong monarchy and for unity in religion. In these matters, his views were not so dissimilar from those of some Protestants, even if each group characteristically defined the basis for uniformity differently — Catholics according to the tradition of their hierarchical church, and Protestants through their interpretation of Scripture.

Raemond's works did not qualify as "universal history," that lofty goal of many sixteenth century historians. For one thing his interests were not truly universal, for he focused primarily on ecclesiastical history. Furthermore, he was too willing to view such questionable factors of causation as climate, geography, national origins, God's will, and (but cautiously) the stars as sufficient causes of historical phenomena. He was without doubt too passionate and too prejudiced. He was also polemical, i.e., subjective in his treatment of evidence. The reader can consider the similarities between a dogmatic Catholic polemicist like Raemond and equally dogmatic Protestants such as Theodore de Bèze or François Hotman. All three were committed to a dualistic notion of good and evil, and equally certain that their religious faction was representative of the good. They all lacked confidence in historical change and sought to interpret changes in the historical past in a way consistent with their hopes for the future.

The last chapter of the book examines Raemond's "shelf-life." A popular author until the late seventeenth century (his books had run to thirty-two editions by 1682), Raemond became the object of several rumors, including one that claimed a Jesuit priest had written his works! Although his religious intolerance was reflected in the national policy of the Revocation of the Edict of Nantes (1685), in the eighteenth century such intolerance appeared increasingly unwise. Rationalists of the late seventeenth century and those of the eighteenth looked disdainfully at the rhetorical enthusiasm which permeated Raemond's work.

The appearance of Tamizey de Larroque's nineteeth-century

biography began the attempt to retrieve his memory from nearly two centuries of neglect. A few historians and men of letters in our own twentieth century have referred to Raemond's history of the Reformation as a work not devoid of interest and value.[1] Raemond's books on Pope Joan and on the Antichrist have attracted much less attention. In recent years Raemond has, on the other hand, been viewed as combative, which he was, and as a forerunner of absolutist monarchy and even of twentieth-century totalitarianism, which he was not.[2]

The fact is that Raemond's religious intolerance was not peculiar to, but standard for his day, and was an attitude shared by all varieties of religious opinion, not excluding Protestant opinion. Totalitarianism was not consistent with the strong monarch Raemond preferred, for he was also aware that a king who was too strong could make it difficult for the Catholic church to function. Since he objected to the Gallican liberties in which moderate or *politique* Catholics put their trust, he had little to buoy him up but a vague and troubled hope that things would work out for the best. He was a conservative idealist rather than a proto-totalitarian, and that idealism was the result of his religious opinions.

These were neither more right nor wrong than those of Protestant polemicists, and certainly not less rational. They were not more rational, either. The serious student of early modern European history will err if he fails to examine the issues that polemicists like Raemond thought important. Such works are valuable sources of the information and misinformation that molded the intellect and shaped the policy of intellectuals, churchmen, and politicians in the era, and not incidentally, gave humbler folk an excuse to obey and a cause for which to endure.

Front façade of Suquet.

Acknowledgments

I am deeply indebted to Prof. Donald R. Kelley for having read this manuscript in an early form and for having offered much encouragement and many suggestions for its improvement. I am very grateful to Prof. Lewis W. Spitz for his careful reading of the original and final versions of the text, his scholarly guidance, and continued interest in this project. During the course of my research I was helped by a good number of archival scholars and librarians, among whom I wish to include members of the staffs of the following research institutions: the municipal archives of Agen and of Bordeaux; the particular director of the latter institution, M. Jean Paul Avisseau, who reproduced many valuable documents and articles and graciously provided a convenient work space for me there; the staff of the Bibliothèque Nationale in Paris, where I worked for many months and required many special services; the library of the University of the Sorbonne, which gave me borrowing privileges as well as research privileges; and the staffs of the municipal archives of Strasbourg and the University of Strasbourg library.

Special thanks must go to the curator of the archiepiscopal archives of Bordeaux, Msgr. Laroza, who kindly introduced me to that extensive collection of nineteenth-century regional and clerical journals and who was willing to share his extensive knowledge of sixteenth-century Bordeaux. I wish to express my appreciation to the staff of the Green Graduate Library at Stanford University, and in particular to Dr. Mary Jane Parrine, who acquired for Stanford volumes of French history necessary to my research and who was always most supportive of my work. I would also like to thank the History Department of Stanford University for granting me the status of Visiting Scholar through the years during which this volume and other scholarly work has been in progress. I would like to thank the Council for International Exchange of Scholars for a Fulbright fellowship, which allowed me to work at the University of Strasbourg and in Paris (1983–84), and also the National Endowment for the Humanities at Duke University, which brought me (summer 1988) into contact with Montaigne scholars from the United States and abroad. Among the former, I wish to thank Dr. Marcel Tetel of Duke University, who provided me with an opportunity to read aloud portions of my chapter on Raemond's affiliation with the Montaigne literary circle in Bordeaux to our Montaigne seminar. Among foreign Montaigne scholars I wish especially to thank two members of the Société des Amis de Montaigne — Dr. Francis Potier-Sperry, a bibliophile and Montaigne scholar, and his friend, M. Richard Chapon of Bordeaux, who spent much time discussing with me the activities of sixteenth-century literateurs. I also wish to thank Inspector Francis Bianco of Agen, who helped me locate Raemond's chateau near the Lot River and who arranged a visit for me, most graciously hosted by the current owners, M. and Mme Pradère (who kindly showed me about Suquet, now beautifully restored). To Dr. David N. Wiley, Director of Susquehanna University Press, and to Mr. Michael Koy, Managing Editor of Associated University Presses, for having seen this book through the publication process, my deepest thanks.

Finally, I wish to thank my husband, a professor of philosophy, William E. Tinsley, who spent many hours listening to me read portions of this book aloud and gave me much to think about in the process. The results of our conversations brought new perspectives to familiar problems, and not infrequently his turn of phrase or insight found its way into my text.

History and Polemics
in the
French Reformation

1
Raemond's Life in Brief

Young Florimond

Florimond de Raemond was born in the river town of Agen, France, around 1540, to a family who traced their descent from the sovereign counts of Toulouse back to the thirteenth century. They had been a prolific family, with six branches, all bearing similar coats of arms.[1] Raemond's branch was that of Quercy, which sometime before 1490 had established itself in the Agen region.[2] Robert de Raemond, Florimond's father, was styled *seigneur* de Villoris[3] and also *sieur* de La Combe-Suquet, an estate located between Sainte-Livrade and Pujol in the *arrondissement* of Villeneuve-sur-Lot. Now called Suquet, this estate was sold in the eighteenth century,[4] and has been extensively restored in the twentieth. Suquet commands a glorious view of the rich and fertile plain of the Lot River, and with its oldest towers dating from the twelfth century, has long been an important part of its peaceful rural setting.

Little is known of Florimond's mother, Marie de Gillis, except that she was of an estate called "honorable"; that she came from the town of Montech; and that besides Florimond, her eldest child, she had three other sons and three daughters. She died in 1570.[5] Perhaps it was she who chose the name of an early regional saint for her firstborn son. Florimond's father, Robert, was a magistrate in the presidial court of Agen, and his son would describe him as a good parent and a pious Catholic — a God-fearing man.[6] The family name Raemond is derived from two nordic words meaning bold protection,[7] appropriate for our subject Florimond de Raemond whose subsequent career as *conseiller* (magistrate) in the Bordeaux *Parlement* was often marked by bold behavior, and who sought to protect his church and society from dangerous "heretic" innovation.

Agen was part of the southwestern region of Guyenne, a word derived from the Latin *Aquitania*, and synonymous with the French *Aquitaine* until the Hundred Years War. During the reign of

Henry IV, it included the present departments of Gironde, Dordogne, Lot, Lot-et-Garonne, with the Bordelais, Perigeux, and Agenais regions as its main parts. The *Parlement* of Bordeaux held jurisdiction over this entire area. It was not an easy region to govern, as it was one of those most exposed to and influenced by the new ideas of religious reform. As Raemond noted in his work on heresy:

> There lies the source of Guyenne's misfortunes, it was the first pawn in the long and painful game which was played out in the disorderly reigns which followed.[8]

In this region infected with "heresy" Florimond grew up with ample opportunity to witness the spread of the new religion. His own father had been a spectator at the burning of the ex-Dominican, Jerome Vindocin, that occurred in Agen on 4 February 1539, and was mentioned by both Jean Crespin, the martyrologist, and Theodore de Bèze, Calvin's lieutenant and later chief of the reformed party.[9] That Robert de Raemond was affected by the sight is attested by his son. Poor Vindocin died calling out upon Jesus Christ so that many who heard him regretted his condemnation, a fact Raemond emphasized in a personal way when commenting on the martyrdom of Anne du Bourg, an event he witnessed in Paris at the age of nineteen.[10]

The town of Agen had, notwithstanding the Vindocin affair, continued to give the reformed religion much support. It had therefore been selected by Calvinist educators as a suitable place for educational as well as religious innovations. Raemond observed that reformed educators had infiltrated the elementary schools:

> Their first concerns were always the regents and school teachers following Calvin's instructions; for just as victory is assured when the chief is felled, so these captains over vanquished youth hoped those little soldiers who marched under their flag would give way and follow the whim of whoever was leading them.[11]

Raemond was not sent to school in Agen, probably because the first two such regents or masters of reformed opinion had recently been exposed.[12] The God-fearing Robert must have felt that his son would be exposed to any of such opinions still lingering in the ivied halls of the Agen school. Furthermore, the family must have wished their eldest son to have as prestigious an education as possible. He was thus sent to Bordeaux for his education, almost certainly to the famed College of Guyenne.[13]

If he were indeed "a little soldier" or scholar at that school, he would have profited from the great attention paid it during the reign of Francis I, when reform minded scholars such as Julius Caesar Scaliger, George Buchanan, and Élie Vinet were on the staff, and the great cities of France vied for their talents.[14] Bright boys like Florimond would have benefited too from the fact that the University of Bordeaux's Faculty of Arts was obliged to hold its own classes on the premises of the college.[15] This must have made the school a livelier, more stimulating environment. Then there is the quotation that enables us to place Florimond against that educational backdrop:

> I recall that in my early childhood a regent named Valois, teaching the sixth form at Bordeaux, began to wean us from the custom of starting our lessons by crossing ourselves. It was, he said, just apish antics, talking to us in private about religion, and all in the easiest manner, so that our youthful understanding might comprehend. That made the first breech in our little souls, all the more dangerous as our first impressions are later uprooted with difficulty.[16]

The mature Raemond recalled some of the reasons why Protestant teachers were able to persuade their students to accept the reformed faith: inadequate knowledge of Catholicism, adolescent tendencies toward daring behavior, and the tantalizing prospect of being able to do as one pleased (eating meat on holy days when it was prohibited, getting out of confession, etc.) all figured largely.[17] Apparently young Florimond was susceptible as well, for he referred to "*our* youthful understanding" and to "*our* little souls." He never denied that susceptibility. More importantly, we know the lad was sent away from Bordeaux to the College of Presles in Paris,[18] presumably to protect him from reformed ideas, though no document or testimony remains to support this hypothesis. But if he were sent to Paris for protection against the new religion, his protection was inadequate. At Presles he was the pupil of Peter Ramus, the brilliant logician who lost his life in the St. Bartholomew's Day Massacre (1572). Raemond had once seen a certain controversial book, the *Trois Imposteurs*,[19] in Ramus's possession:

> I remember that in my childhood I once saw a copy (*Trois Imposteurs*) at the College of Presles in the hands of Ramus, a man well known for his high and eminent learning, (one) who troubled his wits with various inquiries into the secrets of religion, which he handled like philosophy.[20]

Collegiate sympathy for the Protestant cause was not unusual during Raemond's youth, and communicated itself to his friends at Presles. Returning home from the spectacle (1559) of the burning of Anne du Bourg (du Bourg was a Protestant counselor in the *Parlement* of Paris), Raemond marveled at the constancy of the victim in his last extremity: "We burst into tears in our colleges upon returning from this torture, and plead his cause after his passing, cursing those unjust judges who had justly condemned him."[21]

The fact that the son could feel in 1559 the same sense of incredulity and pity for a Protestant martyr as had the father a generation earlier must have worked on his sensibilities. If his father had felt that something was amiss with the burning of Vindocin, Raemond may well have supposed his own outrage was legitimized as by prior consent from his still Catholic parent, but even without parental approval, he would not have felt it unusual for having been drawn toward the reformed religion. The years 1559 to 1565 were a period of explosive growth for the new faith, especially among the nobility. Indeed, in certain regions such as Raemond's native Guyenne, and in neighboring Gascony and in Béarn, Calvinism had made particularly rapid headway. The reformed church of Agen, his home town, had grown to six or seven thousand souls by 1560. The lieutenant general of Guyenne was obliged to give its members permission to assemble in a Catholic church of the city, lest they make good a threat to occupy the Dominican convent.[22]

With so many among the nobility and still more among the *menu peuple* leading the way, it is easy to understand why Raemond was not particularly daring when he assumed the posture of a sympathizer with the reformed faith. When enthusiasm for reform began to cool, as it did sometime around 1570,[23] many people who were not willing to test their own heroism fell away. Raemond was even quicker to put aside his Huguenot leanings, although not before he had drunk deeply of the new wine of reformism at Paris. He recalled hearing Bèze preach with "not uncommon" style, and had seen him mounted on a horse accompanied by a Huguenot prince of the blood-Condé.[24] In 1562 he had heard Bèze preach at the Saint Antoine gate.[25] He was one of a large crowd: "I saw at Paris about the time France was in mad pursuit of these novelties that in a huge crowd of people who had come to the preachment, there was such disorder in their psalm-singing that at one extremity they were singing one verse, and at another, a different one."[26]

So ordinary indeed was flirtation with reform, that Raemond, though he never formally declared himself a convert,[27] felt no compunction in recording his progress into and out of that movement in two of his major polemics written to defend Roman Catholicism. If it were not for his reputation during his own lifetime as a foe of Protestantism,[28] it would not be necessary to consider at length his period of religious experimentation, but his literary productivity and his position as a magistrate attracted so much adverse attention (as well as so much acclaim) that his biographer must hazard a judgment as to the significance of his ordinary and relatively brief experience as a Protestant sympathizer.

The first thing that might be observed about the significance of Raemond's brief Protestant phase is that apparently it was one in which he had few, if any, personal attachments to the reformed nobility. His knowledge of the reformed as a youth seems to have been limited to academic contacts—fellow students and a few teachers. He remained a kind of outsider socially, probably due to an understandable reluctance to jeopardize his family's orthodox reputation. In later life he appears to have had few Protestant friends; the poet du Bartas was the most prominent exception. His knowledge of the reformed was largely determined by his role as a circuit judge, where he was naturally brought into contact with the reformed in their capacity as plaintiffs or as defendants in civil and criminal cases. On such occasions (see chap. 3) his vulnerability to criticism may have reinforced the prejudices of his Catholic faith and of his membership in a professional elite. As a polemical historian, his research into ecclesiastical history tended to emphasize the lowliness in social rank of Protestants generally, and of Anabaptists particularly.[29] His knowledge of the humbler types of reformed people could produce in him a not altogether distorted sense of the social psychology of poor people,[30] though to be sure his understanding of their social aspirations did not make him more sympathetic to their situation. In no more profound way did his brief Protestant period affect his point of view toward the reformed minority than it did in giving him the conviction that ignorance was a major factor in leading folks astray. It could be corrected, he thought, by the will to present the truth, which was to become his self-appointed task as a writer of history and as a defender of orthodoxy.

Sometime around 1563 Raemond went to Toulouse to complete his education at the University as a student of the law. He described that institution as a "school for the children of the best families of

France and the nursery of the finest spirits. This university was the step-ladder which led one to trod a fleur-de-lis-strewn path straight to the highest ranking positions."[31]

Toulouse was a good choice for a young man who traced his ancestry from the independent counts of Toulouse. More importantly, it was the prime university for legal studies. Raemond thought the University of Poitiers the second best school for such studies, and noted that both universities were important centers of Huguenot affairs.[32] While there, he made the acquaintance of many peers who would become his lifelong friends and associates such as Pierre de Brach and Guillaume de Salluste du Bartas,[33] both poets. Here he developed a love of learning and a respect for the learned, especially for men like Guillaume Budé, and his patron Francis I, who had made learning easier by the generosity of his royal patronage. In his major historical polemic, the "History of Heresy," Raemond also took the liberty of criticizing learned men, schoolmasters, whom he dubbed "grammarians," philosophers, and mathematicians. He felt they had neglected the study of theology, and thus caused most of the trouble that afflicted his century: they had erred in placing knowledge above wisdom.[34] Raemond's opinion on such neglect was undoubtedly a reflection of the fact that he was himself painfully aware of the gap in his own understanding of theology, a subject he had never studied formally.

In 1566 Raemond returned to Paris. He may have wished to continue his studies, though presumably not the study of law.[35] His friends were all fellow students. It was in their company that he traveled to Laon, some one hundred forty kilometers northeast of Paris, to view the exorcism of a young married woman of sixteen, Nicole Auberi.[36] Her body had already been freed of numerous demons, and it was now to be exorcised of the last, none other than Beelzebub!

This incident is extremely important in the life of Raemond, for, when he and thousands of other spectators witnessed first Nicole's levitation by the Bishop of Laon, and then the belching out from her mouth of that last demon, Raemond concluded once and for all that the Catholic faith was the only one that could accomplish miracles, and hence deserved his devotion.[37] Nor did he fail to use the story of Nicole's exorcism to persuade his readers of the same truth years later; in fact, he used it twice.[38] In the second telling of the tale he stated that it was this event that had saved him from the jaws of heresy.[39] Although Raemond was given to hyperbolic expressions when he became a best-selling author, there is every reason to believe that his two descriptions of this single event testify to the significance it had for him personally, as well as for his appreciation of the effect his account would have on the minds and hearts of his fellow countrymen. He was never to forget that his soul had been miraculously preserved by the miracle of a Catholic exorcism. Indeed, his whole subsequent life may be viewed as an effort to render thanks to God and to his church for this divine favor.

Florimond de Raemond's insignia was an armillary sphere, three quarters of which was bordered by clouds where there appeared a slogan in a dialect of French: *ARE DU MON NO MUDERA*, which appears to mean: The God of my fathers will not change.[40] This rendering was consistent with the position he would uphold as a Counter-Reformation polemicist for the Catholic cause, a cause he would ever after defend as the result of his witnessing the Auberi exorcism.

Entering the *Parlement*

It cannot be said with certainty how it happened that the future essayist Michel de Montaigne first met Florimond de Raemond.[41] Possibly the families of the two men were acquainted, or perhaps they met some time during 1563, when Montaigne was frequently in Agen to visit his friend and fellow *conseiller*, Étienne de La Boétie, when the latter was working there as a special magistrate. Whenever the meeting occurred, it is certain that Montaigne sold his position as *conseiller* in the *Parlement* of Bordeaux to Raemond on 10 April 1570, that King Charles IX legalized the transaction by letters patent dated July 23, and that Raemond was sworn in as *conseiller* on 2 October 1570.[42]

Not long after he had begun his career as a magistrate he may have spent a few bad moments wondering whether he would have the opportunity to continue as one for he fell into the hands of Huguenots who kidnapped him and held him for a ransom of one thousand *livres*. The incident was referred to in print in 1597 in a book which contained many charges of Protestants against the magistracy, and against Raemond himself.[43] Gilbert Burnet, who knew of the incident, would write at the end of the seventeenth century that after Raemond regained his freedom, he neglected no opportunity to reward himself at Huguenot expense for the ransom and that he even bragged of that fact to others.[44] Raemond's first biographer thought it inconceivable to think that Raemond should have retaliated against his justiciables in such a manner,[45] and

Larroque must surely be right. It would scarcely have aided a magistrate's career to spread rumors about his having sought revenge by means of his judicial authority against Protestants generally. Such overt defiance of justice would have jeopardized more than his career—it would have made his safety problematical.

Raemond's own recollections of his kidnapping are not even vituperative. Indeed, his account began in the mildest of moods, almost as if it had been someone else's ordeal: "While I remained a prisoner of war in their hands."[46] It shows Raemond knew all too well that he had been captured because of the state of affairs—the unrest which followed upon the assassinations of St. Bartholomew's Day in August 1572—rather than because of his own misbehavior. The rest of the narrative account shows Raemond once again surrounded by a crowd of reformed people, a milieu which, if not of his own choosing, was at least not unfamiliar. In any event, he was thrown upon his own resources for entertainment for the brief time of his captivity. He paid attention to their manners and to their life-style—"their mode of living"—as he termed it, and made mental notes of everything he observed. Their religious ritual he described as a kind of colorless form of Christianity.[47] They were perverse because they neglected formulae dear to Catholics. They ate meat on Friday! They prayed standing up! He took it upon himself to argue with them—it no doubt relieved the tedium of captivity—about the meaning of humility. He made it plain to his readers long after the event that he had felt nothing in common with these Huguenot captors, but his experiences with them were not terrible, and did not corrupt his sense of duty and obligation to observe the law.

Dabbling in Poetry

One would like to know how Raemond and his circle of acquaintances and friends in Bordeaux were affected by the political events of the 1570s and 1580s—a period during which the religious and dynastic fate of France was being determined. There is, unfortunately, scarcely a reference to any of these things in his writings,[48] nor do letters exist to tell us what his reactions to such matters were. All we know of him in these decades when he was in his prime is related not to his political activity, but to the affective side of life. Whatever satisfaction he derived from public service, he may not have derived from it so much satisfaction as he did from his private literary endeavors and from the literary circle of friends where he was loved and admired. Not very much remains of the poetry he wrote during these decades, but by 1572 he had earned a reputation for poetry and had been hailed in print for his talent by his friend Guillaume de Salluste, sieur du Bartas,[49] whose sonnet beginning "My dear Rémond" proclaimed the joys of country life, all the more precious in times of civil unrest.[50] Du Bartas's poem suggested that his friend Florimond pursue his own leisure rather than the public's well-being. Despite such advice, Raemond continued to apply himself to his magisterial duties. By the 1590s, after his service as counsellor and judge had been subject to some criticism, this sonnet may have returned to haunt him.

Besides du Bartas his literary circle included Pierre de Brach[51] and Jacques Peletier du Mans.[52] Brach had mentioned Raemond in a sonnet that bespoke the closeness of their friendship and lamented the fact that "Raimond" was often too busy with his paperwork to keep his dinner engagements.[53] The friends who kept Raemond in touch with his poetic side were men of considerable learning and unimpeachable intellectual as well as social connections. They were creative people, but people with marked preferences for what was tried and widely considered true in the light of tradition, especially religious tradition. Most were devoted to the Catholic religion and impatient of innovators and of unrestrained reason. They were men who reinforced Raemond's own conservatism, and while he enjoyed their company and with them he kept abreast of contemporary literary developments, it is doubtful if they offered him any serious intellectual challenges. From time to time he published a poem or two—that it was just an occasional poem he was aware, and perhaps somewhat regretful. Before Brach's first book of poems was published (1576), Raemond wrote him a congratulatory sonnet. In it, he compared the arrival of a book to that of a newborn baby, ending "Happy would I be to father such a son!"[54]

The Price of Prominence

In June 1577, Raemond was a captive again. He was taken prisoner with several men of good families by the Protestant governor of Sainte-Foy. The town was an important center of Huguenot activity,[55] but the precise reason for the men's detention remains obscure. Perhaps their experience was the result merely of Protestant frustrations, and their stature and influence (they were related to magistrates if not magistrates themselves) were simply excuses for harassment. In any event, the period of their captivity was of several weeks' duration.[56] They were released by the intervention of one of Henry of Navarre's most devoted supporters and able captains—André de Meslon. It is possible, but no evidence exists to prove that Henry himself arranged for their release in order to avoid stirring up more overt hostilities between Catholics and Protestants in that area.

While power had its hazards, it afforded some consolations. In 1578, the following year, Raemond took the responsibility for abolishing the celebration of the festival of St. John the Baptist. This was a medieval celebration that was marked by the staging of amateur (artisan performed) dramas depicting Christ's baptism. Wooden stages and elaborate clerical costumes were part of the equipment needed, while real clergymen subjected themselves to indignities such as a "baptism" of water sprayed at them by the actors. The fine June weather permitted large crowds to gather, and these were often exuberant in their enjoyment of the spectacles that were provided in five different areas of the city of Bordeaux. Maintaining public order was a difficult task for the city officials, and Raemond suppressed the celebration to facilitate the keeping of the peace. Furthermore, his actions revealed his anxiety to maintain the dignity of clergy who were apt to be charged by Protestants with having forgotten their real mission, that is, the care of their flock.

Recording the event of suppression, Jean de Gaufreteau, sometime around the turn of the century, applauded Raemond for having put an end to an unworthy, undignified custom.[57] Raemond's action reminds us that the puritan mentality was not a Protestant monopoly.

Love and Marriage

Florimond de Raemond was twice married, the first time to Catharine de Rosteguy de Lancre,[58] a sister of Raemond's fellow counsellor, Pierre de Lancre, sometime in the early 1570s. They had two sons: François, born in 1574, who succeeded him in the Bordeaux *Parlement* in 1601, and who also completed the "History of Heresy" after his father's death, and Jean-Charles, who became abbé de la Frénade after translating his father's *Erreur Populaire* into Latin, (1601).[59] A daughter, Antoinette, may have died in infancy.[60] A second marriage occurred probably in the late 1580s to a woman named Jeanne (or Suzanne) Marin.[61] It certainly took place before Raemond wrote a sonnet to Pierre de Brach intended to console him for the loss of Aymee, his wife, who died in 1587. Raemond urged his friend to do as he had done, remarry, for a new love was, he thought, the perfect remedy for the loss of a former one. Brach remained inconsolable, and in his own sonnet "A Monsieur de Raymond" called his friend unsteady in love.[62] Another son was born from this second marriage named Florimond, on 17 January 1599. It was this child who succeeded his half-brother, François, to the seat in the Bordeaux *Parlement* left vacant by François's death in 1626.[63]

When Florimond de Raemond confronted femininity, he did so from the usual position of sixteenth-century men, that of authority and noblesse oblige. He was fond of feminine beauty, for he was a man of aesthetic taste, a collector of art objects; his portraits suggest that he was a courtly man,[64] one who could compose sonnets to lovely ladies such as the heiress, Dianne de Foix-Candale, darling of her house. True ladies were for him like Dianne (her very name a symbol of chastity, the prime female virtue) "beautiful and virtuous."[65] On the other hand, not all women were virtuous, and for those who were not, he noted there was a garment puffy enough to hide their indiscretions.[66] Raemond's opinions concerning the female sex were the conventional ones of his age. He did not recognize in them the rational quality of men, though he was of course aware that a few well-favored women were capable of great things. Queen Elizabeth was an example, as well as a warning.[67] His conventionality with regard to the fair sex made him mindful of Saint Paul's dictum that virginity was an estate more honorable than marriage, but that it was better to marry than to burn.[68] Still, one must not suppose that because his ideas were ordinary, they were not important. His views of the growth of reform in France were at least in part a reflection of his ambiguous and unflattering opinions with respect to women — opinions shared by the vast majority of his contemporaries.

In Pursuit of the Beautiful

Why should the biography of a polemical historian devote space to his aesthetic interests? What did aesthetics have to do with the subject matter in which Raemond was interested, the growth and development of Catholic tradition, and the rise of a counterfaith, indeed, of a counteraesthetic? In some ways the Protestant Reformation was hostile to the aesthetic traditions of the Catholic past, most notably in the realm of religious art.[69] It was not coincidental that Raemond, whose most consuming lesser hobby was archaeology[70] and the creation of a private museum of Roman antiquities[71] took the Protestants' and especially the Calvinists' iconoclastic propensities as a personal as well as a confessional criticism. The Counter-Reformation gave art the widest possible scope in the life of the church and continued to patronize artists of all kinds as the Catholic church had done since the Middle Ages and throughout the Renaissance. Sensing the hostility of many Protestants to religious paintings and the elaborate decor of places of worship, Rome made art a weapon in the war against heterodoxy.[72]

Works of art deserved man's reverence for the magic of art was to raise man above his own inadequacy, restore his soul, and put him in touch with what was permanent. Did Calvinists reproach once pagan trappings with a certain "mildew" that rendered them odious? They reminded Raemond of men who ignored the works of Michelangelo, Raphael, and Titian because time had dimmed their colors with smoke.[73] Raemond's concern with beauty, secular and religious, antique and contemporary, demonstrates that he, like many fifteenth- and sixteenth-century humanists, did not let their admiration for the antique render them unable to appreciate the modern age.[74] Even if Raemond, like so many of his contemporaries, lamented the decadence of that age in which he was living, he was not opposed to interpreting modern society in its own terms.[75] He was a man who made use of his antique pieces, adapting them to serve his own particular purposes.[76] His reverence for old things did not preclude a certain utilitarianism. If, like so many Renaissance aristocrats, he valued beauty for its own sake, he was also aware that art must serve religion, not do it disservice. On two occasions he was even critical of two works he attributed to Michelangelo, whom he greatly admired. One of these was a figure of Christ on an eagle, which was placed near the choir entrance of Bordeaux's cathedral: "Some conscientious reformer will say that it's a Jupiter we worship."[77] The removal of the other work from the cathedral of Sienna would give him great satisfaction, for it was a bust of the supposed female pope he helped expose as a fraud.[78]

No use to which art could be put was more characteristic of the Renaissance than the construction or reconstruction of churches. On two occasions Raemond involved himself in such activity. The first instance occurred in 1580 when, largely at his instigation and under his direction, the cathedral of St. André received two new galleries.[79] These were added to the nave on either side, extending to the organ at the end of the building opposite the altar. These galleries were designed to provide additional seating for the clergy on the right, along with the pulpit for the preacher, and for the entire *Parlement* of Bordeaux on the left. So popular was this improvement that before long the municipal officials (*jurats*) of the city had a third, smaller gallery built for themselves higher up off the floor and to one side of the organ. The officers of the civil and criminal courts (présidial) then had a similar gallery built for themselves on the other side.[80]

That Raemond's impulse gave impetus to other groups reveals that he was able to take the pulse of the times. He understood his society very well, and this would have its effect on his success as a publicist and as a writer of history. In this matter of church reconstruction, he sensed that the interest of Catholics in attending sermons was greater than it had ever been. The desire for moral edification was no longer a mere Protestant concern. Florimond de Raemond played a major role in promoting the Catholic Reformation in the Bordeaux region. When his books appeared in print,[81] part of their successful reception was no doubt owing to the local reputation of the author.

A second effort to aid in the building of local churches was minor by comparison with the first, involving as it did a gift by Raemond's family of stones for a chapel of the religious order of the *Feuillants*.[82]

Though the last dozen years of his life were busy years of writing and editing, Raemond continued to work as a judge,[83] and also to devote some attention to agriculture and the sale of sparkling wines to England. He was made a "franc-bourgeois" of Bordeaux in 1593, a status exempting him from all municipal taxes, and from payment of the *taille*, or state property tax as well,[84] freeing him of the obligation of paying taxes on his wine sales. His estates were growing in size, for not only had he bought property adjoining Combe-Suquet, but in 1590 he acquired the title to two tracts of vineyard land formerly owned by the abbey of Saint-Croix. For a time his title was in abeyance. The monks claimed he owed them both a money payment of two *deniers*, and a certain portion of the produce itself. As the land was still uncultivated, Raemond asked that the fees be lowered to a more realistic level until the land could be put into production. The suggestion, put by his lawyer, one M. Roque (dated 20 February 1590), contained a warning to the effect that without such a reduction in payment, the suppliant would be obliged to leave the land unimproved.[85] In that case, the abbot would find himself in a worse position.

That Raemond could have afforded to improve his new land

without the reduction in fees is probable, yet the petition reveals that he was determined to manage his property as carefully as he could, hopefully without losing the goodwill of the monastery. In the end, a commission of two monks and several experts in viticulture were sent to the property to study the matter again. Raemond was not blasé about his wine venture—he wrote to his friend Geoffrey de Malvyn that "the wine sparkles and jumps about in the barrels while awaiting shipment for England."[86]

The sale of wine was undoubtedly an important source of Raemond's income. His ordinary quarterly salary as a counsellor was (in 1589) thirty-one *écus*, 15 *sols*, for we have a quittance or receipt signed by him to testify that this was indeed his ordinary salary for a three-month period.[87] He also collected other gratuities for the letters patent pertaining to his appointment indicate that the salary of a *parlement* man was not without fringe benefits. We have no information as to what he may have earned from the sale of his books, but it probably was not a great deal. His son François once remarked that his father did not sell his talents, but donated them. This remark may well indicate that his writing had not made him much richer. It is clear, however, that Raemond's interests were diversified, and that made him a man of the world in a direct fashion for he was involved with the world whose affairs, at least in part, he had to supervise in a judicial capacity.

In September 1592, Raemond's world shrunk perceptibly, for Montaigne died of a "quinsy,"[88] or severe case of tonsillitis, accompanied by suppurations of the throat and high fever. He was without the power of speech for three days before his death, and it is possible that Raemond was in and out of the sick room, along with his friend, Brach, and members of the sick man's family. Raemond refused the task of writing a poem for the literary "tomb" on the grounds that his skills had waned for want of practice.[89] He put a good deal of emotion into his leave-taking "of our Montaigne, never adequately praised."[90]

During the years following Montaigne's death, Raemond was busy with literary projects and with his magistracy, but he found time to interest himself in a third endeavor to expand church facilities in Bordeaux. He was one of a few local dignitaries who were invited to meet with the mayor and municipal council to consider ways and means for establishing a new chapter of Capuchin friars in the city—a pet project of Cardinal de Sourdis. The cardinal little dreamed that a scant three months later one of the lynch-pins of his fund-raising campaign, Florimond de Raemond, would be lying in his grave.

2
Exchange of Views: Catholics, Protestants, and Politiques

Two forces shape the lives of men—events and other men. The last may be their intimates and peers, their patrons, their protégés. They may be bare acquaintances, or complete strangers known to them only by their accomplishments of a public nature. They may be men deemed worthy of emulating, or conversely, men whose opinions are held to be in error, with whom it is a matter of honor to disagree. Events and men are the materials of biography, but where the chronological record is incomplete—and we do not have a complete record of all Raemond's activities—human relationships are the more valuable for the insight they provide the reader into the subject's intellectual formation. This chapter gives the reader an opportunity to examine our subject in the light of his intercourse with four intellectual leaders of his times. The first of these is Michel de Montaigne, his friend and near neighbor, a social equal, but also a preceptor of sorts. The second, Jean de Sponde, was a newer friend, a poet and recent convert to Catholicism, whose relationship to Raemond was that of a dependent to a patron, or of a son to a father. Raemond's correspondence with Philippe de Mornay, the Calvinist statesman and publicist, was not encumbered by any friendship. It offers the reader a glimpse of our subject's satiric humor combined with the tenacity of his Catholic mission. His satire and tenacity resounded in the response of his Calvinist antagonist. Finally, in the letters of the jurisconsult Étienne Pasquier, a *politique* Gallican Catholic, we can deduce what Raemond's views on church-state relations were, and we can compare the range of opinion among Catholics on the Jesuits, whom Raemond admired, and Pasquier despised.

The Montaigne Connection

The lacunae in the evidence that remains of Michel de Montaigne's friendship for Florimond de Raemond are annoying. Our major source for the description of that relationship is Raemond himself. Not only did he make fairly frequent use of Montaigne's ideas in his own works, but several times he waxed lyrical over the respect due a superior thinker.[1] In his own copy of the *Essays* he made annotations that only a close friend of the essayist could have written.[2]

No letters of Montaigne to Raemond, nor of Raemond to Montaigne, exist. That some such correspondence did once exist seems likely, for Raemond scribbled in the margins of his *Essays* a note that indicates that he had had occasion to judge the quality of his friend's letter writing abilities.[3]

Intimate friendships of an intellectual sort rarely exist where a disparity of views on basic issues is too great. Despite stylistic differences — Montaigne's essays are moderate, and his irony gentle; Raemond's style was often bumptious, his irony barbed — the two men were philosophically compatible otherwise they would have gone their separate ways, for Bordeaux did not lack men of culture. In no more important way were they in agreement than in their manner of regarding critics of Catholicism as arrogant, stubborn individuals misguided by their misuse of reason.[4] The whole of Montaigne's *Apology for Raymond Sebond* demonstrates the danger of relying on man's inadequate natural powers (reason), and recommends turning toward God instead for basic illumination. Raemond heartily concurred, for in the second chapter of his *L'Anti-Christ* he urged his readers to refer to the *Apology*.[5] Montaigne's sceptical attitude toward reason was not unique, however. It is not necessary to believe that the essay on Sebond, or any other by Montaigne, was responsible for Raemond's distrust of reason. Erasmus had made the sceptical position part of the humanist tradition,[6] and he was not the first Renaissance thinker to do so. Thus, Raemond could have learned the principles of modern sceptical thought from a variety of Catholic writers whose works preceded the publication of Montaigne's *Essays*.[7] The Catholic Counter-Reformation utilized the new Pyrrhonism to create a reinvigorated fideism.

Raemond was not a consistent sceptic or a systematic philosopher. His attraction to scepticism was a kind of corollary of a less hazardous position,[8] that of Catholic tradition, the espousal of which was as safe as it was orthodox.[9] This was the basic defense of the Catholic party generally. Its appeal for Montaigne was scarcely less strong. Both Montaigne and Raemond let their distrust of human reason reinforce their very basic social conservatism. Both were contemptuous of that arrogance they believed had led to religious innovation at the hands of the Protestant reformers.[10]

Scholars have sought to demonstrate, using Raemond's respect for Catholic tradition as proof, that Montaigne was unimpeachably orthodox in his religious beliefs.[11] This has been questioned by others,[12] but it is not our concern to take sides on the matter. There was in any case enough that was Catholic about his friend to satisfy Raemond, whose closest associates were usually men of his own faith. That there were differences in the degree to which each was moved by his faith is, however, quite obvious. Montaigne was not an enthusiast. He maintained a tolerance toward people of different cultures not typical of Raemond, despite the fact that on occasion the latter could defend religions, which elsewhere, and at length, he had severely belittled.[13] It is also obvious that the two men served distinct and divergent literary purposes. Montaigne's essays were not intended to convince anyone of anything, but were designed to interpret an unknown self for himself and for others.[14] Raemond's purpose was to justify an institution — Roman Catholicism — to his largely Roman Catholic readership; his purpose was polemical and impersonal. Despite differences in tone, form, and function, the writing habits of each of the two men probably served to enhance rather than detract from their friendship. Not only did they share the concerns of writers, but the concerns of their similar social milieu, their professional training (law), their humanist frame of reference, and their party sympathy. These things drew them together more surely than their prose style and intellectual differences separated them.[15]

Jean de Sponde

Jean de Sponde (1557–1595) was a Calvinist poet and politician whose family had strong ties of service to the House of Navarre. Jean himself had studied in Basel and had been praised by Theodore de Bèze for a work on Homer.[16] Employed briefly as lieutenant general at La Rochelle in 1589, Sponde fell out with some of the city's officials and was obliged to resign his post. Although King Henry IV gave him another (at the behest of a Calvinist minister) in 1593, Sponde held it but briefly, retiring in late summer of 1594 to his native mountains of Biscaye. He intended to study theology. He had already converted to Catholicism, due in part to the influence of the famous court preacher, Father Du Perron,[17] who had played a key role in the king's own religious about-face.

At Biscaye Sponde began to write a long rebuttal of a treatise written by Bèze in 1592 on the "marks" of the true church. After several months of work he found it necessary to go in search of source material, and having arrived at Bordeaux for that purpose, he became acquainted with Florimond de Raemond. Raemond became his friend and protector, and after Sponde died, his editor and literary executor. Raemond's large library was to provide Sponde with much of his source material. Sponde's treatise took note of the fact that Raemond's work would also serve as a rebuttal to Bèze's writings.[18] Sponde had read the book Raemond had written on the imaginary female pope, and there is no doubt that his boundless admiration of the older man, along with the similarity of their views on religion, made their brief relationship exceptionally close.

For example, Sponde resented the Calvinists' rejection of Catholic tradition as a regulator of religious forms.[19] Raemond echoed that sentiment in his "History of Heresy" when he wrote: "The old is always the best, and the best is the oldest."[20] Sponde insisted that the Calvinists had not reformed manners and morals at all, but merely masked them with simplicity.[21] Raemond may have remembered these sentiments when he wrote that Calvinists had given up their earlier strict discipline and become more lax.[22] If laxity of morals was a fault, Sponde felt that it was a less serious one than their flawed method of church governance, which led invariably to democracy.[23] Raemond concurred, and wrote later that Calvin had started the dangerous drift away from the divine prototype, the monarchy of Christ; that way lay anarchy — "miserable Anarchie"[24] — a notion he had earlier developed in the *Anti-Christ*, where he attacked Protestantism's affinity to late medieval conciliarism.[25] When Sponde wrote that the Roman church was the only depository of the true faith because the apostolic succession had never been broken, he was making the same familiar argument that Raemond had hoped to illustrate in his *Erreur Populaire* regarding the myth of the female pope. Neither Sponde nor Raemond could afford to ignore the attacks that Protestants made on papal primacy and the purity of the apostolic succession. These were the cornerstones of catholicity.

When Sponde died in March 1595, his *Response* to Bèze was unfinished, although it was over eight hundred pages! Raemond left a touching description of the convert's last moments,[26] perhaps too touching to be wholly convincing. In any event, Raemond's edition of his friend's book went some way to repair the damages to Sponde's reputation that had been inflicted by disgruntled

Calvinists. The leader of that group was Agrippa d'Aubigné, who had accused Sponde of sexual improprieties and even of a failed attempt to poison his wife; d'Aubigné appears to have been fond of such charges, because he also alluded to preposterous rumors that Raemond had poisoned Jean de Sponde.[27]

Devotion to his friend kept Raemond busy as editor and as compiler of one of those literary "tombs" so intriguing to people in the late sixteenth century. Raemond labored to make sure his friend's death—and the last two years of life—would be just what he had told Du Perron they were: a source of credit to the church of Rome, a monument to orthodoxy.

Philippe Duplessis-Mornay

As a popular author, Raemond could hardly escape public disputations over religious issues. Sometimes controversy was thrust upon him; sometimes he sought shelter from it; occasionally he went in search of it. His correspondence with Philippe de Mornay, seigneur du Plessis-Marly, or Duplessis-Mornay, seems to have been an instance of the latter sort. Duplessis-Mornay was a leader of the Huguenot party and one of the chief agents used by Henry of Navarre to negotiate his reconciliation with the last Valois ruler, Henry III, in 1589. Duplessis-Mornay's rewards were the governorship of Saumur and a position as counselor of state. A man who enjoyed religious disputation, he founded a Protestant university at Saumur after his retirement, which began with Henry IV's conversion to Catholicism (1593). In retirement, Duplessis-Mornay continued to serve as the leader of his religious party and was known to the opposition party as the Huguenot pope. Because of Duplessis-Mornay's religious as well as political prominence, Raemond took the initiative to send him in 1597 a copy of the *Anti-Christ* just as it emerged from the press. He sent Duplessis-Mornay the book, along with a brief letter that read as follows:

> Sir, the Lord of Bissouse[28] assured me that you would be pleased to see this book, which speaks to you and of you in divers places. That is why I am sending it to you; and it is fitting that every writer of this century salute you, in view of the honorable place you occupy amongst them. And since God wished you to play an important role in the management of this state, do whatever you can, Sir, so that steel and fire may no longer be the judges of our differences, but books. And, I beg of you, peruse this objectively, as I do everything you write.
> De Raemound[29]

The letter was not without guile, for the various references to the governor of Saumur were all unflattering. Bissouse had very likely praised the *Anti-Christ* to Raemond, but the point in sending it was to goad Duplessis-Mornay into responding, or at the very least, to annoy him. In any event, the Huguenot pope was not one to resist a challenge. Raemond's criticisms pointed up the major differences between Christians who were faithful (to Catholicism) and those who were reformed. The very civil compliments these two men exchanged could scarcely obscure the depth of their differences. That they could maintain civility at all must be noted as a mark of noble rather than vulgar souls.

The first of the criticisms that the *Anti-Christ* contained against Duplessis-Mornay concerned an old cabalistic conundrum[30] to the effect that the word *papacy*, when rendered in Greek, totaled the number 666. This was a number anciently associated with the Antichrist. Irenaeus, for example, in the second century had suggested that the Greek word *Lateinos* (Latin) could be given number values that would add up to the magical 666, but according to Raemond, Irenaeus discouraged contemporaries from taking that kind of game seriously, preferring to wait and see what the prophecy might mean in light of future events. Raemond accused Duplessis-Mornay of "adjusting" Irenaeus's original explanation in order to implicate the papacy as Antichrist. The "adjustments" were "words newly forged," Raemond had written.[31]

His second charge against the Huguenot leader, whom he characterized as an "enemy of the church" referred to Duplessis-Mornay's treatise of 1578,[32] in which he had asserted that Catholics believe the pope to be a god himself, and not a fallible human being. Raemond insisted that such was not the case, and he mentioned that Jean de Sponde had had to endure such distortion of his work. In fact, Raemond said, the Roman church made it clear that the pope was but a man, even though one elevated to great dignity.[33] Protestant detractors such as John Bale[34] and Matthias Flacius Illyricus[35] had "such skinny reasons" with which to pad out the notion that the pope was Anti-Christ that he was reminded of some people who were by nature so thin that they sought to pad themselves out with wadded cotton in order to achieve a more natural fullness.[36]

Third, Duplessis-Mornay had been wrong to say that popes could err on matters of faith. Raemond would stand with Sponde, Bellarmine,[37] and other modern Catholic writers on the proposition that popes were infallible on questions of faith.[38]

Fourth, Duplessis-Mornay and all the reformed writers generally were mistaken in their contention that the papacy was not part of God's plan. Raemond noted that critics of papal primacy[39] blamed the Emperor Phocas (602–610) for having promoted the papacy. Raemond noted that the Council of Chalcedon (451) had dealt with the problems of authority that both the bishop of Rome and the patriarch of Constantinople were claiming.[40] Raemond sought to prove that Chalcedon had unequivocally established papal primacy on the firmest of footings, nor would he accept the Protestant picture of Phocas as the cruel tyrant Protestants were then painting, and with which modern scholars now agree. The charge that "le Plessis" made against Phocas, that he had traded recognition of Rome's primacy (under Gregory I) for Rome's support against his own domestic opposition, Raemond disallowed.[41]

Raemond wished to correct what he regarded as John Calvin's misrepresentation of the antiquity of the papacy. Popes in Charlemagne's time were, Raemond believed, already exercising ancient prerogatives. He dismissed as similarly flawed the disbelief of the Greek Orthodox church in papal supremacy. He thought the Greeks were flattered by the reformed for their ignorance of the matter. He observed with joy that, when in 1574 some Protestant ministers sent the patriarch of Constantinople a copy of their "Augustanian Confession,"[42] he sent it back again with a note saying that the document contained thirty-three errors, and please not to trouble him further.[43]

The last mention of Duplessis-Mornay was the most withering in the *Anti-Christ*. Raemond accused "Le Plessis" of disseminating the erroneous belief that the papacy was doomed to extinction. Our author insisted that as his party's foremost spokesman, Duplessis-Mornay ought not to let his fancy be his guide. Why didn't he leave insults to the less talented men in his party?[44] Why did he feign ignorance of the Roman Catholic victories just now being achieved in Russia and in Poland? Raemond suggested he read the book by Pierre Charron that disproved all Huguenot contentions.[45]

In sum, Raemond's attack on Duplessis-Mornay's religious conceptions was designed to impugn the man's capacity, though not his character. The Huguenot leader's rejection of an early, unambiguous development of papal leadership in the primitive church has remained the basis for modern Protestant theologians and historians of religion. Raemond's view that the papacy derived from the installation of the Apostle Peter by Christ in an eternal office (one that could be continued beyond his own lifetime) has remained the basis of the Catholic conception of papal authority,[46] though a recent study of Catholic opinion on the development of the office of pope has indicated modifications and changes that tend to strengthen the Protestant claim that the primacy was the product of a gradual rather than an abrupt and self-conscious exercise of authority both religious and administrative.

In the course of this correspondence the intellectual prejudices and the emotional pain and resentment of two-thirds of a century are revealed. When Duplessis-Mornay wrote back rejecting Charron's work as an unsatisfactory refutation of facts which he had spent twenty years researching, he was not criticizing one particular Catholic philosopher, but rather he was impugning the validity of the whole Catholic interpretation of church history and spiritual legitimacy. As for the pious wish concerning the evils of fires and swords — "le fer et le feu" — he begged Raemond to realize that his party did not have to be persuaded because they had been the victimized group.[47] As a politician, he had always tried to avoid military conflict. Did the veil, which these gentlemen pulled over their contempt for their religious opponents, not fail completely to mask their true feelings? When Duplessis-Mornay added to his letter that the book he was sending to Raemond would be "inferior as regards form" of which he knew Raemond was a master, but "superior nonetheless as to matter"[48] did he not let drop the veil? In effect, the Huguenot leader was claiming that Raemond had a kind of slick erudition, but did not have the truth on his party's side. The Huguenot party possessed what the Catholics lacked: God's truth. Duplessis-Mornay did not fail to show the same exagerrated courtesy in his close: "what for others may be the subject of contention, shall, if it please you, only strengthen our friendship."[49]

A year and a half later, in January 1599, another exchange took place between them, for Raemond sent a further gift of books to the governor of Saumur. He sent a letter that began with this arresting salutation: "Sir, I fear I shall do as the satyr who blew from one mouth both hot and cold."[50] The "hot" was the gift of books; the "cold" was that our author knew very well that the recipient would not enjoy reading them! These works were by two Jesuits. The first, Fronton du Duc,[51] was the brilliant son of a fellow magistrate in the Bordeaux *Parlement*. The great Cardinal Baronius praised du Duc just as he had praised Raemond in his great *Annals*.[52] The second volume was by Father Louis Richeome, a personal friend of Raemond's and provost of the Jesuit order in the Bordeaux region.[53] There was a wistful quality in Raemond's recommendation of this "Bon père Richeome" whom he said

Duplessis-Mornay would love (despite the fact that the very word "Jesuit" was odious to him). Neither priest was the kind of little scribbler with whom Duplessis-Mornay usually engaged in dispute. These authors would prove a real challenge if only the Huguenot gentleman would read them. Lamenting the fact that he, Florimond de Raemond, found writing hard work — "I always work with beads of perspiration on my brow," he averred — he delivered this "praise":

> You are one of those precise in the cleanly-turned phrase, the method of your works. If you only had the truth on your side! People would sing your praises forever. That will occur when God will make you see that there is no truth nor salvation except in the Catholic church.[54]

The "praise" was the perfect put down. It was an exact parallel to the one delivered by Duplessis-Mornay in his letter of July 1597. Raemond had saved the letter, and he waited until he had just the ammunition (i.e., books) to send so his "friend" could see what the real truth looked like in print.

Duplessis-Mornay wrote back on 3 February 1599. He was not displeased to receive books critical of his, he assured our author. Controversy clarified truth. Yet he was not impressed by the books because they were written in bad faith. Besides, they were not refutations of his own scholarship for they merely skimmed surface issues. Their authors were bent on evasion, pure and simple.[55] He marveled that Raemond could believe that he had much leisure for reading such trivia, but he would still be glad of a gift of Raemond's own works. He did not think Cardinal Baronius as discriminating as he was diligent; he judged according to the convenience of his predispositions.[56] If the cardinal's church did not take reform of its abuses seriously, it would lose its best members. Duplessis-Mornay was not going to admit that the Roman church was winning back its lost sheep. He closed regretting that by law his books were being burned in cities such as Toulouse and Bordeaux.[57] As if recalling Raemond's first letter urging that books rather than fire and steel govern differences in opinion between the two sects, Duplessis-Mornay queried: "How can you allow such a dishonor to your cause, that it cannot defend itself except by prohibitions? that to the light of our reason it has nothing to oppose but flames?"[58]

Did Raemond squirm a little reading this last? Protestant books were forbidden Catholics in all conscience, whether they had or had not yet made their way onto the *Index*. Raemond had been obliged to come to terms with the *Index* when he applied for and received permission to study heretical works in order to win papal approval for his research into heresy. He must have recognized the justice of his correspondent's prayer that God enlighten him, Raemond, as to his preferences for the divine service. It was nothing more than he had wished for the governor of Saumur, after all.

So ended the communication between these two men. But what more could either add? Each believed God disapproved of the other side's view of religion and of history. Neither believed he could be making any errors, nor that the other could have any reason on his side. Each felt God had designed the universe with his very own conception of truth in mind.

Etienne Pasquier

It would be wrong to think that only with Huguenots like Duplessis-Mornay did Raemond differ on matters of religion and history, for he differed with some Catholics as well. His correspondence with Etienne Pasquier, the noted author, lawyer, and publicist, and after 1585, advocate general in the *Chambre des Comptes* of Paris, is a case in point. Only two of Pasquier's letters to Raemond have survived and none of Raemond's to him, but the two existing letters are so explicit, and Raemond's positions so clearly indicated in them, that it is possible to reconstruct his part in the interchange.

Pasquier's career was in some respects similar to Raemond's. Eleven years Raemond's senior, this native Parisian was educated at the College of Presles, too, and studied with Peter Ramus. Later, he attended (for one year) the University of Toulouse, as had Raemond. He was attracted to the lectures in law of Jacques Cujas.[59] Drawn toward literature, he yet accepted the advocate generalcy late in life, and kept it until his retirement. But it was Pasquier's compilation of French historical sources, which he annotated and began (1560) to publish as the *Recherches de la France*, that secured his fame. No more than Raemond did he consider himself a professional historian. Occasionally, he made silly errors, one of which Raemond caught. (See chap. 4.) Typically, Pasquier held very definite views on matters of great significance. Nothing was more important to him than the relations between church and state, for he was an ardent Gallican Catholic and a fierce critic of the Jesuit order. His views on Jesuits won him much publicity and the applause of like-minded Catholics. Raemond was not one of them. He and Pasquier stood on opposite sides of a divide formed by the tradition of the Gallican Liberties of the French church, a divide that had separated Romanists from nationally minded Frenchmen for centuries.[60] The issues were complex. Those who claimed that the French church had ancient rights generally regarded freedom from papal interference in French temporal affairs and from onerous financial exactions the sine qua non of royal and national independence.[61]

Traditionally, the rights of the Gallican church had found their heartiest supporters among members of the *parlements*. During the 1590s, Henry IV's determination to regularize the relations between his government and Rome by publishing the long delayed Tridentine conciliar reforms brought the parlementary opposition to attention. As one authority put it, "The *Parlement* thinks it must defend the king against himself."[62] The conviction that Henry IV was about to imperil his own independence was a common parlementary view, here typified by Pasquier but not shared by Raemond.

It is difficult to say with certainty why Raemond could remain sanguine with respect to the judicial and legislative integrity of the crown when so many other magistrates felt such concern. Perhaps he shared with his king a great confidence that men of good will and conscience could, after so much civil and religious strife, get along with one another under a king determined (as Henry IV was) to give everyone his due. Henry IV had insisted that the publication of the conciliar reforms of Trent not infringe on the temporal rights of France:

> "Now that I am myself the defender of the rights of the crown and of the liberties of the Gallican Church," observed Henry to his councilors, "I fear no disorder; should any turbulent spirit wish to cause some, the means will be lacking. But those of the reformed religion have no longer anything to fear, since a formal clause guarantees the maintenance of the Edict of Nantes, and consequently, their tranquillity."[63]

The ultramontanists, those who rejoiced in the thought that between Rome and France there could be no outstanding conflicts after the publication of the Tridentine reforms, were expecting this victory to take place from the 1570s on, but an opposition made up partly of Huguenots, and partly of Gallican Catholics, delayed the publication and frustrated the ultramontane party.[64]

Pasquier was a friend of Montaigne's, and it is altogether likely that he had met Raemond in Bordeaux. It is certain that he admired Raemond's writing for he cited him as one of four French writers (along with Monluc,[65] Montaigne, and du Bartas, the poet) among Gascony's greatest literary talents.[66] He had in particular liked the great "History of Heresy," which he noted dealt with the "mutation" of religions.[67] When Pasquier read the work it was not yet published, for he noted that it stopped somewhere in the middle of Raemond's treatment of the Society of Jesus.[68] Pasquier had been upset by the fervor Raemond displayed for the Jesuits, to whom he devoted two chapters of his bulky work. He did not agree that the Jesuits were the best let alone the only remedy for a Europe plagued by reform. Indeed, he felt the "remedy" might prove more harmful than the disease. France had a better remedy to protect her against a worse infection (papal domination), namely, the Gallican church. Whenever the Faculty of Theology in Paris felt that Gallicanism was threatened, there was another prescription at hand—an ecumenical council that would correct the erring pope. Such a council in the past had saved not only the Gallican liberties, but the state as well. Councils, Pasquier felt, protected the royal prestige. The fact that they were superior to the pope was firmly established and not at all heretical.

The writer then proceeded to ask why Gallicanism ought to be considered merely French, when in fact the universal church had always entertained similar notions. He had support for this point of view from other *politiques* who wished to expand the Gallican privileges to other states.[69] It was not that Pasquier was unaware of the admirable work Jesuits had done in proselytizing, but he felt Raemond exaggerated its uniqueness. Jesuits were not alone in the field against unbelief, nor could they claim they alone were laboring in the vineyards.[70]

Pasquier raised other objections to Jesuits. He disliked their blind obedience to the pope, and they involved themselves needlessly in international politics, transferring kingdoms about almost at will. Why, they would, he believed, make the French king their slave if they could. Worse, they were murderers! They encouraged "âmes idiotes" to rebel against kings and even to assassinate them![71]

Pasquier's arguments had been fashioned in such a way as to make the Jesuit order appear as a revolutionary rather than as a conservative body. He pointed out that the order was as much a new religion as was Lutheranism, a similarity he insisted upon despite external differences. Both groups fought against legitimately constituted secular authority, opposing such rulers as Charles V or France's own Charles IX and Henry III. The fame of Jesuits as preachers threatened French consciences. They could easily ruin the Gallican church before anyone could stop them. Their most pernicious doctrine, that popes were superior to secular rulers, meant that in the event a pope censured a French king, every Jesuit in France would become an enemy of the state. They could even promote civil disobedience in the populace: "Because the Jesuits will have taught them that it is part of our Christian faith to believe that the pope can whenever it pleases him dispose of every kingdom."[72] Pasquier sought to strengthen popular support for kings against popes; he believed this to be the conservative position. Raemond, however, believed the conservative position could only allow popular, royal, and papal cooperation for the protection of the church, when and if it were threatened. He was probably not able to consider a French policy opposed to papalism, for he denied the legitimacy of any differences between national policy and papal policy.[73]

Pasquier did not agree with Raemond that Luther was the primary cause of the Reformation. Instead, he believed that the ill-advised policies of Pope Leo X were to blame. Leo had properly proclaimed a crusade against the Porte and a sale of indulgences to finance it, but after the death of the aggressive Selim I (in 1520), the need for the crusade disappeared, and the sale of indulgences became a convenient method for financing nonspiritual projects. Pasquier pointed out that the pope was not the sole party to benefit from such traffic. Francis I and several other princes had also pocketed monies collected for spiritual purposes. Leo X, "Pape facile et debonnaire," was egged on by his *Curia* and abetted by regional prelates whose avarice was unrestrained.[74] Such men preached that the amount of money donated stood in direct proportion to the amount of pardon a sinner could anticipate. Luther was not all wrong to preach against indulgences. He got out of hand only when he began to attack papal authority on general grounds. A weak pope, a passel of flattering scholars, ill counsel and abrogation of the Pragmatic Sanction[75] all contributed to weaken Roman prestige and good discipline in France and in other countries as well.[76]

Pasquier resented the politicization of religion, and believed the Concordat of 1516,[77] signed by Francis I and Leo X in Bologna, had unfortunately produced a situation that contributed to it. He bitterly regretted the fact that Leo X and secular princes had sacrificed the spiritual needs of the faithful to politics, appointing "gens de nulle valeur" — married men, wenchers, militarists, and even Huguenots to church positions.[78] Pasquier wanted strong monarchs to promote able, reform-minded men to the church, foregoing the temptations of a kind of spoils-system mentality, which he believed had brought on the Protestant Reformation.

Although the Tridentine reforms would give too much power over clerical appointments to Rome, he could not be sure the crown's candidates would be any more devoted to spiritual matters. He appears to have trusted no one. Probably he would have wished to give the French church preponderant power over French clerical appointments, i.e., to return to the system that had prevailed prior to 1516. Since that was not feasible, Pasquier's letter to Raemond ended on a desolate note. Given the fact of a "generale desbauche" in the church, it was not likely that a truly reform-minded papacy would ever emerge to give heresy the coup de grace. The pope should reform — or the king should. He was quite dubious that either would in fact do so, or that mere writing would do much good.

Against Pasquier's general indictment of the venal papacy and its worldly clergy, Raemond's optimism stands out. Raemond quite agreed that Leo X had willingly shed the burdens of church governance for the "plaisirs du repos,"[79] but he preferred to shift the major blame from Leo to his *Curia*. He wrote of that pope that "he was poorly informed about the disorders in Germany, and heard only one side of the matter."[80] Raemond preferred to speak as well of popes as possible, and when not possible, to accuse personalities rather than institutions. His history of the reform differs from Pasquier's analysis chiefly in the fact that Pasquier was more concerned with institutions and their effects on religion than was Raemond, who stressed the weakness of men in their individual capacities. Whereas Pasquier mourned the passing of particular legal structures which had guaranteed Gallican liberties, Raemond never alluded to laws, concordats, or the rights of the French church. The decay of religion was inevitable to him. It was not a function of structure, but of nature: "There is no discipline so well-established, even in God's house, which does not in the end change and degenerate. Vice grows stronger as laws grow older. It's the way of the world; here everything gets worse."[81] There was still hope, for heresy would be laid to rest[82] through the efforts of the Jesuits, whom Raemond hailed as the order of heroes, which would sweep the field against heresy or Protestantism.[83]

Less than a century later, Louis XIV would revoke the Edict of Nantes and declare the nation of France to be wholly Catholic. Raemond's prediction would come true. It would not make France a better country, certainly, nor a more victorious one. Indeed, uniformity of religion in France during the seventeenth and throughout the eighteenth century coincided with a rise in anti-clericalism and in secular thought that would have distressed both

Pasquier and Raemond.[84] Neither papal reform, the patronage of reformed royalty (during the reign of Henry IV), nor the persecution of unreformed royalty would prove successful in keeping religious enthusiasm (or intellectual inquiry) amenable to discipline imposed from an arbitrary state or by ecclesiastical fiat in subsequent centuries.[85]

3
Pen and *Parlement*

Raemond's first career began in 1570 with the purchase of his *conseiller*'s seat in the Bordeaux *Parlement* from his friend, Montaigne. It was a career that brought him provincial fame and respect. He seems to have earned it, for he devoted long hours to his magisterial duties. Being in the public eye meant that he was liable to the penalties as well as the prerogatives of his position, and he was illegally detained for political reasons on two occasions. As is the case with every judge, not all his decisions at the bench were popular, yet he reaped more advantages than criticism from his thirty-one years of public service. Had he exercised just this one occupation, he would have enjoyed a modest place in the history of his adopted city and in Guyenne as a man of learning, a devotee of the arts and beautifier of Bordeaux, and as a conservative judge who performed the often tedious chores of a *conseiller* without stint of time or energy.

But Raemond took upon himself the burden of a second career. He became, with the publication of the *Erreur Populaire de la Papesse Jane* (1587),[1] a writer of polemical history, a defender of Catholicism in the grand manner of the Counter-Reformation: devout, dogmatic, didactic, and dedicated. It was this second rôle for which he trained on the job, as it were,[2] that made him not merely a figure of provincial interest, but of national stature. Florimond de Raemond became a best-selling author[3] and a star in the eyes of co-religionists for whom the ultimate success of their cause was, in the 1580s and 1590s, still a matter of doubt, and for whom the Edict of Nantes represented a definite defeat.[4] In these years the *Erreur Populaire* and the *Anti-Christ* (1597) served as defensive historical weapons for a Catholic polemical arsenal, which was forged mainly in Latin[5] (except for ephemeral literature), and thus useless to the majority of literate faithful, limited as they were to reading French. For a time it was not wholly clear that the old religion would be capable of reasserting itself in the spiritual dimension after a prolonged period of disorganization, caused in part by a syphoning of its energies into political activities. Of these, the dubious and self-interested program of the Catholic League had compromised, if not the spiritual credibility of Catholicism, at least its ability to tap the energies of its most intelligent and talented adherents, the *politiques* and the Gallican Catholics.[6]

Raemond's greatest publishing success was his posthumous "History of Heresy" first published in 1605. Unfortunately, he did not live to find satisfaction in its eighteen appearances in print during the seventeenth century.[7] It may be pertinent to note that of those appearances, only two occurred during the reign of Henry IV, whose policies with respect to religion have been termed "undulating"[8] and "vacillating,"[9] but which were certainly intended to effect a conciliation between the two parties.[10] Henry IV's political instincts were of greater significance than his religious beliefs; they told him that while religious uniformity might be more appropriate for monarchic rule, France could not permit itself the "luxury" of uniformity. France needed tranquility; Henry IV tried to tranquilize it. The precarious balance maintained by him for political reasons was, also for political reasons, deliberately tilted by the subsequent reigns of Louis XIII and Louis XIV. Against the erosion of Protestant privileges, Raemond's last historical polemic must be assessed. It was obviously the book for the times. The title itself predicted the demise of heresy; the intense pressure that absolutism brought to hear on dissidence prepared the market for brisk sales, though the royalties that accrued were to be paid posthumously.

Pope Joan, the Popular Error

In 1587 an anonymous sixty-eight page volume entitled *Erreur Populaire de la Papesse Jane* was published in Bordeaux by the firm of S. Millanges. The next year the same title, still anonymous, emerged again, but this time with one hundred forty-four pages; and when the work was printed for the third time in 1594, it comprised three hundred and sixteen pages and included the name of the author: Florimond de Raemond, "conseiller du roy au Parlement de Bourdeaus."[11] The increased length was a reflection of the acute interest in the topic of a female papal reign having occurred in the ninth or perhaps tenth century. The printer himself had seen fit to address the "friendly reader," informing him that the author had found the subject on everyone's lips before deciding to treat the matter.[12] Raemond felt rather uncomfortable about the length of the completed book, observing that it was the fault of the subject, which was itself so fertile. Although it had seemed on the face of it to be a sterile topic, he had found that was not the case. In the author's "Note to the Reader" in the 1594 edition, Raemond confided that aside from the complexity of the legend, he had been obliged to expand his original draft because it had been challenged by a man to whom he referred as R. T. of Béarn. He insisted that because of R. T.'s temerity he, Raemond, had been obliged to abandon his preference for anonymity. While he refused, by way of revenge, to publish R. T.'s name, he did identify him as a minister and, somewhat surprisingly, did not scruple to publish the man's objections to his *Erreur Populaire*.[13] Raemond's painful admissions of inadequacy (at one point he called his research a series of "little abortions")[14] and his rather servile inclusion of R. T.'s hostile review of his book, point to a lack of confidence, a fund of insecurity that dogged the efforts of this devout warrior for the Counter-Reformation. We cannot fully understand Raemond unless we remind ourselves that the Catholic party of the 1590s had no way of knowing the very real success their religion would enjoy in the era that followed the civil war period. Only one year before the expanded *Erreur Populaire* of 1594 appeared in local booksellers' windows had the king finally decided to which religion he belonged—for the second time! When Raemond chose his weapons—verbosity, irony, satire, and a tone of supreme confidence—was the last not intended to cloak the fears he entertained for the welfare of the body politic and the cultural milieu of which he was a spokesman and for which he was an apologist?

Monluc's Editor

In 1592 Raemond put to press the first edition of the *Commentaires* of the Catholic commander Blaise de Monluc. It was the first of two works he would edit or publish that were written by men he admired.[15] A modern critic has called Monluc's memoirs a kind of modern statue, more closely approaching the cinematographer's art than the historian's, for Monluc was very free in his attitude toward historical evidence.[16] As we have already seen, Raemond had certain tendencies in the same direction.[17] He had, however, a strong sense of duty that the living have toward history and an antiquarian's sense of reverence for the past, which served him in very good stead as an editor, and in some ways, as an historian.

Certainly he brought to the task of editing Monluc's memoirs a great deal of enthusiasm. To Raemond, Monluc was a great hero and worthy of emulation. Like Montaigne, who rather regretted the passivity of a modern nobleman's normal (i.e., peaceful) lifestyle,[18] Raemond admired the military mode and Gascony's military heritage.[19] He introduced his subject as a model of restraint and prudence, and a devoted servant of the state.[20]

In considering Raemond's performance as an editor of Monluc's memoirs, two major facts emerge: one is that Raemond's adulation of Monluc, the loyal servant of his king, had an inevitable impact on his own reputation as a fire-eating, intolerant kind of Catholic; the second is that Raemond proved himself to be a basically honest, if not wholly disingenuous craftsman.

To the younger generation Raemond introduced Monluc as a man who had been tireless in his service to France:

> Here lie the bones of such a one—
> Monluc! whose work was never done.[21]

To Raemond's Huguenot compatriots, however, it was not Monluc's unflagging energy that most distinguished him, but his gratuitous cruelty toward them in the civil wars of the southwest. Monluc had become a symbol of calculated sadism to the reformed, a commander who boasted that hanging Huguenots by their necks along the roadsides was a certain inducement toward loyalty, that he had hanged seventy such in the market place of Targon, and had "rounded the number off" by hanging thirty from the trees nearby. Though Monluc grew more reflective and more pacific in his later years,[22] his exploits were not forgotten by the victims' co-religionists. Even though Raemond's admiration for the old soldier was not unique, and was, indeed, shared by Henry IV[23] one need not wonder that the French Huguenots must have been appalled by Raemond's opinion that the *Commentaires* were "a good lesson for any soldier, and still more for a captain of troops."[24] It is all too apparent that Raemond enjoyed a vicarious thrill of adventure as he studied the account, although it was mildewed and crumbling from excessive neglect by Monluc's heirs. He could not help comparing the literary efforts of Monluc to record history with his own. The difference between them was that of the participant's firsthand recollections and the gentleman's secondhand research: "One cannot help but observe what a difference there is between a history written by an idle fellow comfortably and delicately nourished on the dust of books and records, to that written by an old captain and soldier, raised in the dust of armies and of battles."[25] Military exploits appeared to him not just good reading, but good living as well. His own years had been devoted to books and art, to court dockets and paperwork of the most tedious sort even though his family history was Gascon and military. What was this scion of the Counts Raymond of Toulouse doing if not writing history amid the dust of his own library, while his fellow noblemen were glorying in (if not actual battles) the fond memories of battles fought by their fathers and grandfathers? Fortunately for posterity's sake, Raemond accepted the task of editing Monluc, snatching the brittle pages from "the nonchalence of the Monlucs who had let the manuscript moulder."[26]

The conditions of his editing labors were not solely due to the poor state in which he found the manuscript; his inability to check the details (especially with regard to Italian names) of Monluc's foreign exploits troubled him. He did not have at his disposal adequate source materials for Italy. If, as Henry IV once remarked, the *Commentaires* were the soldier's Bible, then like that text it, too, had to be taken on faith.[27]

The more serious problems for Raemond were those presented by the nature of the material. He urged his readers to rise above their own prejudices and not to get upset by Monluc's faithful self-portrait—"not perhaps to your particular taste"—as he blandly observed to his readers.[28] Despite the extreme naïveté of this plea and the chilly reception that his Protestant readers must have given it, many of his compatriots were aware that civil war atrocities had been committed by both sides. In fact, Raemond was not above recognizing that war brutalizes men and causes them to forget their Christianity. In his *Anti-Christ* he commented wryly on the fact that the reformed had given the Catholics excellent training in every kind of cruelty, with the result that the faithful (Catholics) had become masters of cruelty themselves.[29] Such admissions were not forth-coming in his edition of the *Commentaires*, however, and it remained a monument to an untarnished hero in the eyes of the least tolerant Catholic readers.

Two modern editors of the *Commentaires* have turned their attention to Raemond's capacity in this connection. The first, Alphonse De Ruble, whose second edition appeared in 1864–1872, believed Raemond had taken pains to protect himself from criticism by suppressing some vignettes of the wars and by softening certain of Monluc's opinions.[30] He thought the fragility of the text had caused some of the editorial changes made by Raemond, but those that bothered him most were changes he felt Raemond had made in Monluc's virile original, substituting correct but insipid phrases for the old soldier's rugged, but colorful, prose. The motive De Ruble ascribed to Raemond in this kind of activity was a desire to make a rough personality more attractive to a later, more refined sixteenth-century taste.[31] If De Ruble was right, then Raemond emerges as a politic editor less concerned with honesty than with his own welfare or the book's salability.

The second modern editor of the *Commentaires*, Paul Courteault, disagreed with De Ruble's harsh judgment of Raemond. He pointed out that the changes in Monluc's writing were made by none other than Monluc himself in the soldier-author's continuous revision of his memoirs between the years 1571 and 1577. Courteault portrayed the old soldier as a man whom age made wiser.[32] Monluc's second manuscript had taken on an altogether different tone from his first, and thus, his first editor was not guilty of cosmetic surgery. Courteault took the trouble to point out passages that appeared in the first edition which were unflattering to Monluc. Had Raemond been merely high-handed in his approach to historical materials, Courteault reasoned, he would never have included them, given his admiration for Monluc.[33] Only once did Courteault find Raemond guilty of taking self-preserving measures. The occasion was Monluc's reference to Catholic priests—Italians—whom he had forced to take up arms on behalf of Francis I. Since Henry IV was, at the moment Raemond was wrestling with his work, prosecuting some clerical obstructionists, members of the Catholic League in Bordeaux, Raemond omitted the incident. Apparently the issue of clerical conscience versus clerical patriotism was considered too sensitive by him. He may not have wished to compromise himself with League sympathizers.[34]

In other instances Courteault found Raemond guilty of suppression of Monluc's material, but his conclusion was that the suppressions were dictated by collegial loyalty on the part of Raemond vis-à-vis his fellow *parlementaires*. Monluc, for example, had criticized the Bordeaux magistrates and those of Agen for inadequate subsidies for repressive measures taken against the Huguenots of Blaye, a town some thirty-three kilometres northwest of Bordeaux on the Gironde River. On another occasion, Monluc had charged that newcomers to the Bordeaux *Parlement* sided more often with Huguenots than with Catholics on certain issues.[35] Again, Monluc had attacked a member of the magistracy, one Herman de Sevin, member of the *Presidial* of Agen, and a close friend of Raemond's friends, the Malvyns.[36] These incidents did not make their way into the first edition of the *Commentaires*, nor did several others relating to the *gens de robe*, more familiarly known as the *robins*.[37] Courteault found a half dozen incidents suppressed in Raemond's edition, and very few changes made in an effort to improve the original manuscript's style, grammar, and diction. Stylistic changes he attributed to the *ambition littéraire* of Monluc himself.[38]

Courteault's careful study of Raemond's editorial activity provides useful indices with which we may begin to judge his performance as a historian. Through Courteault's study of Monluc, we learn that Raemond was concerned to record most facts faithfully, loathe to sacrifice Monluc's rougher diction to please a gentler age, distressed by limited source material, and willing to present evidence not flattering to a man he regarded as a patriotic hero. We are also alerted to Raemond's tendencies to suppress information when it seemed prudent or politic to do so, or when his sense of particular loyalty (as to his fellow magistrates) excused him in his own judgment from telling the whole truth.

Prudence in the context of sixteenth-century France is most understandable; an irritated king could prove more damaging to an author's welfare than negative reviews to a modern scholar's. Besides, when Raemond set to work on the Monluc material in 1591, France was still in the throes of civil war. Particular loyalties, in this case to his fellow public servants, are similarly explainable in a country not yet accustomed to the uniformity which absolutism would oblige during the next century. The corporatism of medieval France lived on in the independent attitudes of its *parlementaires* and its regional dignitaries. Prudence and particularism: Are they not still temptations for journalists? Politicians? Writers? Historians? And insofar as they succumb to temptation, do they not abandon the trust that their positions of responsibility carry with them? Raemond was not a bad editor of Monluc, in Courteault's opinion, or an incompetent historian in ours. Yet, every time he suppressed a pertinent fact, he reverted to a kind of polemic, for polemics are rooted in half-truths. Whether Raemond was unusual in this respect will be explored more thoroughly in subsequent chapters.

Antichrist

Between 1594 and 1596 Raemond was hard at work on his second original work, *L'Anti-Christ*. The legend of the Antichrist (see chap. 5) had enjoyed a splendid revival during the sixteenth century, and even its own reformation; Protestants were bent on associating the papacy with the bogey of Jesus's great enemy. Frenchmen who were well-educated in the Latin tongue could arm themselves against the insistence of Luther, Bale, Calvin, and other Protestant works which incontrovertibly proved that the pope was Antichrist by choosing Catholic works (fewer in number, but equally in Latin) which proved definitively that he was not.[39] The only book in French on the subject was one written by a Calvinist, Lambert Daneau.[40] Raemond had achieved considerable publicity and favorable response from his Catholic audience for the *Erreur Populaire*.[41] There was no reason to think the Antichrist legend would not produce a similar effect, yet he needed some encouragement before plunging once more into the inevitable maelstrom of critical response.

Encouragement came from his friend, Geoffroy de Malvyn,[42] to whom Raemond had dedicated one of his Tertullian translations.[43] Malvyn had lavished so much praise on Raemond that our author felt genuinely embarrassed. In a letter dated 5 November 1596, Raemond disclaimed any especial writing ability. He compared his literary voice to that of a broken reed. Whereas Malvyn wrote with the sweetest style, he reproached the "saltpeter and sulphurous strains" that "fell in great droplets" from his own pen.[44] He expressed anxiety over the fate of the *Anti-Christ*, which he awaited momentarily from Lyon.[45] He expected the usual insults and calumnies from his enemies.[46]

Benchmarks

Fifteen ninety-four was a very productive year for Raemond.[47] The next year saw the appearance of his edition of Sponde's *Reponse* to Bèze, and he was finishing the *Anti-Christ*. He had been thoroughly hooked by his writing career, whatever he might say to the contrary, and he was casting about for another subject. He had several in mind that never came to fruition.[48] It is possible that in the later 1590s Raemond went to Germany to gather materials for his next book, the "History of Heresy," for in the 1599 edition of the *Erreur Populaire* (or *L'Anti-Papesse*) he mentioned having recently returned from Wittenberg.[49] He did not neglect his magisterial duties, however, and these could not have been easy to perform. In the 1590s France was a country of divided loyalties. On several occasions he must have wished himself still in Germany, comparatively free from the ordinary cares of the bench. His career became a matter of public controversy toward the end of his life when the pamphlet of reformed grievances was published (1597) naming him as one of their causes for discontent.[50]

This popular edition of complaints had been compiled several years earlier by the reformed party when Henry IV was on the point of converting to Catholicism. The Huguenots were dismayed by the possibility of his abandoning their interests, and they prepared a detailed list of their major problems. One of the most troublesome was the incursion of Catholics into government offices (*charges*) at the expense of Huguenots who felt more deserving in view of their unimpeachable record of loyalty to Henry of Navarre. They pointed to the spotty record of Catholics, many of whom had supported the Guise family and the League during the civil wars. They were chagrined that the king seemed to be favoring a formerly rebellious group against his own best interests. While Henry made fair promises to his erstwhile comrades of the reformed faith, he was not able to assure that those promises would be honored by locals or even by the government's own servants.

In the early 1590s, the Huguenots drew up grievance lists or *cahiers* that were to be submitted to the king. The *Plaintes*, (1597), similar to the *Gravamina* or grievances of the Conciliar period, was a document of over two hundred complaints of Huguenots against people or circumstances that troubled them. Three of these were complaints about Raemond. The first of them stated that he had tried to extort funds from Protestant defendants in order to recoup his loss in ransom money paid in 1572 during the kidnapping incident. Raemond's first biographer dismissed this as impossible to believe.[51] His opinion is persuasive, for there is no evidence that Raemond sought revenge on Protestants in this peculiarly mercenary manner. The other two grievances deserve closer inspection,[52] not merely because of the obligation to write the most complete life of Raemond possible, or even because the charges might be untrue and the historical record deserves to be cleared. Both considerations merit a close scrutiny of evidence. Still, it is the task of this study to assess fairly Raemond's performance as an historian and polemicist. If the compilers of the *Plaintes* had offered convincing evidence that he was a corrupt judge, one who deprived Protestants of their legal rights on account of his own religious beliefs, Raemond would deserve to be condemned for perverting his office. It would be more likely that such a judge would conduct his writing of history with a mind predisposed to condemning those with whom he took exception. Since, however, the *Plaintes* do not provide evidence of malfeasance, the task of determining how fair an historian Raemond was ought to be considered on its own merits.

The question to ask, then, is how the process of writing even polemical history was a function of shared public perceptions, rather than of private and personal experience. To shed light on this matter a detailed analysis follows of the two remaining charges, both of which were subsumed under the seventeenth-century dictum: *Judicat sine conscientia*.[53]

Before turning to the two remaining charges, it is helpful to review the social context that gave rise to the *Plaintes*. The whole configuration of reformed grievances amounted to what we now could term civil rights issues. These included rights of employment, selection of living space, securing educational facilities, obtaining justice in law courts, and so on. Religious issues were, of course, prime. No issue was more troublesome than that of securing burial grounds. Beginning with the Edict of Saint-Germain-en-Laye (1570), the state sought to make separate provisions for Protestant burial by obliging magistrates to provide Protestants with separate burial sites in the various towns of France. In the 1590s the situation deteriorated due to the influence of the Catholic League. Civic obstruction and popular prejudice produced situations that made decent Protestant funerals almost impossible. The despised sect, refused burial in its own parish churches and cemeteries on the grounds that they were Catholic parishes and Catholic cemeteries, was now being refused the necessary sites for its own cemeteries. Those already granted to them, were increasingly wrested away. The result was that many Protestants were obliged to make long journeys to find burial places for their dead. Unpleasant incidents attendant on funeral processions were numerous. Unwelcome attention from local toughs and even from normally law-abiding Catholics led by zealous priests, produced frightful scenes and aggravated civil unrest.[54]

Under relentless pressure from their Catholic neighbors and their religious leaders, in the 1590s Protestants began to protest exclusion from the local Catholic parish cemetery or from burial in the local Catholic parish church itself. They named two groups of Frenchmen particularly responsible in their eyes for their suffering — the clerics and the magistrates.[55] While we need not trouble ourselves here over the demands they made of the state with respect to religion,[56] those they made with respect to judicial procedure concern us directly. They asked for "non-suspect judges," and for courts made up of Protestants as well as Catholics.[57] They cited the *Parlement* of Bordeaux for having ousted a Protestant *résidial*[58] in the town of Bergerac and given his office to a Catholic. This was a typical kind of injustice[59] — one that cast gloom over the prospects of the reformed for obtaining justice. While many other *parlements* were named for their unfair and harsh practices, the Bordeaux body was among those mentioned most frequently as an offender, along with their counterparts at Toulouse and Rouen. The Bordeaux *Parlement* was accused of illegalities as well as brutalities, prompting the seventeenth-century Protestant historian of the Edict of Nantes, Élie Benoist, to exclaim: "The *Parlements* did more harm by their ill will, than the king could by his good will remedy."[60] In particular, the Bordeaux *Parlement* had offended by passing a law sometime in 1595 or 1596 making it legal to disinter a Protestant corpse which had been buried for less than ten years in a Catholic cemetery.[61] In fact, similar laws had been passed by the *Parlements* of Rouen, Paris, and Toulouse, and in the districts of Angers and Touraine, but only oblique references were made to those places in the *Plaintes*.[62] In addition, only Raemond's name was mentioned as one who had ordered such disinterment.[63] Hence, the *Parlement* of Bordeaux bore the lion's share of responsibility in this publication, and Raemond the largest share of its guilt. He chafed considerably over this:

> It was the main reason for the capital hatred which the whole Calvinist party conceived against me, for having pronounced the judgment before the court for disinterring one of their religion. I am not trying to disavow my opinion, but it was not my judgment; it was the Court's: nevertheless, some of them ever afterward try to destroy my name, setting their teeth into my reputation, and blackening it with their malice. Which prompted me to respond in a little pamphlet, prepared by my hands to save me from theirs.[64]

Despite the fact that Raemond was no more responsible than the collective group, his position in the eyes of the Huguenots may well have approached the diabolic. After all, vampires were widely believed to dig up dead bodies, and ghouls and vampires were regarded popularly as minions of the devil. In an age in which both Catholics and Protestants eyed each other as the devil's helpers, it was not to be supposed that the reformed would view Raemond's role in the disinterment in the same detached way he did.

In order to appreciate Raemond's exasperation with what he termed the unreasonableness of the authors of the *Plaintes* and of the reformed party generally, one must begin by reviewing his feelings about Calvinist attitudes regarding death. Of course, as a recent historian of the subject has remarked, death is a taboo subject, and coming to grips with it is difficult indeed.[65]

Raemond devoted a whole chapter in "The History of Heresy" to death and its observance.[66] He pointed out that Jews, Muslims, and Catholics all considered proper funeral ceremonies reasonable and appropriate. He tried to show that all except the reformed buried their dead in hallowed ground. Calvinists were worse than Lutherans and Anabaptists, for they had eschewed all pomp and ceremonies and prayers.[67] Although Raemond erred in his contention that John Calvin had outlawed all burial services,[68] he was correct in surmising that there was indeed a tendency within Calvinist thought to pare such ceremonies to an absolute minimum. As a modern commentator on Calvinist funerary tradition has observed, "In the Reformed tradition it is often a question of discussing the absence of any burial rite rather than the nature of the rite itself."[69] Although Calvin's disciple, John Knox, would have preferred to dispense with any and all ceremonies, not even he interfered with congregations that continued to use graveside sermons and prayers, and such groups persisted in Calvinist churches in Scotland until the 1630s.[70] It is quite likely that the vestiges of a Catholic and more ceremonial past lingered among the French Huguenots as well. In matters of mind and the heart it has been noted, "l'evolution des mentalités se fait lentement."[71]

Raemond wrote primarily to enforce the Catholic "mentality" or viewpoint, and he did so by underscoring a kind of mechanical homogeneity of practice among Calvinists. He also wished his readers to believe that these reformed people were devoid of respect for their own dead. This was far from true, as Calvin and Knox and their followers attested repeatedly. One senses the dilemma in which Calvinists found themselves, torn between a sincere wish to avoid what they felt to be Catholic superstitious practices and their own emotional need to recognize the grandeur as well as the transitoriness of the human condition. Raemond's account of his behavior with respect to the disinterment (his insistence on collegial responsibility for it) was technically correct. On the other hand, his feelings of outrage and contempt were the product of a mentality that could not contemplate religious pluralism with equanimity, even though he recognized that for the present a policy of toleration was indicated: "The unfortunate fact is that in this kingdom it is still necessary to tolerate diversity of religion."[72]

In the work on "heresy" he was incapable of presenting the whole story of Protestant concern over burial of their dead. He was right to say that the reformed did not believe that some soil was more sacred, hence more suitable for burials, than other soil. They did indeed wish to avoid what they considered a superstitious practice — the sanctification of church ground by means of certain ceremonies and "incantations." It was true that Calvinists resorted to garden burials in order to avoid what to them was mere superstition, but Raemond did not mention the fact that not all Calvinists wished to resort to backyard burials. Some wanted to be buried in their parish churches or parish cemeteries, even though these were Catholic, because their ancestors had traditionally been laid to rest in those places.[73] He deliberately avoided mention of the fact that Protestants would have preferred in most cases to accompany their dead to their resting place. He deliberately hoped to persuade his readers that mourning the dead was considered un-Protestant. In reality it was not. His insistence that the reformed had always preferred their own gardens for burial until the 1590s, when the devil made them change their tune, was a gross distortion. The fact was that continual persecution from the Catholic zealots made them more aggressive in their demands to be permitted to use parish facilities.[74]

Raemond justified the position his court had taken in connection with the disinterment on canonical and historical grounds. He reminded his readers that the Catholic church alone had determined who could and who could not be permitted burial in its designated burial sites. Even the pagans, he argued, gave full control of cemeteries to priests, a policy Gregory of Tours had, he said, reaffirmed for the Christian church.[75] The church had traditionally excluded certain people, for example, heretics and the excommunicated. Tradition gave magistrates such as himself only the power to enable the church to enforce its own will. Magistrates were policemen at the service of the ecclesiastical authorities.[76] Apart from such traditional use of the magistracy, Raemond argued that the case was one of property rights. The Catholic church was the owner of its cemeteries and, hence, had proprietary rights over their use.[77] If that argument was not sufficiently persuasive, Calvinists ought to remember that Catholic practice included many rites that the reformed considered abominations. For that reason Catholics were not allowed to share the same cemetery with Calvinists. Separated in life, Raemond reasoned, the two groups naturally had to be separated in death.[78] Anything less would contaminate the church. Arguments such as the last were clearly designed to wound, and wound deeply, for no group could easily tolerate a bald assertion that its members are offensive by their very presence, more so dead than alive![79] Yet Raemond's other arguments were not unreasonable or even incorrect. The church had traditionally been permitted to decide whom it would bury on its own grounds, and the question was indeed a matter of property rights as well as of religious propriety. The *leit-motif* of both the historical and the proprietary arguments was that the established custom of a homogeneous Catholic, ultramontanist and provincial, rather than national past, was sacrosanct and not subject to review. Such assumptions were appropriate, as Raemond believed, to pre-Reformation France. They were not appropriate for the sixteenth century with its aggressive national monarchy and its religious diversity. The juridical appropriateness of Raemond's arguments was correct. The ethical inappropriateness of those same arguments escaped his notice wholly. Nevertheless he did make one argument which, had it been his only one, might have permitted contemporaries to consider more calmly the benefits of toleration which Raemond viewed unenthusiastically as a mere necessary evil: "Laws must be equalized and weighted according to one and the same standard. It is no longer permissible for you, really less, to trouble the Catholic in the exercise of his religion. The curate has no more obligation to share burial facilities with Calvinists than the minister does to share the sacramental supper of his table with Catholics."[80] Such sentiments were also present in the Edict of Nantes. Laws were to guarantee all Frenchmen the opportunity to practice the religion of their choice and an equal chance to partake of civil life. Though the Edict was widely criticized by a majority of Frenchmen, and its liberal posture impaired by the servants of absolutism, the idea that law must be equal for all remained the essence of subsequent modern constitutional practice. That was not Raemond's vision, or yet the private (much less the public) vision of many men of his time. It was, unfortunately, but the last of a string of defenses he used to make his part in the disinterment appear reasonable. He would have preferred to see "heresy" disappear entirely.[81] His was not the endorsement of a tolerant man for social pluralism, but the wail of a conservative man who regretted the loss of a past he imagined had been a tranquil one because it had been religiously homogeneous.

The second charge made against him by the authors of the *Plaintes* concerned his service as *Rapporteur* (judge advocate) in a murder trial in which he condemned an innocent Calvinist to death.[82] The defendant was later discovered to have been innocent, possibly the victim of perjured testimony on the part of (presumably Catholic) "false witnesses." The account in the *Plaintes* is not sufficiently detailed to enable us precisely to determine the extent of Raemond's irresponsibility or culpability, although both his detractors and his defenders make much of the fact that he later apologised for his error.[83]

Taken in their entirety, the *Plaintes* offered ample proof, if proof were needed, that the Huguenot minority labored under gross social injustice to achieve the dignity and to obtain the respect of their fellow Frenchmen. They do not prove Florimond de Raemond made it his business to persecute them for their beliefs. From the vantage point of the present we perceive that the injustice of their situation was due to institutions and modes of thought that antedated the Reformation and that were sadly in need of adjustment.

To some extent the Edict of Nantes provided the reformed with such adjustment. It was designed to establish a new normalcy for a society which had outgrown the religious and legislative equipment dragged down from simpler and more homogeneous times. Yet what is clear to us would not have been clear to Raemond's contemporaries. His co-religionists must have felt, had they chanced to read the *Plaintes*, that the Huguenots were needlessly obstreperous and patently unwilling to abide by good old laws that they deemed serviceable still. Calvinists, on the other hand, would have read the *Plaintes* with the conviction that both the laws and their administrators needed replacement.

There was another case that was not contained in the *Plaintes*, but which was revealed by Raemond in the "History of Heresy," and it provides additional insight into the kinds of tensions that marked his long service as a judge. This case involved the adulterous relationship the Calvinist governor of Castillon (Perigord) had with a married woman. From the affair arose considerable controversy concerning the type of body before which such a case might properly be tried. While the governor's wife had persuaded her errant mate to go before the Consistory of their church, the married woman and her husband, members along with the governor of the same Protestant church, insisted that the matter was one of calumny, not adultery, and preferred to present themselves before the court of the *Parlement* of Bordeaux when it met with Raemond as senior counsellor presiding at La Tournelle. Raemond sided with the aggrieved couple, believing that the Consistory had overstepped their jurisdiction. In ruling that the church court had erred, Raemond succeeded in getting the reformed party to carry the governor's case to the royal privy council. There Raemond's decision was overturned.[84] This reversal, coming in 1597 at a time when Raemond's name was already on the lips of many as a result of the publicity he had received in the *Plaintes*, was undoubtedly a cause for chagrin on his part. Why he felt it necessary to rehash the whole affair in his history is a matter of speculation. Perhaps he felt it was an important piece of contemporary evidence to the proposition that the reformed party was dangerously aggressive when its own interests were involved. He must have believed that the reformed consistories were threats to the judicial independence of provincial *parlements* as well as to the individual's enjoyment of civil rights undisturbed by private parties such as the Calvinist church elders. At the very least, his inclusion of an incident, which had been embarrassing to him in his professional career, puts Raemond in a new light as a man who was willing to take some personal risk in order to protect his conception of judicial honor.

Heresy and History

What turned out to be Raemond's last book was his "History of Heresy," or his history of the rise, development, and eventual ruin of that form of "heresy" called Protestantism. The plan of the book was ambitious, and it dragged on to the point where its author lost patience, skipped half of Book V (on Jesuits, the Inquisition, Germany), and wrote nothing of the sixth but left a memo that it was to treat of the English schism. He could not wait to launch himself on the chapters pertaining to France,[85] but apart from a very detailed account of the beginning of reform in France and especially of John Calvin and of Calvinist religious practice, he failed to give much information on French affairs in a political way, or even to treat of religious affairs generally. He might have done so had he lived to present the additional two chapters on France, which he said he wanted to do before he "set sail" to the new world.[86] The fact that he found writing this history more time consuming than he had anticipated and more difficult is plain. He compared himself with the apprentices of a great sculptor who took more trouble on the plaster work than their master did on the marble. He felt his major difficulty was the fact that few historians had written on the subjects that interested him.[87] The remark is indicative of the kind of research that Raemond was given to — namely, the reading of secondary sources. He did a good job of reviewing large numbers of these sources, but he had little time for archival work. Even had he used archival sources, it is doubtful that a man whose major concern was to defend Catholicism from those "roaring lions, famished wolves, monstrous dragons and biting snakes,"[88] by which he referred to various Protestant sects, would have interpreted archival evidence differently than secondary materials. Cardinal Baronius, whom Raemond so greatly admired,[89] and who greatly admired him as well, used archival sources, as did the authors of the *Magdeburg Centuries*.⁹⁰ Were their histories free of sectarian prejudice? Raemond's history was popular and reflected the prejudice of the mass of Catholic Frenchmen. In this he was, as in so many other ways, typical of his age.

Rites of Passage

The Secret Registers of the Bordeaux *Parlement* record Florimond de Raemond's death in the following manner: "On this day, November 17, 1601, the Hon. Florimond de Raemond, Counselor in the Court, and a very great man, passed away."⁹¹ A further note informed the members that he was buried in the church of the *Feuillants*,⁹² which had benefited considerably from the charitable donations of the Raemond family, that the *Parlement* attended his funeral obsequies *en masse*, and that the young Cardinal François de Sourdis delivered the funeral oration in the church of Saint-Seurin.⁹³ The cause of death is not known, but it came about unexpectedly, rather than as the result of illness or any obvious incapacity. His son and literary heir, François, wrote in a prefatory letter to Cardinal de Joyeuse that "a too hasty death halted the perfecting and completion of his history of the Reformation, and cut short his anticipated lifespan."⁹⁴ He busied himself with civic duties and literary ones until the eleventh hour. His passing affected his best friend, Pierre de Brach, profoundly.⁹⁵

It was only natural for an old friend to miss another after a lifetime of shared experience. The fact was that Florimond de Raemond was missed by the whole Catholic party in Bordeaux and beyond. Cardinal de Sourdis attempted to take upon himself the direction and patronage of the remaining Catholic writers, including François de Raemond⁹⁶ and Jean-Charles de Raemond, later abbé de la Frénade;⁹⁷ but he observed that their efforts were as *la monnaie* (small change) to Raemond's gold. They bore the stamp of the original, but were not of equal value.

Mourned publicly as well as privately, the "very great man" who had been Florimond de Raemond would have been pleased that his funeral was as elaborate as a ceremonious age could devise. François, who dedicated the third Book of the history to Cardinal de Sourdis, was careful to express his gratitude for the magnificence of the occasion.⁹⁸ He averred, however, that his father's greatest monument would be the books he wrote for the defense of that bride of Christ, the Roman Catholic church. Those, he prophesied, would prove more lasting and durable than any tomb of bronze.

We must now examine these literary remains, the not-so-durable products of an age that inflated the value of sectarian certainty. What were these literary "monuments" on which the dust of subsequent centuries gathered so thickly that every commentator on Raemond has had to retrieve them and their author not only from the dust, but indeed, from the dustbin of history?

4
Pope Joan

The thirteenth-century literary tradition that a female had once reigned as pope was frequently retold in sixteenth-century Europe by Protestants anxious to destroy the validity of the papacy. They attempted to do that by insisting that her reign had made an irreparable breech in the heretofore uninterrupted (and male) apostolic succession from St. Peter. To disprove this charge, Raemond wrote the *Erreur Populaire*,[1] which appeared anonymously in Bordeaux in 1587 as a short essay of forty-four pages. The next year's edition, three times as long, was followed by a third edition (1594) that was over three hundred pages in length, and bore, for the first time, the author's name on its title page. This exposé of the popess myth went through fifteen editions between its first and last appearance in 1691. Despite some minor flaws and factual errors, the book made it difficult to resurrect the popess myth without offending the rules of humanist literary criticism, historical accuracy, and plain logic.

Given the problems posed by religious schism during the seventeenth century, it cannot be said that Raemond's *Erreur Populaire* dissolved old tensions. It can be demonstrated, however, that the legend had been put to good use, for Joan was a hard worker even if she were a figment of the medieval imagination. The best use to which Joan (with Raemond's help) was put was that she aided in establishing a firmer, more historically accurate foundation under ecclesiastical history. This involved a more deliberate analysis of old medieval documents, especially of medieval chronicles that had been altered since the thirteenth century to include Joan.

In the process of this analysis, Europe's serious, but not formally educated readers were initiated into the mysteries of historical methodology. Even before the efforts of Raemond and his Counter-Reformation predecessors, the myth had been used to vent the frustration of reform-minded Catholics. After their work had been done, Catholics possessed polemical works on Joan with which to defend their doctrine against Protestant polemic. Exposed as myth,

Joan became a defender of her faith, Roman Catholicism, rather than the defense of Protestantism against Catholicism. While Joan's exposure was used to teach Catholics not to apologize for their faith, this same exposure had ecumenical potential—it freed Protestants from the trammels of myth, enabling them to use the new history and reason in their own defense.

The fable had all the makings of a soap opera. A girl of twelve named Joan, Agnes, Jane, Marguerite, or Geliberte had run off from home in Mainz[2] having quarreled with her folks. She may have been seduced by a monk or servant who accompanied her to an English university, or to a convent in Fulda, so that Joan, in male disguise, could be educated. That English universities did not yet exist—Oxford, England's oldest, dates from the thirteenth, not the ninth century[3]—seems not to have troubled medieval chroniclers. Having earned her *baccalarius*, another thirteenth-century invention, Joan and friend went to Athens to study science and philosophy. Not until the sixteenth century did the Augustinian friar, Onofrio Panvinio (Panvinius)[4] object that ninth-century Athens was not yet equipped with schools that could provide such instruction. Athens was still in barbarian hands so that Joan could not have furthered her education in such hostile surroundings. Panvinius's work was only five pages long, but upon it Raemond, and everyone else who wrote to refute the myth, could build.

After Joan's lover died, presumably of natural causes, Joan went to Rome. Employed there as a lecturer, or reader of Scripture in the church, she made a rapid rise up the clerical ladder. Some sources say she became a cardinal; all agree she was soon elected pope. The Roman mob had elected her by public acclamation because of her learning and piety. Unfortunately for Joan, one of her staff had penetrated her disguise. Whether this staff member was a cardinal or a mere clerk in the Curia was always a matter of conjecture. The result, however, was plain to see. Joan delivered her child while officiating at Mass, or on horseback, or while marching in a Corpus Christi Day procession. Raemond objected that the latter supposition was impossible. Corpus Christi was not in existence during the ninth century. Pope Urban IV had instructed its observance only in 1264.[5] In any event, Joan's delivery was also her public humiliation, and it proved fatal—not to her, but to her reign. Deposed, Joan was variously dealt with.

Although Protestants would try to fasten Joan's story to the eleventh-century *Chronicon* (1082) of Marianus Scotus, Joan really made her debut in Jean de Mailly's chronicle of 1250.[6] She appeared in other chronicles afterwards, each time with changes that Raemond felt made her reign improbable.[7] One detail of her "career" never changed—she was always deposed for fornication. Giovanni Boccaccio (1313—1375) was the earliest Renaissance man of letters to retell her story. His *De Claris Mulieribus* (1353) cited Joan and other women famed for their prowess in literary or martial arts. It has been remarked that Boccaccio, who seemed to admire his unique female subjects, carefully recorded the gross humiliations most suffered for their uniqueness.[8] His feelings toward bold and learned women were not unmixed. In the next century, Jan Hus referred to Joan at the Council of Constance shortly before he was burned there for heresy. Before his condemnation, he urged the church to clarify its position regarding the status of the primacy after, and because of, Joan's interruptive reign.[9] Joan was a weapon in Hus's effort to question papal authority. Since no one at the Council objected to his having raised the issue, it seems likely that conciliarists found Joan a convenient means for strengthening their case. Conciliarists hoped to substitute an ecumenical church council for what they believed was damaged papal authority.

The first doubts raised about Joan's authenticity were those of the fifteenth-century humanist, Aeneas Sylvius Piccolomini, later Pope Pius II (1458—1464). In a letter to one of his bishops, Juan de Carvajal, Aeneas recounted an interview that he had with Nicholas, bishop of the Taborites. He had told Nicholas that he did not believe Joan's reign was an error on Rome's part and that it did not break any tenet of faith or of law. It was only a sign of the church's ignorance of the real status of Joan. He thought the whole story was far from certain.[10] Aeneas did not publish his doubts, and he did not reproduce the story in any of his historical works. Nevertheless, the early seventeenth-century Lutheran theologian and polemicist, Johann Gerhard (1582—1637), said he had seen such a work, published in 1493 in Nuremberg. What he had really seen was not Aeneas's work, but Hartman Schedel's illustrated *Chronica Universalis* or *Nuremberg Chronicle* (1493). This book did contain generous portions of Aeneas's *Historia Bohemica* (1475) and his manuscript *Europa*; Schedel used these for his contemporary reference. But Schedel did not get his popess information from Aeneas. Gerhard's memory betrayed him, perhaps because the prestige of Aeneas Sylvius as an historian was greater than Schedel's, whose profession was medicine, not history. Gerhard would have found it peculiarly useful if a respected scholar (and pope) could be shown to have affirmed Joan's existence. He was led astray by his own reluctance to put aside the (by then) long discredited myth. There was, of course, no lack of popess sources that Schedel had at his disposal. One of his chief sources, Giacomo Filippo Foresti of Bergamo-Bergomensis (d. 1520), had written of Joan's existence in his *Supplementum Chronicarum* (1493).[11] A still more influential source for Schedel (and countless other authors) was the account of Platina.

Bartolomeo de' Sacchi (Platina 1421–1481) had personal reasons for disliking papal authoritarianism. Pope Paul II had abolished the Roman Academy, and Platina had led a protest movement against the closure. The protest was against a loss of income, but Paul believed that Platina and his colleagues were conspirators. Since many of these men had written admiringly of pagan gods and goddesses, Paul began to believe them capable of heresy as well. Platina was imprisoned twice on charges of conspiracy, but was also charged with the greater crime of heresy. He disavowed heretical ideas, saying that he had lived as a Christian, and had gone to confession and to communion once each year.[12] Platina took his revenge on Paul by incorporating antipapal polemic, including the popess story, into his popular *Lives of the Popes* (1474).[13]

The French theologian and humanist, Jacques Lefèvre d'Étaples (1455–1537), a Catholic reformer whose piety was attested by practical deeds of church reform as well as by scholarship, edited a work by a medieval friar named Robert of Uzès. This book, *Liber Trium Virorum et Trium Spiritualium Virginum*, published in Paris in 1513, concerned a dream that Robert said had permitted him to visit Rome. There he had seen the object that would become the most notorious reminder of Joan's reign — the perforated porphyry chair on which the *probatio sexus* was said to have been administered immediately after a papal election.[14]

On the eve of the Reformation several of the uses of the myth had already made their appearance. The story had been told to entertain. Misogyny permeated western culture, and the notion that women might achieve power or intellectual distinction made monkish chroniclers laugh. If their humor was barbed, hiding clerical resentment of papal power, their brief entries offer little certain evidence. During the Renaissance, Joan's tale was used by men of letters to indicate, albeit tentatively, that new standards for civility rendered ignorance in either sex less than desirable.[15] Civility offered new standards of social conduct, and new interest in sexual misconduct — the story was alluring for its pornographic aspects. Raemond believed Boccaccio had capitalized on the grossness of the story for the sole purpose of expanding his readership.[16] Raemond's contention would seem borne out to contemporaries familiar with early fifteenth-century editions of Boccaccio's work, many of which contained illustrations of Joan's public parturition. Such illustrations continued to appear during the sixteenth century as well. The fact that Joan's story always ended in such public humiliation or punishment offered a justification for reading unsavory material.

If Renaissance literature was sometimes ribald, the late fifteenth and early sixteenth century seethed with spiritual unrest. Many people longed for reforms of a church grown worldly and an administration grown insensitive to that longing. Joan became a symbol of papal immorality, and also of papal fallibility. Conciliarists, who wished to substitute ecumenical councils for papal leadership, used Joan as an example of papal misconduct. Her story was a reproach to popes and their curial officials, but was not commonly viewed (except by Hussites) as a wholesale condemnation of the Roman church. Some pious Catholics mentioned her so casually they seemed not to have been disturbed by the possibility of the story's most dangerous use — the denial of spiritual validity to the church hierarchy.

With the onset of the Reformation that kind of denial had become common. The Protestants charged that Rome was not merely error-prone (fallible), but totally bankrupt spiritually. Joan's reign was a case in point, and they insisted that it had fatally interrupted whatever claims to legitimacy it once had. Martin Luther said that in 1510 he had seen a monument to the popess (Agnes) in the form of a stone tablet on which she appeared in papal garb, holding a child by the hand.[17] He concluded that the papacy had become so callous it had not bothered to destroy the incriminating monument. John Calvin said one would need to "pass over Popess Joan" in order to preserve an interrupted apostolic succession.[18] Joan's "crime" was unique. She was a woman.

Once the Reformation was well under way, the pursuit and exposure of the female pontiff became for Catholic historians a political necessity and a religious obligation. Although the basic refutation was composed by Panvinius, it was Florimond de Raemond who proved to be Joan's real nemesis. He transformed Panvinius's brief outline of debating points into a lively, yet systematic book over three hundred pages long. Since he wrote in French, the literate but not learned among his countrymen could profit by the scholarship of the Counter-Reformation. Latin and Dutch translations appeared in the course of time.[19] Raemond surveyed much of the medieval literature, soliciting friends and booksellers for examples of rare manuscripts and printed works. Though he was handicapped by the limitations imposed by a provincial city, he nevertheless examined an impressive number of sources. To forestall criticism of his conclusion, he cited the work of the "all knowing Pithou,"[20] whose diligence in documentary research had not yielded any reference to the popess.

Chronicles that mentioned Joan varied. Although researchers like Raemond knew this, not many of his contemporaries did. He aired difficulties with which scholars were familiar, but that ordinary readers must have found surprising. Even after the printing press made standardized copies of medieval manuscripts available, the amount of misinformation was not reduced. It probably increased. This was due to the fact that many printers set in type chronicles that they did not carefully edit. Raemond knew that not all the additions to original manuscripts were of Protestant manufacture. Along with Panvinius, he cited the case of the chronicle of Sigebert of Gembloux (d. 1112). Panvinius had attributed its alteration to include the popess to an English monk, Galphridus of Oxfordshire who died (1356) over two hundred years after Sigebert.[21] Panvinius's judgment has been borne out by a nineteenth-century scholar.[22] But while Raemond knew that Catholics had altered many such chronicles, he vented his wrath principally upon Protestant printers and editors who failed to exercise adequate caution in their work: "So if afterwards, these annotated books fall into the hands of some printer, he does not fail to make what the commentator has added appear the work of the first master's hand even though innocent of all errors."[23] In Raemond's haste to condemn Protestant printers, he made some errors. For example, the same Sigebert, replete with references to Joan, had been printed in 1513 by the Estienne press. He attributed this edition to Robert Estienne, the reformed printer who in 1550 fled from Paris, where he was printer to Francis I, to Geneva. Robert had been the victim of Catholic attacks, but in 1513 Robert was still a child. He did not assume the business that his father Henri (d. 1520) had founded until 1526. Henri was no Protestant. In attributing the edition of Sigebert to the reformed son, Raemond's passion seems to have got the better of him, even though he warned his readers against the violence of emotions that distort truth.[24]

Raemond's suspicion of Protestant printers led him to villify Johann Herold of Basel, a Protestant who had migrated to Switzerland from Burgundy. Herold was a great admirer of Erasmus, and like that humanist continued to hope for religious unity between all Christians. A pastor for some years, Herold satisfied neither his parishioners nor his superiors, all of whom considered him a covert Catholic.[25] Herold was forced to turn from pastoral work and to rely solely on printing for his living. Among his printed works were the two medieval chronicles of Marianus Scotus and Martin of Troppau, or Polonus. Raemond said he had deliberately falsified Polonus by omitting the term *dicitur* (it is said) used by Polonus to indicate that he doubted the story of the popess.[26] Herold's 1549 edition was followed in 1574 by one from a Catholic printer, Suffridis Petri of Louvain, whose edition also contained the persistent legend of the popess. Whatever Raemond felt was the case, the religious preference of printers was not the determining factor in the reiteration of this myth. Not until the next century was an edition of Polonus, who larded his chronicle with many fables, to appear minus the popess.[27]

Although Raemond was harsh on Herold, whom a modern critic has excused from altering Scotus,[28] he was right to say that "Jean Oporin Lutherien" (Johann Herbster, or Oporinus) of Basel had printed an inaccurate edition of the fifteenth-century Greek scholar, Calcondile. The original had not mentioned Joan, but Clauser, the German who translated it, had. Oporinus said he knew no Greek, but he was disingenuous, for he had taught Greek at the university in Basel, and Latin in the local Latin school. Oporinus, formerly the employer of young Johann Herold, was not Lutheran, but a Zwinglian.[29]

The acceleration of religious unrest, in part a result of the revolution caused by printing, was also a cause of its success. The availability of copies shaped public opinion. If "typographical fixity" perpetuated positions once taken, it did not slow down the invention of new positions.[30]

The sixteenth century was beginning to interest itself in the discovery of antiquities.[31] Often its enthusiasm outstripped its expertise. Luther's "identification" of the stone tablet was no unusual case. A statue of another woman and child, rediscovered around the time of the *Erreur Populaire*'s first appearance, and now thought to represent Juno nursing Hercules, seems to have been described in a fourteenth-century book as the statue of the popess.[32] Raemond ordered a sketch of this statue to be forwarded to him. He agreed with the verdict already rendered by Panvinius that the subject was classical, not Christian.

The sculpted bust of Joan could be found in the sixteenth century, together with those of other popes, along an interior cornice frieze in the Cathedral of Siena. Raemond included in his twenty-second chapter of the *Erreur Populaire* an appeal to Clement VIII to have this offending sculpture removed. He must have been pleased when he received sometime in 1600 a letter from Cardinal Baronius, the same man who had lavished fulsome praise on Raemond's book on the popess in his *Annales Ecclesiastici*.[33] The cardinal wrote to tell him that the Grand Duke of Tuscany had ordered the bust removed. It was later to be transformed into the likeness of Pope Zacharias and replaced on the cornice in that guise.[34]

More troubling than the sculpture, which only a few could actually see in the cathedral at Siena, was the story of the porphyry chair with the hole in its seat, a rumor everyone who knew about Joan was likely to repeat. This perforated chair had first been described, as we have seen, in the thirteenth century. Platina had included the first reference in his *Lives of the Popes*, but gave his readers another interpretation of the use of the chair. He said that rather than the means for performing the *probatio sexus*, the chair was simply a toilet seat, or *stercoria sedes*. Its use during papal installation ceremonies was simply as a reminder that God, who had elevated the candidate to such high office, left him subject to all the ordinary vicissitudes of human nature.[35] Raemond thought the whole business of the perforated chair of porhyry was "so gross" that the only possible response for Catholics was to laugh at the Protestants' folly in repeating it.

The mystery of this chair has only recently been solved. In fact it was a *sella obstetrica*, or parturition chair, used by women in antiquity during childbirth, and in papal installations to symbolize *Mater Ecclesia*, or Mother Church.[36] Although to my knowledge no explicit comments were made by reformers linking this maternal concept of the church to Joan, the mother of an illegitimate child, it is certainly possible that sixteenth-century readers made such inferences themselves. Apparently, Pope Urban VIII (1623–1644) took steps to restore the nobility of this concept to the church by commissioning Bernini to depict labor pains on four female faces that decorate the Bernini baldaquin in St. Peter's. He also hired two historians to write repudiations of the popess myth.[37]

One of the many lamentable features of the popess myth to Raemond's mind was its acceptance by Catholics as well as Protestants. Raemond knew a Franciscan friar who had used the story of Joan as sermon material until he disabused him of the story.[38] Since friars were not frequently well educated, Raemond found it more disturbing when an acquaintance of unimpeachable cultivation perpetrated the same error. This was the case of Etienne Pasquier, eminent jurisconsult and prolific historian, and like Raemond, a friend of Montaigne, the essayist. Pasquier had several times referred to Joan in his popular *Recherches de la France* which began appearing in 1560. Raemond reproached him for this. In the

Erreur Populaire he wrote that "he who had given France his *Recherches* ought to have searched more carefully for the truth, and not to have sullied his lovely pages with such filthy stuff."[39] Pasquier, in a letter to a friend years later, said that he was much obliged to Raemond for having lifted the seals from his eyes.[40]

In the process of disabusing his readers of their belief in Joan, Raemond undertook to analyze certain aspects of early medieval history. He used Joan to expose the tactics of his Protestant opposition. He said the Protestants had made heroes of the eastern emperors and saints of their patriarchs in order to put the papacy in the poorest light. Three popes, Nicholas I (858–867), Hadrian II (867–872), and John VIII (872–882), were cast as villains for refusing to give their blessing to one of the emperor's men, Photius, a candidate for the patriarchate of Constantinople. Although John VIII[41] did eventually recognize Photius and give him his blessing, he was no more popular with Protestant historians than his predecessors. As for Catholics, John VIII was an embarrassment for having given in on the Photius issue, thus weakening, or so they believed, papal authority in the East still farther. Cardinal Baronius believed that John's critics (who eventually bludgeoned him to death) gave rise to the myth by their portrayal of this pope as a weak, womanish creature.

Although Raemond frequently followed the lead of more famous Catholic writers, he could display independence on other occasions. He rejected Baronius's theory about John's character. Photius had simply been adopted by Protestants because he was perverse, and though a learned man, had "spit up a thousand insults at the Roman church."[42] That was why, according to Raemond, he was the idol of Lutheran writers. But Photius had not mentioned the popess while petitioning Rome for its blessing. His failure to do so proved Joan's nonexistence for, mused Raemond, why would Photius, who could have made his own qualifications for high church office glitter by comparison with Joan, have failed to mention her disgrace? Although this kind of argument (from silence) is generally regarded as invalid, in this case it was not unconvincing. The significance of the controversy over Photius is meaningful when we learn that it was mixed with the growing tendency of the Roman church to insist on spiritual and political primacy throughout the Christian world. A matter of spiritual tension between East and West was the exact manner in which the Holy Spirit was believed to operate. The West claimed that it proceeded through the Father and the Son (the so-called *filioque* clause); the East did not. Political tension derived from Rome's contention that it should have the direct jurisdiction over Illyricum, when in fact Photius believed that belonged only to Constantinople.[43] In championing Photius, Protestant writers believed they were demonstrating their dissatisfaction with the extent of Rome's claim to total authority over all spiritual and temporal matters with that kind of caesaropapism so inimical to reformers such as Luther. The irony of the sixteenth-century debate over Photius was that John VIII's eventual recognition of him was conciliarist in nature and conciliatory in spirit, for it was given in a council at which papal legates met with representatives from the patriarchates of Jerusalem, Antioch, and Alexandria.[44]

Raemond used the myth to appeal to French chauvinism, largely anti-German. Germans were presented as immoderate by their very nature, preferring strong drink and weak women.[45] He said they had invented Joan because they preferred secular to spiritual leadership, because their kings were often heretics, and because their bishops imitated their monarchs' religious heterodoxy.[46] He did not mention the Gallican Liberties that gave the French church immunity from some of the inconveniences of papal monarchy, and gave French kings some of the powers German princes hoped to obtain. He did not mention spiritual discontent on the eve of the Reformation either, except in connection with heresy.

Raemond claimed that the Germans had used Joan to symbolize their detestation of chastity; she was the symbol of temptations that inevitably befell celibate clergymen, a kind of occupational hazard that resulted from inappropriate vows. Raemond was an admirer of the controversial works of Cardinal Robert Bellarmine, among which was a discussion of celibacy. This the cardinal regarded as apostolic law.[47] In fact, celibacy had been a matter of debate as late as the Council of Constance (1415) and that of Basel (1432). The subject was not interesting only to Germans, as Raemond's readers might have been led to conclude. But celibacy was a subject more distressing in German-speaking lands than elsewhere, and early in the Reformation treatises on the problem were written by Andreas Carlstadt (1521)[48] and by Luther (1521, 1522).[49]

Against those German historians, the Centuriators,[50] whose *Septima Centuria* had contained the popess myth they claimed had damned all subsequent popes, Raemond made a serious accusation. He said that these writers, concerned more with the defense of Lutheranism than with historical truth, had invented a correspondence between Nicholas I and a German monk named Hildaric who opposed celibacy.[51] Raemond said the correspondence was impossible on several grounds: first, the two men were not contemporaries. Furthermore, the letter purported to have been written by Hildaric never mentioned Joan, whose adultery might have given him support for his case, i.e., the renunciation of a policy (celibacy) that had produced such a notorious lapse.

Apart from the theological issues of apostolic succession, primacy, infallibility, and celibacy, and apart, too, from any consideration of historiographical method, the popess was used to reinforce Renaissance misogyny, a theme that appeared in this and in Raemond's last great work, his history of the Reformation.[52] That the myth was not intended by its monkish creators to invite commentary on the role of women in society is obvious. Raemond thought the story was intended merely to amuse. After all, there were no learned women to speak of in the thirteenth century, and of female philosophers, there were none at all. A few women in the middle ages achieved clerical prominence within their own orders,[53] but none attained Joan's universal authority.

Research into feminine history indicates that medieval attitudes toward women were predominantly misogynist, but that a softening of opinion occurred during the Renaissance and persisted into the Reformation.[54] Still, women remained under the stigma of a supposed inferiority to men.[55] There were few acceptable outlets that educated women in the sixteenth century could find to justify the expense of their education. The patronage formerly given by great ladies to authors of poetry or romance had long since become impossible. Religious struggle replaced the artificial struggles on tournament grounds, once the focus of romance. Humanists turned their talents to more pious uses. Learned ladies turned theirs as well, but found religion at least as restrictive as it was liberating. The scope that noblewomen had for patronizing serious scholarship, and even on occasion, engaging in it themselves, was not unlimited. A Marguerite of Navarre could, it is true, exercise her pen as well as her patronage, but there were risks she ran which only the services of a king (her brother, Francis I) could obviate.[56] While the involvement of women in religion — a role pioneered by Joan — has frequently been studied in terms of the stimulus given by Protestantism to feminine education and liberation,[57] recently research has taken the opposite direction with indications that Catholicism offered more educational opportunity than was formerly thought.[58] Women's history seems to attract a growing number of historians, and the subject certainly bears further exploration.[59]

The questions that concern us with respect to feminine roles in the Reformation are of a more restricted nature since they are limited to the subject of the popess. To what degree might it be said that Joan influenced feminine advance or was influenced by it? Was popess polemic useful in advancing the cause not only of women, but of humankind in general?

If the *Erreur Populaire* of Florimond de Raemond was representative of late sixteenth-century opinion, and its brisk sale indicates that it was, it could not help but reinforce misogynist opinion at a time when misogyny was being threatened by feminine assertiveness and increased involvement in political and religious life.[60] Raemond reminded his contemporaries that feminine achievement, however possible, was always undesirable. The real popess, he wrote, was Elizabeth I of England, to whom he devoted two chapters. While he admired her diplomatic skill and her authoritative style (he especially liked the decisive way in which she dealt with Puritans), he was appalled by the active role she took in the Anglican church: "That certainly is unnatural to see one who was created for obedience, wilfully command; and one who by Scripture is excluded from any performance and administration of ecclesiastical things, bind and loose the most holy and sacred mysteries of religion as she pleases."[61]

Joan probably did little, if anything, to encourage women to go into religion or to challenge the prevailing prejudice against their sex.[62] She may, however, have reminded her readers that some real women had overcome hierarchical limitations and in this way fed the fires of feminist dialogue.[63]

Despite her charisma, and maybe because of it, Joan could not prevent a number of Protestant writers from refusing to abjure their belief in her. Pierre Bayle recorded a number of such diehards[64] who refused to follow the lead of more rational members of their faith. Pierre Bayle was not one of Raemond's ardent admirers, but he was able to say that on the whole, Raemond's *Erreur Populaire* was the best refutation of Joan that had ever been written.[65]

Though Joan could not disabuse all sixteenth- and seventeenth-century folk of the inferiority of women, or her own historicity, she had nevertheless performed several outstanding services in the course of the late Renaissance and during the Reformation period. These made her story serviceable. In the earlier period, Joan provided some solace to reform-minded Catholics who tried, by means of ridicule (next to revolution the most powerful of social tools) to promote change within the Roman church. During the Counter-Reformation Rome did change, taking upon itself the investigation of its own ecclesiastical history. Such research taught Catholics not to apologize for the major tenets of their faith, and Protestants not to devalue theirs by resorting to myths of less scrupulous centuries. Joan's hands were raised over everyone. By the time David Blondel's refutation was published in the first half of the seventeenth century, fair-minded Protestants could accept what he proffered by way of consolation, that the popess had not, after all, been a Protestant myth, but a Catholic one.[66]

In sum, Joan was herself a reformer, a charismatic personality who stimulated many people to think and reason their way to new intellectual and spiritual positions. Though she could not teach everyone to read history more carefully, she could justifiably claim, along with Florimond de Raemond, that she had been used to instruct Catholics and Protestants in one great truth: that men do not have to defame another religious establishment in order to justify their own. In the Enlightenment, Protestantism no longer needed Joan to survive, and Catholics were no longer embarrassed by her. Even if Joan were only a fictitious popess, she was, in addition to being a great reformer, a great ecumenicist. She distributed even-handedly blessings to Protestants and Catholics alike, encouraging them to investigate their common historical roots and to subject written history to rigorous analysis.

5
The Antichrist

Belief in Antichrist[1] for medieval Christians was no idle exercise in biblical exegesis or in literary criticism. Would the "Man of Sin" against whom St. Paul warned the Thessalonians[2] and who was understood to represent Antichrist, the prince and very principle of evil, prevail against the faithful? Antichrist commanded enormous respect in the middle ages, and belief in him was part of the conservative, orthodox eschatology throughout the period.[3] That belief was the result of faith and the fragility of life in this world. Faith compelled credence in all the Bible texts that prophesized Antichrist, while the application of those prophecies to the present and future seemed a helpful means of preparing the faithful to cope with contingent events.

The legend had its inception in Babylon. A rebel goddess of darkness was overcome by a son of the gods and giver of light. The story migrated to Canaan, and later its political as well as spiritual implications were preserved by the Israelites. In Daniel the idea that the godly were to be punished for their sins by unbelievers reached a climax. Prophets such as Ezekiel (38:1–9) hinted that God would smite the enemies of his people, Gog and Magog. The Messiah would appear at the end of time as a deliverer, but the Antichrist would be a personal opponent to Him. The political aspects of the story were to fade in the *New Testament*, where spiritual ones predominated. Early Christian comment portrayed Antichrist as a purveyor of false doctrine (Origen). Contradictory elements as to Antichrist's identity abound in the Bible. In Matt. 24:24, the Son of Man is opposed not by a personal Antichrist but by many pseudomessiahs or false prophets; in John 2:22, Antichrist is a single individual and a liar. However, Antichrist was not to be limited to the one or the many. He was also dual, as Satan and his son, Antichrist, or Rome and the East. Although the idea of his duality receded in the middle ages, Luther revived it, identifying Antichrist with the Turk and the papacy.[4]

Antichrist was early associated with the Jews, a fact that, at the hands of St. Paul (I Thess. 2:14—16), produced a distinctly anti-Jewish interpretation. During and after the Crusades, the Muslim was also regarded as an Antichrist. That the pope was so regarded was cultivated by Franciscan monks who disparaged papal wealth as a desertion of the ideal of poverty. From them the idea spread to followers of John Wycliffe and to the Hussites. Eventually the pope/Antichrist theme was restated by Martin Luther and elevated to a tenet of faith, having been incorporated into the Schmalkald Articles.[5]

The reiteration of the charge that the pope or even the papacy as an institution was Antichrist appeared in thousands of broadsides, in theatrical performances, in sermons, and in monographs in the course of the sixteenth century. It was the denouement of a painstaking exposition that had been developed gradually during the later middle ages from an infra-structure of far greater antiquity. Much of the imagery for Antichrist derived from an unknown scribe who, in the second century before Christ, recorded the prophet Daniel's dream of the Babylonian Captivity. It was this source that provided the first extended biblical account of a monster later associated with Antichrist.[6] Daniel's dream was inextricably mixed with the scribe's own fears for Jewish survival. The Syrian king, Antiochus IV (d. 163 B.C.), had outlawed the Hebrew religion, and thus was identified with the fractious "he goat" Daniel imagined dictating to the heavenly host,[7] prospering until "the indignation should be accomplished" and himself destroyed. The practice of associating disagreeable rulers with Antichrist was strengthened when St. John Chrysostom (d. 407) designated Nero as a forerunner of Antichrist.[8] Later, Frederick II in the thirteenth century was called "that limb of Antichrist" by his foe, Pope Gregory IX; Frederick retaliated in kind. Hussites identified Emperor Charles IV with Antichrist,[9] and with the growth of papal wealth and political power, it was not surprising that Joachim of Fiore, the Cathars, Albigensians, and Franciscans took up the practice. Even the papacy as an institution, with its doctrine, traditions, and hierarchy, was thus villified before the Reformation,[10] though critics had not yet begun to advocate its abolition, merely its reform.

After the advent of Luther, Rome grew more sensitive to criticism of its popes and practices. That reformer got off to a rather hesitant start, but the conviction once formed that the pope (and the Turk) was Antichrist remained ever after a major preoccupation.[11] He believed that the primitive church had been able to repel much corruption until the advent to the papal throne in 606 of Boniface III.[12] Boniface had persuaded the regicide Emperor Phocas to recognize his primacy over all other bishops and hence achieve the universal power that corrupted the whole Roman church. This evoked biblical prophecies concerning Antichrist's power[13] and promoted heresy among believers. With regard to heresy, the reformed faced problems. The Roman church had traditionally regarded heretics as forerunners of Antichrist, even if it preferred to think *the* Antichrist would be one person yet unborn.[14] Luther had become increasingly aware of his debt to certain late medieval heretics, and particularly to Jan Hus, whom he came to regard as one who, like himself, had been persecuted by Rome for preaching God's word.[15] He concluded that the papacy was not a divine but a mere human institution.[16] Like the unspeakable one in Daniel, it had taken unto itself control and dominion of every kind of temporal power[17] while the pope assumed the air of a god on earth or put himself even above God.[18] Because of these misdeeds, the church had committed itself to heresy.

Luther's insistence on the pope as Antichrist encouraged other reformers to publish works on the theme.[19] Catholic refutations were sporadic rather than systematic, and were not very frequent. The best known were those of Nicholas Sanders and Cardinal Bellarmine.[20] However, until Florimond de Raemond published his work *L'Anti-Christ* (1597), there was not a single source in a vernacular tongue where a full-scale treatment of the subject could be read with confidence by Catholics that their convictions would not be compromised.

The major battleground of the Antichrist controversy was the issue of papal primacy, as Cardinal Bellarmine stated in his work on the subject.[21] Raemond relied heavily on Bellarmine.[22] The reformed attempted to undermine the significance of St. Peter and hence of the primacy. Some denied that Peter had ever visited Rome,[23] while others questioned the Roman claim that he stayed there twenty-five years.[24] John Calvin denied that Peter might have established a bishopric in the eternal city, though he admitted that Peter once visited it.[25] Bellarmine thought the length of Peter's stay there was unimportant, but Raemond insisted on twenty-five years. He thought the figure derived from testimony of St. Mark, Peter's companion.[26]

Having lodged Peter at Rome, Raemond proceeded to investigate his preeminence over the other apostles. Aware that the Protestants insisted on the equality of all the apostles, he hedged, admitting that the other eleven were equally apostles, but insisting that Peter was more equal than the rest, since "on him the church was founded."[27] Tertullian was the first to interpret the passage "Tu es

Petrus" to mean that the church was Peter's special foundation, but he also made provision for the whole church to enjoy the powers Christ conferred on Peter. Raemond chose to ignore this fact.[28] Luther interpreted this passage to mean that the rock (*petram*) was Christ, not Peter, and that the foundation of the church was perceptible by faith alone.[29]

Another key passage of scripture was Luke 23:31−32 where the Lord tells Simon (Peter): "I have prayed for thee, that thy faith fail not." Raemond objected that the Centuriators had stated that Christ prayed for Peter out of respect for his age, Peter being the oldest apostle. He felt the passage meant Christ was going to guarantee the purity of church doctrine down through the ages. Luther had once averred that the Lord could scarcely pray for the faith of faithless popes.[30] He pitted against Luke, the passage from John 17:18: "Father, I pray for all who believe in me" as evidence that Christ prayed not only for Peter, but for the whole body of faithful. Luther urged these faithful to trust the secular princes and church councils to maintain ecclesiastical order.[31] As for John Calvin, he regarded Peter's keys metaphorically, believing that they stood for the gospel. The powers of binding or loosing had to do with reconciling men to God by teaching them faith,[32] which ought to have been the task of popes. He cited St. Paul as having contested the primacy of St. Peter: "He that wrought effectually in Peter to the apostleship of the circumcision, the same was mighty in me towards the Gentiles." (Gal. 2:8).[33] Calvin conceived of no power greater than the Word, and thought Peter had accepted on behalf of all the apostles Christ's gifts.[34]

In part, as modern scholars have observed,[35] the inability of Catholics and Protestants to arrive at the same view of the papal primacy resulted from the complexity of scriptural evidence and historical traditions, a complexity neither side fully appreciated. Modern research attests to the slowness with which the notion of primacy developed. The problem was not even widely noted until sometime between the late fourth century and the Council of Chalcedon in 451.[36]

At times the Antichrist legend made it difficult for Raemond to defend primacy, for it presented a monster of tyranny to which the reformed referred when describing the pope. Both Luther (see note 12) and Raemond recognized that Gregory I had refused the title of universal bishop: "The pope does not regard himself as universal bishop, nor do we call him such, as if he alone were the only bishop the Church had."[37] Each one drew a different conclusion from this fact. Raemond denied any inconsistency between papal leadership and the religious leadership of national bishoprics. He failed to understand that a power such as confirming bishops could be political as well as confessional. He knew Antichrist exercised both kinds of power, and thus he tried to spare popes from the appearance of similar tyranny. To preserve local and national political integrity Luther had insisted on German-led consistory courts, and on free ecumenical councils.[38] Against papal primacy the reformer had waged a revolution.

The crisis of the Reformation from the Catholic standpoint was both institutional and doctrinal. To defend its institutional legitimacy, the church sought to validate papal primacy. To defend its doctrine, it emphasized papal infallibility. Since Antichrist preached the wrong doctrine, Catholic controversialists had to establish that the pope's was error free, preserved from mistakes by the Holy Spirit. Whereas historians most frequently write of the unfolding of infallibility doctrine, a new interpretation is that infallibility was developed all at once by a Franciscan friar named Peter Olivi, who was appreciative of Pope Nicholas II's ruling in favor of poverty as a means of salvation.[39] Wrapping itself in the doctrine of infallibility, the sixteenth-century church sought protection against the Protestant blast, the insistence that only scripture was reliable. The church of Rome hoped to dignify itself with what had once been disavowed as the doctrine of Antichrist.[40] In this matter Raemond turned to the *Controversies* of Cardinal Bellarmine, though the cardinal was not the first to attempt a rehabilitation of infallibility.[41] Raemond was obliged to adopt a softer tone than his mentor, denying that popes were infallible as individuals or where morals were at stake, and insisting only that they were infallible in matters of doctrine.[42] To adopt a more uncompromising position might have strained further the relationship between France's Gallican Parlement and the papal Curia and jeopardized what loyal churchmen were most anxious to promote, the registration by France of the Tridentine religious legislation.[43]

To assert infallibility, Catholics had to clear every pope of any charge of error or heresy. There were many such cases, most of whom were popes in the early centuries of the primitive church. Pope Zephyrinus (d. 217) was excused of the heresy of Montanism[44] by Raemond on the grounds that he later abandoned it. Such an admission, however, was scarcely compatible with asserting that popes were infallible. Jacob Latomus of Louvain excused some heretic popes because they did penance for their mistakes, as had St. Peter himself. Raemond further explored the possibility that some popes had been subjected to intimidation. Popes Marcellinus

(d. 304) and Liberius (d. 361), for example, could be shown to have feared their respective emperors. Because of such fears, Raemond absolved Marcellinus of heresy, saying in so many words that his soul was willing even though his flesh was weak.[45] Unfortunately, this was not a very convincing argument in a century where martyrs ran to the stake rather than disavow their faith. A similar excuse was made for Liberius. This pope had defied the emperor, Constantius II, and suffered exile for two years. When he returned to Rome, he submitted to the emperor, who favored Arian doctrine. After the death of Constantius, Liberius reasserted orthodoxy. Although this pope was scarcely a man of great resolution, Raemond found six authorities to praise him for his otherwise fine record.[46]

Sometimes Raemond followed where Baronius led, giving credence to suppositious historical "evidence" when dealing with heretic popes. Such was Pope Felix II (now considered an antipope), whose Arianism was forgiven when a specious carving on a tombstone discovered in 1582 seemed to indicate Felix had damned his Arian patron, Constantius II.[47] It was this monarch who had set Felix upon Liberius's vacant throne.

Sometimes the reformed were unfair in their treatment of erring popes, as when John Calvin found John XXII guilty of heresy for considering that souls received the beatific vision only after the Resurrection.[48] As Raemond pointed out, the church had not finally pronounced on the matter, which was first pronounced dogma only during the reign of John's successor.[49] But Catholics could not deny that some popes had made mistakes regarding doctrine, and that made the doctrine of infallibility less than convincing. It only took one error by one pope to disprove (to Protestant satisfaction anyway) the very idea of an infallible pope. The fact that Protestants found a number of popes who had erred in faith lent strength to Luther's conviction that the pope was an arch heretic, a "heresiarch," or leader of heretics.[50] The notion of heresy was reassessed in the sixteenth century after Luther admitted his indebtedness to Jan Hus. Those late medieval heretics became martyrs for the reformed, just as the early Christians who perished at the hands of the pagan emperors. Martyrologists such as Jean Crespin and Simon Goulart established an identity between Protestant martyrs and those victims of the Antichrist popes. Into the seventeenth century Protestants reiterated the idea that heretic popes had persecuted faithful Christians and had sheltered ancient heresies.[51] The absorption by the papacy of false opinion made the pope a concrete evil power, whereas the Catholics, who held

Antichrist to be an as-yet-unborn individual, were limited to a mere abstraction. For practical purposes and for dramatic ones, however, the Roman church spoke more often of Antichrist's helpers or minions than of the Antichrist not-yet-arrived. There were still outbursts of passion when Catholics labelled Luther and Calvin and other reformers Antichrist or collectively, Antichrists. The scriptures made a multiplicity possible in the war of epithets:

> "You were told that Antichrist was to come, and now many antichrists have appeared." (I John 2:18)
> Jesus warned the disciples on the Mount of Olives: "Take care that no one misleads you. For many will come claiming my name and saying, 'I am the Messiah.'" (Matt. 24:4—5)

The plurality of Antichrist — the idea that he had minions who were loosely termed antichrists — enabled the Catholic church to associate heretics, pagans, Jews, and Muslims with Antichrist.

The Jewishness of Antichrist was part of the medieval tradition. Antichrist was of the House of Dan, and Dan was an accursed race defined in Genesis (49:17) as a "serpent" in Deut. (33:22) as a lion's whelp, and in Jeremiah (8:16) as "strong ones" who devour the land. Since that was believed, it was considered by medieval people that the Jews would be the first to welcome Antichrist, and that the ten lost tribes of Israel, long associated with the figures of Gog and Magog (Ezekiel 38 and 39) would serve as his armies. Raemond's book reflects the deep-rooted Christian fear of Jews: "We believe as did the ancients that this miserable people, who repulsed the truth, will embrace the Lie: who crucified the son of God, will raise up the son of the devil."[52]

Since the Protestants called the pope Antichrist, Raemond reasoned, only Catholics were left on guard against the evil one. Jews would flock to him because his doctrine was already familiar, including as it did circumcision and Saturday sabbath. Christianity would become a shambles, thanks to heretics who "Judaized."[53] Because the Jews were people of the Book, and the reformed preached nothing but the Word, Raemond lumped them together. These Jews and Protestants were Antichrist's helpers. An interesting analysis of why Jews are permitted by God to survive is resolved by Raemond's assertion that their misery promoted the Christian's spiritual welfare.[54] The Jews were a good example of a bad example!

Another Jewish aspect of Antichrist's career had to do with the two witnesses, Enoch and Elias (Elijah). These were considered Christ-types since the death of neither is asserted in the Old Testament. In the Book of Revelation, they prophesy for three years before the beast rises up and "kills" them. But they do not die. Instead, they are revived by God after three-and-one-half days and called home (resurrected). In the middle ages these witnesses preached against Antichrist and converted the Jews to Christ.[55] While Raemond thought the two prophets would convert the Jews at the Tribulation, he felt their first duty was to encourage the faithful, that is, Roman Catholics. He deeply resented the reformed assertion that was made by one Theodore Buchman, or Bibliander (d. 1564), to the effect that the prophets were Luther, Zwingli, and Calvin. He deplored the statement made by Bullinger that Protestant ministers served as Enochs and Eliases. He well knew that Luther was called the second Elias.[56] Two chapters of his book *L'Anti-Christ* were devoted to these biblical prophets to demonstrate the distortions of Protestant exegetes. Since, he reasoned, neither Luther nor Calvin had in fact converted the Jews *en masse*, neither could claim to be the equals of these prophets. He insisted that the Roman church would ultimately baptize all the infidels — Turks and pagans as well as Jews.[57]

The Jews had, in fact, done the papacy a great service. By refusing conversion, they refused to recognize the pope as leader. Since Antichrist was said to be a Jew followed by Jews, the pope, ipso facto, could not be the Antichrist. Such reasoning proved for Catholicism an eschatological necessity. It released them from the political tradition linking the Roman Empire and its capital to Antichrist.[58] It has been demonstrated that Catholic writers put new emphasis on Antichrist's Jewishness in the seventeenth century.[59] They did so to protect the pope from Protestant efforts to persuade the masses that he was the Antichrist. Protestants, on the other hand, found it useful to deny Antichrist's Jewishness. For them, the pope was the Man of Sin. In France, where the reformed were a declining minority, the exculpation of Jews from this heinous charge was not as popular as it was in Protestant England. To refute those reformed writers who denied Antichrist was Jewish, Nicolas Vignier[60] wrote *L'Antichrist Romain opposé à l'Antichrist juif du Cardinal Bellarmine . . . et autres* (1604). It is intriguing to think that if reform had expanded in seventeenth-century France, the intensity of antisemitism there might also have been reduced. Instead, Jews in Catholic countries bore the whole burden of guilt for being Antichrists or at least his followers rather than the popes, papists, and Turks who were thus charged in Protestant lands.

Raemond denied what Protestants (and some Catholics) thought was true, i.e., that the Turk was Antichrist. His reasons were largely a reflection of scriptural assertions to the effect that the Jews would worship Antichrist and that he would be of their race and would call himself God. In chapter 15 of his *Anti-Christ* he insisted that Mohammed could not be Antichrist because he had never called himself God or set up a seat for himself in the Temple of Jerusalem where St. Paul (II Thess. 2:4) thought God's temple was located, but had chosen Mecca instead. He ignored the fact that the Dome of the Rock was constructed (691 A.D.) over the very site of the temples of Solomon and of Herod. Like the majority of Roman Catholics, Raemond urged the Jewish origins of Antichrist.

Luther, by way of contrast, had linked the papacy and the Turk to the Antichrist.[61] Although he became convinced that the Turk was the little horn in Daniel 7,[62] he preferred to regard this enemy as an agent of a greater power, a lesser danger than the papacy. Luther believed Gog (Ezekiel 38:16) represented the Turk, and Magog (Ezekiel 38:2) the pope.[63] Since the pope was the enemy from within the church, while the Turk was merely that from without, the pope was the more dangerous of the two.[64] Both were associated in that "double abomination of the last time" on which Melanchthon[65] and reformed writers like Lambert Daneau, a French Calvinist, had elaborated. Daneau had devoted two chapters in a book on St. Augustine to a discussion of the similarities between the pope and Islam. He believed the Muslims had incorporated into their own doctrine the mistakes of many other heretics, including the heresies of papists.[66] John Calvin, however, in his *Commentaries on Daniel*, disagreed. He refused to associate the little horn with either the papacy or the Turk. He thought the sequence of events described in Daniel had been twisted out of context, and that by them God had declared only what would happen before Christ's first coming, not afterwards.[67]

Most Lutheran writers equated the wars of Gog and Magog with the crusades, though Luther felt these wars would be the double scourge of pope, joined with Turk, to effect God's punishment of wayward Germans.[68] Raemond objected that the wars of Gog–Magog would be fought against God's saints, as the Bible suggested, rather than against the Turks. He accused Lutheran writers such as David Chytraeus and Theodore Buchman of having believed that the church of the middle ages was made up of Turks, and that God's saints (i.e., Catholics) were Saracens.[69] He pleaded that the wars of Gog–Magog were difficult to understand due to the scanty scriptural references to them.

When Cardinal Bellarmine and King James VI of Scotland (later

James I of England) debated the identity of Gog–Magog, the cardinal claimed that Gog was Antichrist, and Magog his followers, "the nations," while James insinuated that Gog was the pope and Magog the Turk.[70] At the end of the sixteenth century, Luther's dual Antichrist was still yoked to usher in the last days, though his identity remained an object of controversy.

Although neither Catholics nor Protestants wished to be thought soft on Turks, and although the Turk threatened both equally, neither side could claim a consistently aggressive stance against the scimitar. Catholics might well blush when recalling that even though the Turks had been menacing their Danubian provinces and southern shores since the fourteenth century, the willingness of Catholic Europe to unite against them had often been imperfect. A Holy League composed of Venice, the papacy, the Empire, Spain, and Lodovico "il Moro" Sforza of Milan to combat the danger had become a bone of contention between members. Early in the sixteenth century it turned its forces against French Christians rather than against Muslims. Europe's inability to coalesce against the danger of Turkish incursion was apparent before the Reformation began. It was, for example, considered scandalous that the French king, Francis I, had allied with Suleiman I in order to weaken the Holy Roman Emperor, with whom Francis was at war. Nor were the French the only Christians who had used the Turks to pursue their own ends. A king of Hungary owed his crown to cooperating with the Turks instead of battling against them. His Christian predecessor died (of drowning) while retreating from the same Turkish enemy.[71] Throughout the sixteenth century, the French sought and won commercial treaties from the Turks[72] while at the same time they engaged in the bloodiest of civil war against their own reformed Christian countrymen.

On the other hand, the Catholics felt Protestants were unwilling to shoulder their fair share of the burden of defending against Turkish invasion. Raemond recalled Luther's unwillingness to engage in an anti-Turkish crusade.[73] In fact, it was Luther's conviction that the Turk would usher in the apocalypse, which made him passive before the attack of Suleiman's forces.[74] In the final analysis, the Protestant party owed much to Suleiman's anti-imperial assaults in the 1530s. Had it not been for that peril, Charles V would have been free to crush the heretics (Protestants) as the Catholic princes at the Diet of Augsburg (1530) had threatened. Apocalypse or no, Luther had been willing to sanction a war effort against the Turks when the emperor agreed to a religious peace (Peace of Nuremberg, 1532), which gave the evangelicals some important concessions.

Raemond reminded his readers that the Protestant princes had stood aside with crossed arms when Charles V attempted to defend Hungary, and, of course, the Protestants had done so because Ferdinand, Charles's brother, meant to re-catholicize Hungary anyway. Again, at Lepanto (1571), Raemond recalled the Protestants had refused to help the papal, Venetian, Genoese, and imperial fleets, an act that resulted in the freeing of twelve or thirteen thousand Christian galley slaves and the capture of 177 Turkish ships.

Although Raemond was justified in portraying the papacy as having led the fight against the Turk, the Protestants maintained that the reverse was true — that the Turks survived because of papal support. Their position was not dependent on the truth of their charge, but on the receptivity of their audience. Both sides agreed that the Turks' religion was offensive, but not all could be counted on to take the offensive against them. No matter how boldly both sides assumed a virtue vis-à-vis the Turk, to some degree some of its members were lacking it.

The Antichrist story, like religion, was a construction of visible and invisible elements, a mixture of material and spiritual symbolism. Raemond felt that the rejection of the visible use of the cross, whether in signing oneself, or in the decoration of one's home or church with crucifixes, was a rejection of Christ himself. He recalled that the ancient heretics had hated the sign of the cross because they disbelieved that God had been so ignominiously killed. Those who did not honor crosses would inevitably bear the mark of Antichrist instead, which the Bible said was to be some sort of symbol left by the evil one on the hand or forehead of his own.[75] He resented very much the statements made by Theodore de Bèze at the discussions of Poissy to the effect that Catholics had turned a noble sign into a mark of superstition by the excessive nature of their reverence for it and that they had substituted the crucifix for the Crucified.[76] The controversy was as old as the commandment that forbade the Hebrews to make graven images. It reared its head during the early days of Christianity, as St. Paul had warned the Philippians (3:18). It reappeared during the iconoclastic controversy in the eighth century, and was in fact an enduring problem that the Reformation reawakened but did not invent. Raemond blamed the reformed anyway. They were no better than Jews, who were now called a race of vipers because vipers, alone of all snakes, hide the sign of a cross under their lower jaw.[77]

Not all criticism of outward symbols of the faith had been made by Protestants. Erasmus, who was highly regarded by Raemond, had once chided Catholics for confusing things spiritual with things visible, for imagining that the presence of "a copper cross hanging from the neck" was consistent with "perfect religion."[78] Luther took the sign of the cross rather prosaically to mean the symbol of Christ's suffering. Calvin viewed it as a symbol of his suffering and of his church, and frequently preached the necessity of "bearing the cross" and of preferring "affliction under the standard of the cross"[79] to a life of ease. Since these were scarcely opinions disrespectful of the cross, Raemond was obliged to note that the reformed often said that they loved Christ but secretly rejected him. He was sure that the duplicity of Antichrist was reflected in their reluctance to display the sign of the cross. Who, asked Raemond, follows more closely in Antichrist's footsteps: you (reformed) who are horrified by the sign of the cross, or we (Catholics) who adore it? You who boast that you see only the spiritual cross, or we who have it always before our eyes, in Church, along our highways and by-ways, in our homes (and in) our bedrooms, so that it might be vividly engraved on our hearts?[80]

When sixteenth-century Catholics reflected on the evil that Antichrist was supposed to accomplish in this world, they remembered that he had taken away the daily sacrifice, and had cast down the sanctuary.[81] They could well imagine that the Protestants, having abandoned the daily sacrifice of the mass and having turned so many religious houses into schools, had also spurned the cross, Christ's symbol. Were they not anti-Christian? Were they not minions of Antichrist?

Although the Antichrist story provided a host of details that could be turned to the advantage or disadvantage of Catholics and Protestants, limited only by the ingenuity of the *raconteur*, both parties were drawn to the fascinating additional exercise of trying to predict, by means of the mystical number 666 found in Revelation (13:17–18), Antichrist's name and the date of his coming. Raemond referred to these mysteries as "*Arithmantie*" and noted that numbers had been used by the Hebrews, Chaldeans, Assyrians, and by Pythagoras and the Sibylline prophetesses for prediction.[82] He believed the dates of Christ's birth, death, and resurrection had been found in the first book of Moses (Genesis), and that Pico de la Mirandola, the fifteenth-century Platonist, Johannes Reuchlin, Melanchthon's son-in-law Caspar Peucer, and his own contemporary, Jean Bodin, had been adepts at mathematical prediction. His twenty-first chapter on numbers reveals his sympathy for the subject, but also his wariness. He began the chapter by referring to the trackless sea, the thick shadows, the profound abyss that such a study at once suggested. He also cautioned the reader against the Protestant error of thinking that the mystical number 666 could be used to stand for the year of Antichrist's coming. He pointed out gleefully that attempts to do so by Martin Luther, Heinrich Bullinger, John Bale, and Lambert Daneau had produced widely divergent results.[83] He insisted that the number 666 was an indication of Antichrist's name, not his arrival date. However, when applied to the searching out of his real name and identity, the number was no more productive than when applied to the date of his coming.[84] Raemond said that Irenaeus, the second century bishop of Lyon, had warned against taking the results too seriously.[85] Yet Bullinger, undaunted, had sought Antichrist's name in one of the Sibylline texts.[86] Duplessis-Mornay had tried to get it by building on Irenaeus's work,[87] and the Bernese theologian, Nicolas Colladon, had taken liberties with a Greek transcription in order to condemn the papacy as Antichrist. Raemond consulted some lecture notes he had once taken while listening to one Jean Dorat, a royal lecturer in Greek. He concluded that Colladon's argument was thoroughly discredited by a superior linguist, and he proferred Lambert Daneau's opinion, which coincided with his, to the effect that the holy spirit was not to be constrained by cabalistic devices such as 666.[88] None of these various efforts was definitive. Raemond said he would not conclude that Luther's name meant Antichrist even though in Latin, Greek, and Hebrew the letters of his name added up to 666. He would not so conclude even though the names Jean Hus and Theodore de Bèze also totaled 666.[89] He was too much of a linguist to ignore the fact that language can be manipulated, and "proofs" established linguistically that have no reference to nature or to historical fact. He was too much of a polemicist to restrain himself from mentioning that the names Hus, Luther, and Bèze produced the fateful number 666! His sense of mystery was such that he was reluctant to press for definite answers to problems better left unsolved. Christian scepticism combined with Christian credulity in him, as in his friend Montaigne, many of whose philosophical positions he freely drew upon in his own writing. The effect of Raemond's reluctance to jump to conclusions based on numbers and the superstitious use of numbers helped to create an intellectual climate more circumspect and rational. Despite the fact that Raemond's penchant for verbosity and bellicosity in other connections was unfortunate, it did not altogether undermine his contributions toward moderate, rational discourse.[90] It must also be pointed out that just because religious polemicists and commentators of the era did not indulge in bellicose language to the degree that Raemond did does not mean that they were inherently more rational. An example of this type might be the Calvinist writer Lambert Daneau, who posited a gradualistic, rather than a cataclysmic, defeat of Antichrist. Another example might be Nicholas Vignier. Both these authors have been described as rational because they do not resort to violent expression.[91] Yet Daneau was nevertheless as firm a believer in Antichrist as anyone else of his century. So was Vignier. But the notion of Antichrist was scarcely rational, whether it was couched in the more peaceable rhetoric of Daneau, or in the assumption (held by Vignier) that history is bound to repeat itself. Given the universal acceptance of the belief in Antichrist's coming, which typified the sixteenth and seventeenth centuries, it must be concluded that that legend was a potent barrier to rational theories of causation in a historical context. The habit of rearranging and manipulating historical facts and religious customs was as typical of one as of the other side in the period. During the lifetime of Raemond, economic, moral, and political uncertainties seemed to intensify, rather than to reduce, man's irrational propensities. Within two years of Raemond's death, the reformed church in France, meeting together at the Synod of Gap in October 1603, decided to include belief in a papal Antichrist as part of their Confession of Faith.[92] They cited by way of explanation for their action the arrogation by the pope of all ecclesiastical and temporal authority. They expressly identified the papacy with Antichrist and associated that figure with that "Son of Perdition predicted by the Holy Prophets, that great Whore cloathed with Scarlet sitting upon Seven Mountains" described in the seventeenth chapter of the Book of Revelation.[93]

Belief in Antichrist was the product of a common Judaeo-Christian heritage which, among other things, stressed the unregenerate and rebellious nature of mankind and the likelihood that misbehavior would bring punishment. Indeed, that mentality shows alarming persistence even in the twentieth century.[94] Antichrist was then, and some would say is still, God's secret weapon; the great traitor; the borer from within; the beast on the border. Antichrist was man's collective bad conscience.

6
Luther and Lutheranism

Florimond de Raemond was a popular writer in terms of writing style and sales. He acknowledged these facts readily: "My works are common and popular books"[1] he wrote in *L'Histoire de la naissance, progrèz et décadence de l'hérésie de ce siècle*, adding that scholars ought not waste their oil, labor, and precious time reading his works.[2] His modesty was clearly *pro forma*. In fact, learned men read his books with interest. He did not avoid difficult subjects and referred his readers to the best research available on them. Nonscholars read his books, which dealt with significant issues in an appealing style, one more popular than academic. His subject matter and methodology were respectably historical, though not invariably accurate. His books were polemical, combining history with Catholic piety in a manner not unusual for his times.

His "History of Heresy" was informed by the same dynamic as his first two works, i.e., the superiority of Catholicism, culturally as well as religiously. Unlike the earlier works, however, the "History of Heresy" was not a monograph. His subject was the development of Protestantism throughout Europe in the sixteenth century. His first chapters, with a wealth of symbolism and prognostications, concerned the religious upheaval in non-European areas of the world, such as Persia, Africa, and America, all of which he believed had sustained spiritual revolutions simultaneously. Such events presaged the onset of Europe's religious Reformation guided by an Unseen Hand.

His choice of subject matter—principally religious history and ritual—together with his audience, for the most part nonscholarly and Catholic—made Raemond a historian of the heart and spirit. He had a genius for explaining human behavior with respect to religious doctrine. Although he had paid some attention to the history of institutions (especially to ecclesiastical institutions) in his earlier works, his history of the Reformation affords scanty information as to basic causation of a political or an institutional kind. Nevertheless, this history deserves attention for several reasons.

First, it dignified the century or more of religious change by focusing on the importance of doctrine and ritual in the lives of ordinary people. Raemond's major preoccupation was the seriousness of religious affiliation collectively, on a national basis, and individually, in the realm of man's psychological as well as spiritual well-being. Second, his book was original rather than derivative in its pursuit of the varieties of religious experience available to sixteenth-century people. Few if any historians exhibited the interest he had in documenting the origins, spiritual formulations, style, and proliferation of dozens of radical splinter groups. Raemond was not only an historian in his determination to flesh out the development of Protestantism, but something of a cultural anthropologist in his perception of the significance of such developments. Third, Raemond's history merits study because it was often published in the seventeenth century and must certainly have encouraged Catholic readers—the vast majority in France—to regard Protestantism as a religious phenomenon doomed to extinction for its errors. Although Raemond was not an innovator in terms of historical theory or methodology, and though his works appear to modern scholars to be marred by religious intolerance and polemical distortion, he had an uncommon ability to assess the effect of religious forms on the behavior of individuals and groups of individuals. He is quite possibly the earliest French historian of *mentalité*.

The motives that impelled Raemond to write his history are clear. He wished to expose Protestantism (heresy) as inimical to God and man. He hoped such exposure would produce the demise of all Protestant sects. He tried to appear confident that such heresy was on the wane, and that a Roman victory depended largely on better communication of facts to the public: "All that remains for their final reduction is to portray them as they really are, and they will no longer be; to demonstrate their errors is enough to refute them."[3]

Raemond was devout and sincere, an ideologue willing to use his ideology and his humanist methodology to undermine a religious revolution and to re-establish religious uniformity.[4] He was convinced that the world had been better off before Luther and would be once again after the heretics returned to Rome. He was a cold warrior for his faith when the religious wars in France had barely cooled. To establish religious truth and to achieve social harmony, Raemond turned to the writing of history. The Counter-Reformation encouraged a dynamic history because it had to fight for truth on two fronts: scriptural and historical. Since not all Catholic practices were provable by Scripture, historical circumstance or tradition was used to explain and to justify many things.

If history was the field on which the war for men's spirits could be won, it was also a war that had been declared by the Protestant party. The chief opponents of a Catholic view of history were the authors of the *Magdeburg Centuries*,[5] and reformers like Luther, Calvin, and Bullinger who wrote about ecclesiastical history, nor can one ignore the influential Johann Sleidan, whom Raemond called the "Tite-Live" (Livy) of Lutheranism. Such sources our author felt were prejudiced, written by men who were ignorant of what really happened in history. They were motivated by a desire to hide the light of the real church—Rome's—from the world.[6]

The humanist tradition of textual analysis of original documents was a legacy for all sixteenth-century historians. Raemond's model was Caesar Baronius, who, as we have seen, had already been attracted to our author's works on the popess and on Antichrist. Like Baronius, Raemond wrote to confirm the fact that Catholicism incorporated historical as well as religious truth in its experience and traditions.

Intellectual Framework

Raemond was guided by a set of themes that comprised his conceptual underpinning. He was convinced that God is strictly unaccountable to man. He shared the common belief of his contemporaries that natural phenomena such as storms and marvelous events, not explainable by natural means, were expressions of God's inscrutable will. Since Satan delighted in duping mankind with right-seeming but false notions, Raemond fell back on a certain scepticism, and on occasion, to obscurantism, when he was at a loss for an explanation. His attitude might be contrasted to the more positive, but not necessarily more correct, posture of certain Protestant writers who believed that Scripture, properly understood, offered a certain guide to past, present, and future history.

Raemond held the common fideist point of view that his era offered striking evidence of material and spiritual decline. Such decline produced social instability, so that the wise man placed his trust in the Catholic church; it alone possessed infallible knowledge. Not only could the church assure salvation in the next world, but adherence to it would produce harmony in this one. Raemond felt that his church was particularly sensitive to human needs in a way that Protestant churches were not. Catholic rites were superior because they were designed to meet the needs of all people in all times.

In his attempt to account for heretical belief, Raemond stressed the arrogance of individuals and to a lesser extent, the failures of institutions. Both individuals and institutions were guilty of greed and sloth, and Rome had been lulled into complacency by a long era of good times. More persuasive to Raemond than a detailed analysis of papal or monarchical governance was the moralistic argument that God punishes societies which fail to perform their religious duties by sending civil calamity, i.e., the Protestant Reformation. He refused to recognize the fact that the Reformation had been the response to a deep spiritual unrest and to unmet spiritual longing. If people were dissatisfied with the performance of the church, he held it was due to their weak understanding and will. He was especially sensitive to the impetus given heresy by weak-willed women, such as Marguerite of Navarre. Along with women, the lower classes attracted his attention as having contributed to the success of heresy. He cited "masons, carpenters, book peddlers and tinsmiths" as having been the first parishioners of the first Protestant minister (a former wool-carder) of Meaux.[7] Once the *menu peuple* had tasted of liberty and license, civil disorder and new heresy was inevitable. Heresy spawned heresy, for heretics found cooperation and agreement impossible. Their differences were institutionalized and became capable either of resisting or of initiating further change.

The Scene Is Set

The bulky "History of Heresy," published posthumously (1605) by Raemond's son, François, begins amid a plethora of melodramatic devices that impress on the reader the stability of the Catholic church on the one hand, and on the other its fragile maintenance of unity vis-à-vis its historic enemies, heretics and demons. A rapid sketch of the religious turmoil in Africa, Asia, and the New World demonstrates the interrelation between God's plan and man's fate. Man is tempted by greed, but rewarded for his loyalty to Rome by the expansion of his military and moral authority. He exulted in Catholic success in Mexico, Peru, and Cochin China. The defeat of pagans and idolaters in those far-off lands suggests the ultimate defeat of unbelievers closer to hand.[8] God watches over his own. Even when Christian kings failed to deflect the Muslim threat by diplomatic and political means, they were protected from Muslim conquest by an all-merciful God.⁹ God triumphs over nonbelievers and will help man re-establish religious uniformity.

Such scene-setting was important to Raemond, for he had set himself the task of describing the spread of Protestant belief throughout Europe. Although French Protestantism was in decline after the failure of the Colloquy of Poissy (1561),[10] its ability to resist the established religion impressed the Catholic party. They needed to remember, and Raemond sought to remind them, that the new religions were doomed.[11] The lesson was all the more valuable for, at the time our author was writing this history, the French monarchy was promulgating the Edict of Nantes (1598). That document guaranteed the survival of a religious minority. Catholic readers had to believe — and Raemond hoped to persuade them — that the Edict was but a temporary setback to the triumph of Romanism. His very title obliged him to maintain that Protestantism was decadent in Europe.

The remainder of this chapter explores Raemond's position on Luther and Lutheranism. This simple schema requires that we ignore dozens of interesting topics and many anecdotes that are illuminating even when outrageous.[12] The material has been selected to give the reader insight into the *mentalité* of pious Catholics concerning Protestantism.

Luther Himself

Raemond thought Luther was revolting. He introduced him with so much unflattering detail to indicate clearly that the German was a man of negative moral stature. For example, he noted that Luther's astrological chart indicated that he would fail in his faith.[13] He said that "Ludder" meant one who mocks, scoundrel, or carrion in German.[14] If one spelled the name Lauther, it totaled 666, the sign of Antichrist. Raemond informed his readers that Luther's career was presaged by three moons over Germany in the year 1514, and tossed off his reform movement as the mere product of jealousy between Augustinian and Dominican monks.[15] Yet, Raemond admitted that Luther had some good, as well as bad, qualities. He observed that his person was not ungraceful, and that he had a ready wit, an excellent memory, the ability to explain things well, and he excelled at public speaking. He also ascribed to the reformer a prodigious capacity for hard work and immense learning.[16]

In his treatment of Luther's faith, Raemond tended to shift

positions. On the one hand, he claimed it was a patch-work of heresies which had long troubled Christianity. On the other hand, he was impressed with Luther's preservation of the form and some of the content of Catholicism.[17] He frequently alluded to the relative conservatism of Luther's views when comparing Lutheranism to Calvinism. When he wasn't comparing the two, but concentrating on Luther's reforms only, he stressed Luther's heretical tendencies.[18] Luther's admission to Dr. Johannes Eck that he did not condemn all of Hus's beliefs confirmed Raemond's conviction that he was primarily a Hussite.[19] Other heretical elements in Luther's system included the denial of free-will from Simon Magus; the belief that secular authority must govern the church from Athanasius; that faith, and not good works, is justified from an Arian heretic named Junonius. This last idea was basic to Lutheranism, thought Raemond, because that reformer had condemned five of seven sacraments, along with almsgiving, fasting, and orisons. Luther's views on many issues were borrowed. He shared with Peter Abelard the idea that all events are by necessity, which made God the author of evil. His rejection of fasting was all one could expect from a German, for Germans, as everyone knew, were great eaters. Vaudois heretics had criticized indulgences.[20] Armenian ones had refused to regard marriage as a sacrament. The Lutheran concept of an invisible church was a Donatist invention, as was the notion that only the good are in the church.[21] Greeks had insisted on communion in two kinds long before Luther.[22] Raemond did not have to produce his own list of heresies. The idea that heretics were forerunners of the Reformation was an old argument of Catholic controversialists. As early as 1521, the Faculty of Theology at the Sorbonne had condemned Luther's theses for repeating the same errors made by Wycliffe, Hus, and others. Bishop John Fisher and Dr. Johannes Eck pointed out the similarities between the reformer and more ancient heretics. This literature enjoyed a vogue in the sixteenth century and a special name: catalogs of heretical belief.[23]

It is interesting to note that those heretical influences are not the ones modern historians think prime in shaping Luther's theology. That such factors as the Scriptures, the German mystics, William of Occam, Saint Augustine, Saint Bernard, Gabriel Biel, Lefèvre d'Étaples, and Pierre d'Ailly had an important effect on Luther, Raemond did not mention, nor did the other authors on whom he frequently relied.[24] Scripture was embarrassing to Rome where it contradicted Catholic tradition, while none of the men on this list had actually been declared to be heretics.

Although Raemond admitted that abuses did exist in the church, he thought Luther would have served Christianity best by working within the church for reform.[25] Instead, he had used the exaggerated claims of indulgence peddlers to accuse the papacy of complicity in a dishonest sales drive. Finally, he had rejected papal authority altogether.[26] He blamed the historian Johannes Sleidan for giving the impression that Dr. Johannes Eck had been bested at Leipzig by Luther, when the reverse was true. Sleidan had not mentioned that Luther believed in purgatory at that time and admitted so during that same debate, a damaging concession.[27] He accused Sleidan of distortion. Nor was this the first occasion that Sleidan's account was duplicitous, for he had reported Luther's examination by Cardinal Cajetan, which occurred in autumn 1518, without mentioning the fact that Luther had abjured many faults that he later reiterated.[28] Such at least was Raemond's contention about this examination. He was quite correct about the distorted report of the Leipzig debate; he was quite wrong about the "abjuration" Luther had made to Cajetan. In fact, Luther did not abjure.[29] Raemond recognized the polemical nature of Lutheranism's favorite historian. His own bias, however, was not always clear to him, and led him to commit errors and distortions of his own.

Luther and Anabaptists

If, in the course of writing his chapters on Luther, Raemond necessarily dwelled on those issues that divided Catholics from Protestants, it is not altogether surprising that he forgot or rather, overlooked, a problem that united them: a mutual abhorrence of the principles of the Anabaptists. Luther did indeed abhor Anabaptist views, and Zwinglian ones. Raemond's assessment of the cause of Anabaptism must have been extremely distasteful to Lutheran readers, who were able to read *L'Histoire* in German as early as 1614.[30] According to Raemond, Luther and Zwingli were the two main sources of inspiration for, and thus causal factors in, the emergence of Anabaptism.[31] Raemond was aware of the Swiss theologian's tergiversation with respect to infant baptism.[32] Luther was to blame for encouraging Anabaptist views because he had preached that it was better to leave little babies unbaptized than to baptize them without faith.[33] Both Zwingli and Luther were concerned that baptism be followed by instruction in the faith, but neither one was prepared to substitute adult baptism for pedobaptism. Luther expressly rejected delaying this ritual, one of only two sacraments that he had salvaged from Catholicism. Since Zwingli broke with more radical-minded followers who went on to found the first Swiss Anabaptist church,[34] and since Luther could not endure Zwingli's religious position and came to view all Anabaptists as imitators of false prophets such as Thomas Müntzer of Zwickau,[35] what did Raemond mean by suggesting that these two men, Zwingli and Luther, had inspired the Anabaptist movement?

Despite the fact that Anabaptists had, like streams, run out in different directions from the sources (Luther, Zwingli),[36] Raemond believed common principles united them all. One was Luther's biblicism, with its accompanying suspicion of Aristotelianism and scholasticism.[37] Luther's emphasis on the Scriptures revealed to Raemond an anti-intellectualism basic to Lutheranism and copied as well by Anabaptists. This unwillingness to accept authorities other than biblical resulted in a deep distrust of civil authority: "Anabaptists reject civil authority and had long disputed its power, using the Bible for reference; so too with Luther. All his books, *On Secular Authority, On the Babylonian Captivity* ... sing the same song."[38]

Many Anabaptists had turned away from Lutheranism after having identified with it. One case in point was Balthasar Hübmaier (d. 1528), whom Raemond believed had been inspired by Luther's statement that no sacrament was effective if faith were absent.[39] This idea, so important in Luther's conception of the sacrament of baptism,[40] is in fact revelatory of a deep spiritualism which Luther held in common with Erasmus and Zwingli, and which many religious radicals including Anabaptists carried to even greater lengths. It must be recalled that Luther tempered the external signs of a sacrament with faith that he believed was bestowed only by God's grace. Without grace, Luther felt the external signs to be worthless.[41] Motivated by the polemical need to implicate the father of the Reformation with having given rise to religious radicalism (both Anabaptist and Sacramentarian)[42] and aware of Luther's spiritualist tendencies and their reflection or intensification at the hands of these same radical leaders, Raemond insisted on their linkage to Luther. His assertion that Anabaptists, Sacramentarians and Confessionists were all three inspired by Luther[43] has been reiterated in the scholarship of the twentieth century[44] even though the necessity of examining the precise local circumstances, which helped form a variety of heterodox groups and their leaders, remains an imperative of historical research.

The Lord's Supper

If baptism was the second most trying problem for Christians to resolve during the Reformation, the first was surely that of the Eucharist, communion service, or Lord's supper. It was the sacrament which affected most people most often. Raemond wrote that Luther believed in the real presence of the body and blood of Christ in the communion bread, but unfortunately added to this orthodox belief, a heretical view (Wycliffe's) that the bread, once consecrated, becomes the body of Christ while still remaining bread.[45] In Raemond's opinion, this confused Christ's divine nature with his human one. Luther's rejection of the sacrificial aspects of the service and his "refusal" to elevate the bread for fear of making of it an idol annoyed Raemond. On this point he was not well informed, however, as Luther continued to have the consecrated host elevated until 1542, if only to preserve the concept of the true presence against its critics, of whom Carlstadt was the first.[46]

Andreas Bodenstein von Carlstadt occupied a whole chapter in Raemond's book. He was characterized as the first Sacramentarian, father of Zwinglians and Calvinists (Luther was the grandfather or grandmother) because he was the first to deny the real presence of Christ in the communion rite, saying instead that the bread offered was but the sign and symbol of Christ, not his body.[47] Just as Raemond wrote that Luther was the departure point for Anabaptists with respect to baptism, so too did he stress the affinity between Carlstadt and Luther.[48]

In the course of the struggle to define the basic meaning of the Eucharist and to determine its ritual, Raemond named the Silesian nobleman, Caspar Schwenckfeld, as the father of a new and detestable sect or heresy that called into question the authority of the Bible itself in determining the substance of holiness. Schwenckfeld has been analyzed in terms of his having taken over from Luther a doctrine of justification by faith before turning it into a doctrine of "progressive justification."[49] Raemond was right in saying that Luther thought Schwenckfeld a Zwinglian for having inverted the ordinary rubric "This is my body" (Hoc est corpus meum) to read "Corpus meum est hoc."[50] He was wrong, however, to believe Luther, for Schwenckfeld was no Zwinglian. Schwenckfeld certainly thought the inverted words conveyed a spiritual meaning only, not a literal one. When Christ said "My body is this," he meant merely that like bread, his body was also food, only food for the soul. Christ similarly taught the apostles that his blood was a spiritual drink for a thirsty soul. Schwenckfeld regretted the fact that Zwingli had interpreted the verb is (*est*) to mean symbolizes. The Silesian came to reject the idea that this spiritual mystery of communion should be dependent on material bread and wine. Despite the fact that Luther had dismissed Schwenckfeld's interpretation of the

Lord's supper as Zwinglian, Raemond blamed Luther for the spiritualist excesses of the Silesian's interpretation, which he considered a prime threat to church ritual and to the purity of the Evangelical message:[51] "Oh, Luther, base born man. For, as we have seen, it was he who first forged and whetted the knives of this juggernaut."[52]

Although Luther's views on the communion service were mistaken, there was still much in Lutheranism that Raemond thought unexceptional and even good. Lutherans still retained Latin in parts of their church service; they decorated their altars with lovely chalices; they knelt to receive communion, etc. Their beautiful churches were totally unlike the plain ones that Calvinists maintained.[53]

Lutheran Marriage

The question of marriage, like baptism and the Eucharist, was another divisive issue separating some Christians from others. Raemond quoted a tract Luther had written in 1522 entitled *On the Estate of Marriage* in which the reformer claimed that it was not within his power as a man to do without a woman, or in a woman's to do without a man, and this was because God had commanded men and women "to be fruitful and multiply."[54] Raemond had prefaced his quotation of this passage with his own statement: "God commands one and all." This addition led his readers to think Luther had made no provision for those who would prefer to remain celibate.[55] This was not true, for Luther had provided for three categories of men—the impotent, the castrated, and the clergy—the choice of celibacy.[56] Raemond was scandalized by the fact that monks and nuns had married, and he felt Luther's own marriage had set a bad example.[57] Actually, Luther was not the one who had first set such an example. Many of his friends and admirers were priests or monks who married before Luther did himself. Raemond also criticized Luther's permissive attitude toward divorce.[58] The reformer believed it was allowable on scriptural grounds, for Christ had permitted divorce where one spouse was adulterous, so that the innocent party might remarry.[59] Man's sinfulness after the Fall made divorce necessary, according to Luther (who quoted Christ). Luther hoped a more permissive policy would reduce the sins that a less permissive one encouraged. Although divorce was to be obtainable in his scheme on the widest possible basis, remarriage for Christians was to be permitted only on a somewhat more restrictive one.[60]

Raemond condemned Luther as a man of incontinent appetites and no self-discipline. Luther's benign attitude toward marriage as a source of help and companionship, a shelter from temptation, most valuable because of the children who could be taught to love God, was ignored by Raemond.[61] Instead, he dwelled on the physical side of marriage, comparing it unfavorably to a virginal or to a chaste life acclaimed by Catholics from time immemorial.[62] The reduction by Luther of legal impediments to marriage and divorce, and even more so, his hearty endorsement of married life as a happier, but also a healthier state, made Raemond view Lutheranism as a principle of liberty that was sure to produce license.[63] He wrote that Luther condoned adultery with maidservants and referred to a famous passage in Luther's sermon on marriage in which the reformer quoted a well-known proverb in his effort to warn wives concerning the dangers that they provoked by refusing to perform their conjugal duty. This proverb said "If you won't, someone else will."[64] Raemond followed other Catholic writers who misinterpreted Luther's use of this expression concerning maidservants coming in to do what wives would not.

The disparity between the Lutheran and Catholic view of sex and marriage was great. Luther was as accepting of the physical needs of men and women as Raemond was suspicious. The German acknowledged the sexuality of mankind as "a natural and necessary thing," an irresistible urge because it had been instilled in both sexes by God with only a few exceptions, and those exceptions were mostly "eunuchs" of one kind or another, incapable of reproducing anyway. These God excused from that duty and consolation.[65] For Luther, marriage was an "estate," a special status that was replete with comforts and not below the celibate estate. It was the equal of celibacy and, when those who professed celibacy were not single-minded in devoting their surplus energies to God, superior to it.[66]

For Raemond, there was no proper estate of marriage. At best it was inferior to celibacy: there were more thorns than roses in marriage.[67] He rejected the idea that men and women could not dispense with one another. He upheld the medieval Christian view of the superiority of virginity and chastity to sexual intercourse: "God, wrote St. Augustine, does not command that which is impossible to do; but in commanding, insists that you do what you can, and ask for help in what you cannot do. Granted that the vow of chastity is not easy ... still, it is not impossible. ... Nothing really fine is easy: virtue is not virtue if it is not difficult."[68]

Both the Lutheran and the Catholic view of sexuality took as their departure point the fallen nature of human beings. Luther admitted that "Intercourse is never without sin," but he reminded his followers that God's grace excused the sin and blessed the estate of marriage.[69] For him, the ordinary goal for men and women was a happy marriage and the enjoyment of one's humanity.

For Raemond, on the other hand, and for his church, of which he was a self-appointed defender, moral grandeur was attainable at the cost of subduing one's sexuality, of living chastely in God's service. Because the Lutheran view of sex and marriage more nearly approaches the modern attitude than the medieval, Catholic ideal of Raemond, one may view Luther as an harbinger of change. Yet both Catholicism and Protestantism continued to accept as fundamental the moral depravity of the fallen human race, and their different views of marriage were but different responses to a common heritage.

Lutheranism, First and Last

When Florimond de Raemond called Lutheranism the grandmother of all the major and minor Protestant sects,[70] he was doing something more than referring to the chronology of reform. He was not suggesting that Luther approved of them all—he knew Luther did not. He was not saying that he had been personally involved in drawing up their confessions, or even, that he was acquainted with their founders. Carlstadt was exceptional because he had been a colleague at Wittenberg. Raemond was totally informed of the theological differences that divided the Protestant sects; he knew they were historically derived and generally nonnegotiable. He was sensitive to the variations in sectarian rubric and even in church architecture because he knew these had encouraged sectarian proliferation. That "heretics" were stubborn and prone to disagree about these matters he believed to be their most characteristic trait.

No, the "grandmother" had not been a role-model for her brood. He knew that Zwinglians had an independent origin, anyway, and that serious doctrinal chasms divided the Swiss reformation from the German one. What Raemond meant by his "grandmother clause" was that Luther had left a spiritual legacy to Protestants that ran deeper than history, right down to the bedrock of faith, where it drew its strength from an individualistic, antilegalist, antitraditional source of faith—spirit.[71] It was Raemond's sensitivity to religion that provided him with this insight into the nature of the bond between Luther, the radicals, and all other Protestants.

Many scholars of the sixteenth-century Reformation may discount such insight as superficial and mere hyperbole, but it was more than idiosyncratic, and has of late been reflected in the studies of some specialists. Luther has been called a "provisional Spiritualist" by one of these, while another gives the spiritualist contributions of Luther prime significance when observing that "in Luther in some respects these traits are more pronounced than in the fanatics."[72]

One of the most fascinating aspects of contemporary research into the Lutheran reformation is the increasing recognition given by Roman Catholics to the movement once considered merely heretical. Catholic scholars are now able to view Luther as devoted to God and Scripture in a deeply personal, subjective, way albeit with some "emotional impulsiveness" that resulted in an excessively individualistic interpretation of Scripture.[73] This view is at once more politic and more respectful than the dictum given by Raemond, who described Luther as "entrenched in his own opinions, under the influence of some poorly understood Scriptural passage, impervious to reason, tradition, or authority and not by them to be persuaded."[74] The difference in tone between these two Catholic opinions, one modern, one ancient, is not to be minimized, but then neither is their point of contact.

Notwithstanding Raemond's regret that Luther had perverted Christianity by ignoring those elements of faith not compatible with his own interpretation and inspiration, he was painfully aware that Luther's church was more Catholic than Calvin's, observing that "Lutheranism makes some truce with Catholicism ... but with Calvinism, it's all-out war."[75]

7

Calvin and Calvinism

France and the Coming of Reform

That France was a happy country before heresy crossed the Rhine at Strasbourg was a basic premise for Raemond's introduction to the reform movement in his native land.[1] He may have been thinking of her recovery from the Hundred Years' War, for the economy had begun, sometime in the last few years of the fifteenth century, to recover from that struggle.[2] Raemond could also rejoice in the intellectual recovery of France, which had begun to equip herself for a literary renaissance. The patron of this intellectual renewal was Francis I, Raemond's favorite king, whose favors to well-intentioned scholars like the classicist, Guillaume Budé, and to Erasmus, Raemond approved. Unfortunately, Francis was taken in by more unruly academics, many from Luther's Germany, or Zwingli's Switzerland, men routed through Strasbourg by a meddlesome Martin Bucer. Such foreigners influenced French scholars like Jacques Lefèvre d'Étaples,[3] Guillaume Farel,[4] Michel d'Arande,[5] and Gérard Roussel,[6] members of the famous Meaux Circle. There, under the guise of scholarship, they tried to make a religious revolution of a "Luthero-Zwinglian" sort.[7] "Lutherans from Meaux," said Raemond (quoting Theodore de Bèze), grew to be a proverbial expression that Raemond felt accurately described the majority of scholars there. Bishop Guillaume Briçonnet, however, was unfairly accused of Lutheranism. He found him guilty only of an imprudent curiosity.[8] As for Lefèvre, he offended by retaining the guise of Catholicism while fantasizing a new religion at Navarre. Raemond refused to define its precise nature, but believed that the humanist-reformer had sewn doubts and scruples in all who listened to him.[9]

After Lefèvre, Gérard Roussel was the most troublesome of the Meaux group according to Raemond. He was Marguerite's confessor, and to him she entrusted first the abbey of Clairac, and then the diocese of Oléron. Like Lefèvre, Roussel never formally abandoned his Roman allegiance. Raemond's feeling toward him reflected the respect many people had expressed for his elevated sense of Christian piety and morality; "above reproach" was the expression Raemond used to describe these traits. Yet Roussel's excessive individualism in celebrating the divine service and in interpreting basic doctrine made of him, in Raemond's opinion, a "Rousseliste" more certainly than a Catholic. Roussel erred principally, in our author's view, by disregarding all authority that contradicted his private opinion. Raemond asked his readers to consider what confusion would result if everyone decided to be his own interpreter of **Scripture**. Roussel is the man whom Raemond fingered as having set up an alternative religion for the mountainous regions near Guyenne.[10] Because Raemond was convinced that the religion one was "suckled" on was ever afterwards the most likely to maintain its hold on the imagination, he regretted the influence Roussel wielded in Navarre. He was particularly distressed that Guyenne, his own province, had been obliged to bear the effects of heresy longer than any of the other regions of France.[11] Although John Calvin would later blame Roussel bitterly for having deserted the Evangile for the chains of Rome,[12] Raemond did not for a moment consider Roussel a deserter of the evangelicalism which our author considered basic to the Protestant reform movement. He persisted in viewing Roussel's position as unorthodox despite that cleric's episcopal dignity. Raemond's stubborn estimation of Roussel as a (Protestant) heretic is consistent with that which Roussel's biographer found characteristic of his doctrine and practice.[13] Although Raemond regretted the influence that Roussel had exerted over Marguerite, who shared the "imbecility" of the female sex, her ultimate rejection of Protestantism reconciled him to her memory.[14]

The reformers of Meaux have been rather circumspectly treated by historians bent on distinguishing what was native to the reform movement there and what was derived from the Lutheran reform movement to the east. Raemond did not anticipate the chauvinist and largely Protestant drift of nineteenth-century historians who regarded Briçonnet and Lefèvre as the originators of the Reformation in France independent of Lutheran influence.[15] He believed that Lefèvre was infected with Lutheranism first. In turn, he did his best to infect his former pupils at Meaux, of whom three — Briçonnet, Roussel, and d'Arande — became Roman Catholic bishops, and only one, Farel, became a Protestant. Raemond devoted no space to speculation about this extraordinary turn of events, however. Such facts did oblige a gradual but accelerating change in the historical analysis of the French reform movement.

Twentieth-century historians of what Augustin Renaudet termed the "Pré-réforme" in France have increasingly tended to confirm the fact, which Raemond and his Catholic contemporaries felt was self-evident, that is, that the turmoil in sixteenth-century French religious life was caused by the importation of Lutheranism, and not by the dogmatic, individualistic, and mystical "precursors" of reform such as Briçonnet and Lefèvre d'Étaples.[16]

Even though the dynamics of Lutheran influence were appreciated by Raemond, his unwillingness to consider the extent of Catholic reform activity prior to the German Reformation must be considered a real deficiency of his otherwise fascinating, often illuminating narrative. He did not even hint at the disciplinary reforms effected by Briçonnet and Lefèvre at Saint-Germain-des Prés in Paris, or of those in and around Meaux. The former, to be sure, were consistent with the monastic reforms of prior centuries, but the latter were intended to provide the parish of Meaux with a reasonable supply of resident clergy who would and could be expected to preach Scripture to their flocks. Since the hunger for the Word of God, for the *Bible*, was well-rooted in France at least as early as 1513, and well before Luther's own translation into German of the *New Testament*, Raemond might have acknowledged this fact.[17] He did not. Instead, he contrived to make the translation and proliferation of Bibles in France appear to be a non-native concern. He did, it is true, attribute what he mistakenly thought was the first translation of the Bible into French to a Frenchman—John Calvin's cousin, Pierre Robert, generally called Olivétan. But he made it appear that Olivétan was responding to a foreign influence, that of the Vaudois heretics, at a time when the Vaudois was governed by the counts of Savoy and the prince-bishops of Lausanne.[18]

By failing to identify evangelicalism as a native and significant preparation to the successful spread of the reform movement in France, and by turning a blind eye to the implications of a native Catholic reform movement, Raemond made the success of John Calvin's theology at once more unaccountable, and more impressive.

Raemond's Calvin Sources

Florimond de Raemond was proud of the fact that he had amassed a certain amount of original material in his effort to treat of John Calvin's early life and religious career in France:

I will write nothing of him (and if I touch on several things which have never yet been written it is because the subject requires it) that I have not obtained from a reliable source; and from people who knew him from his earliest youth, about which I am particularly well informed; that is, from their own testimony, and from several small leaflets which the new Reformation swallowed up as soon as it started.[19]

Since Calvin was born in 1509, it is unlikely that Raemond first started to collect information about him when he began his "History of Heresy" in the late 1590s. By then anyone who had known Calvin in his youth would have been ninety years old or more when they were interviewed. It is more likely that he began collecting pamphlets and recording information from knowledgeable people who had been close to Calvin or who had participated in the reform movement when Raemond was himself attracted to it, sometime during the 1560s. Even then, the memories of those Raemond interviewed may have betrayed them with respect to certain facts, and certainly with regard to a precise chronology.[20] Because he relied very often on the reports given to him by eyewitnesses, Raemond's account was vulnerable to treacherous memory as well as to political and social pressures. This was so because his witnesses — many of whom had compromised themselves during the reform by abandoning their church before it was either legal or prudent to do so — were similarly vulnerable. Other inaccuracies were almost certainly derived from Raemond's use of published sources, many written by men whose own religious persuasion, whether Catholic or Lutheran, made them hostile to some or even to most of the positions that came to be associated with John Calvin and his followers. Such men were usually professional theologians, though not always — some were merely pastors with a bent for polemical writing. Among the Catholic sources Raemond consulted were individuals he was afraid to name because he knew them to be motivated principally by hatred rather than by love of truth.[21] Those he did name included Antoine du Mouchy, the Sorbonne theologian at the Council of Trent (Demochares); William Lindanus, a biblical scholar from the lowlands who tried to reconcile tradition with Scripture; Lawrence Surius, a Cistercian monk whose works included rehabilitating St. Leo from the effects of Protestant polemic; Victor Palma-Cayet, the royal historian of Henry IV and former Calvinist minister converted by Father Duperron; Claude de Sainctes, a critic of Bèze's Eucharistic theology; Gabriel Dupréau (Prateolus), a theologian and professor at the College of Navarre and a foe of Farel; and Reginaldus, a Jesuit critic of Calvin.²² Last, and quite possibly least in stature, was Jerome Bolsec, a renegade Carmelite friar and *quondam* medical practitioner who had migrated to Switzerland in admiration of the reform, then fallen out with Calvin and taken his revenge by writing a slanderous biography (1577). Bolsec was eventually reconciled with Rome.²³

Other than these, the major Catholic sources, Raemond consulted several Lutheran ones. Besides the historian Sleidan, he relied on Tileman Hesshusen (Hesshusius), a gnesio-Lutheran theologian and professor at the University of Heidelberg, and on Joachim Westphal, a pastor at Hamburg. Both of these men had running controversies with Calvin over the Eucharist. One can assess in some measure the probable animus of these writers when one learns that of the Catholics, three were men who had been temporarily won over to the reform (Cayet, Bolsec, Raemond), while another (Sainctes) had been suspected of heterodoxy.²⁴ Shattered illusions added to their contempt for Calvinism, while the desire to win approval after a temporary *lapsus* might account for the heightened acerbity of their rhetoric. Two of the three Lutheran sources named were gnesio-Lutherans (ultra-conservatives), a group that jealously preserved theological differences between Lutherans and Calvinists. Such sectarian division was heightened by political considerations, for Lutheranism in the last half of the sixteenth century lost ground to Calvinism in some areas of western Germany (the Palatinate) and in central and eastern Europe (Poland, Hungary, Transylvania). Raemond's writing, drawing heavily as it did upon secondary sources, could only reflect some of the tensions and prejudices — political, theological and even psychological — that shaped their authors' points of view.

Naturally he availed himself of a good deal of published works by Calvinist authors. There are frequent references in the history to Calvin's *Institutes* and to certain other of his works, including the autobiographical sketch which the reformer wrote as a preface to his *Psalms*. He referred as well to Bèze's biography of John Calvin, and perhaps to that of Nicholas Colladon as well.²⁵ The ecclesiastical history, which Bèze helped to write and which bears his name, was also one of Raemond's sources of information.²⁶ From time to time he was privileged to obtain or to study official documents, and, more frequently, private documents that came his way — all the more frequently it appears, since by the time he was writing the "History of Heresy," he had achieved a reputation that was certainly national and, to some degree, international.

Calvin's Conversion

The biographers of John Calvin's youth and early reform activity have long struggled to give a convincing and precise chronological account of his religious development, particularly of his "conversion" from Catholicism to Protestantism. Some observers have attributed the initial influence with regard to such a conversion to Calvin's cousin, Pierre Robert (Olivétan), an influence attested by Bèze and Colladon in their biographies of the reformer, which was published after his death and echoed by a number of other authors on the subject, but not by Raemond.[27]

Although Raemond's failure to mention Olivétan's possible influence appears on the surface to be a grave over-sight, when one examines the problem more closely, this omission seems due merely to carelessness. It can be seen that by no means did all of Calvin's biographers attribute great spiritual significance to the friendly relationship maintained by the two cousins, and some have denied it altogether.[28]

Aside from Bèze and Colladon, who claimed that Olivétan had been the first to set Calvin's feet along the path of reform, biographers of the reformer have Calvin's own references to his conversion with which to work. The most important of these is the Preface to Calvin's *Commentary on the Psalms* (1557). In addition, there are the two letters, replies of Calvin to his critics (Sadoleto and Westphal), which are generally assumed to include autobiographical information. Although of late this notion has been subject to revision, what is not debatable is the fact that in none of these statements was Calvin specific with regard to the people instrumental in any conversion, or to the precise moment that conversion occurred.[29]

In attributing Calvin's conversion to the German classicist Melchior Wolmar, Raemond initiated a controversy that continues to this day.[30] Unlike the question of Olivétan's influence, Wolmar's is not attested to by Bèze, nor did Calvin acknowledge such spiritual indebtedness. What is known certainly is that Calvin studied Greek with Wolmar for a while, perhaps at Orleans, more likely at Bourges.[31] His studies were interrupted by his father's final illness (1531), and after Calvin's departure from Noyon, he went to Paris to resume his literary education. Neither in his letters to Wolmar nor in his dedication of his *Commentary on II Corinthians* (1546) to this old professor of Greek did Calvin refer to the spiritual influence of his former teacher and friend. Such silence on his part has led many scholars to deny Wolmar was ever the prime influence over Calvin with respect to his conversion.[32]

Given the lack of evidence other than Raemond's own narrative, it is not surprising to find that a certain number of Calvin scholars still follow Raemond in asserting the prime role Wolmar played in shaping Calvin's spiritual destiny. For Raemond's biographer it is important to attempt to account for the decisiveness with which our author named Wolmar as the mediator of the reformer's conversion. It is always possible that Raemond had acquired some inside information from his living sources regarding the matter, but it seems rather unlikely that this was indeed the case. He was usually quick to point to such sources by name, and did not do so in this business about Wolmar.

A contributing factor to Raemond's assertiveness seems to have been his own juvenile experience at school, although he does not tell us so. It seems an unlikely coincidence that Raemond began his introduction of Calvin with a disquisition on the "Regents" and "Masters" of schools who had sown doubts about religious truth by openly discussing the works of Luther, Zwingli, and other reformers. In search of certainty concerning religion, they succeeded only in establishing Lutheranism in France according to Raemond. We know of course that he was himself susceptible to the reform attitudes he described as characteristic of several of his masters. It is thus quite possible that he read his own life story into the educational history of John Calvin, even though he lacked written documents that could unequivocally support such conclusions. It is less likely that Raemond's position on Wolmar was due mainly to a desire to establish Germany rather than France as the source of Calvin's heresy,[33] for he had already made that quite clear in connection with his treatment of the Lutheran penetration of the Circle of Meaux.

In naming Wolmar as Calvin's conversionary mediator, Raemond was operating in the context of the historian more than the polemicist, though with some admixture, certainly, of polemical intent. The fact is that he was trying to make such ambiguous and incomplete evidence as was available to him explain the events that did, in fact, take place in and around Bourges when Calvin was Wolmar's student. Using Calvin's own Preface to the *Psalms*,[34] Raemond attempted to apply it to Calvin's situation in Bourges. When Calvin mentioned his obstinate addiction to papal supersititions, Raemond believed him implicitly. Hence, he rejected the secondhand testimony of Bèze and Colladon concerning Olivétan's influence, accepting the firsthand but retrospective testimony of Calvin instead.

In other words, Raemond accepted Calvin's statements that he had been a staunch Catholic as he had interpreted them from the Preface to the *Psalms*, but he did not attempt to apply to the problem of the conversion such information as might be gleaned from the two letters to Sadoleto and to Westphal.[35] Yet, even if Raemond had used the letters, it is hard to see how he could have avoided the essential problems which the letters, along with the Preface to the *Psalms* pose; namely, the problem of a gradual, intellectual preparation for an eventual change (conversion), and the quick realization that change had at some point been accomplished.

The problems can be illustrated by the Preface to the *Psalms* alone. Calvin's most important statement in it is his mention of "sudden conversion" and of being "subdued" and "reduced" to "docility" by God. Raemond did not wish, evidently, to legitimize Calvin's conversion by attributing it to God. Instead, he took Calvin's further statement, that he had been the recipient of "some taste and knowledge of true piety" to mean that he had been instructed in these matters by Wolmar. Calvin then proceeded to say that he had given more attention to religious matters after that conversion, while not abandoning his legal studies altogether.[36] Thus it was not, in the short run, correct for Raemond to assume that Wolmar had convinced Calvin to abandon law for theology, although in the long run that proved to be the case. From the Preface Raemond was able to say that Calvin was of a melancholy, retiring personality,[37] even though the reformer admitted that "before a year was out" he was sought out by evangelically minded acquaintances to preach or teach what he had only begun to learn himself.[38] Raemond believed that Calvin began to preach after leaving Bourges for Paris (in June 1531), while studying law.[39] He also wrote that Calvin's main energies were now turned to religious pursuits, and that Wolmar encouraged him for this "enterprise," not only by letter, but also with gifts of books purchased in Germany. Raemond added that despite this encouragement, Calvin never said a word about Wolmar in connection with his new vocation.[40]

What can we deduce from such testimony? First, Raemond's comment about Calvin's having silently received Wolmar's encouragement was factual. Calvin did not admit to Wolmar's religious influence. Second, the reference to letters and books sent by his former master does not establish a date prior to the time when Calvin was publicly committed to Protestantism. The correspondence between the two men was lifelong, and would have an entirely different meaning after Calvin threw in his lot with reform than it would have had before.[41] Raemond was guilty of manipulating what he knew about Wolmar, after Calvin went public, in order to strengthen his point about that classical scholar's significance in Calvin's religious life. And yet, the thesis continues to be defended and may be true without being provable. A key to determining to what degree Calvin was or was not a Protestant during 1531 (or for several years thereafter, since historians do not agree as to when his conversion was accomplished) would be the existence of his early sermons and other teachings. The records do not exist. It may well be that his teaching was consistent in fact with Catholic teaching at any time before he committed his system (*The Institutes of the Christian Religion*) to paper, between 1533 and 1534.

All we can say of Raemond's view of Calvin's conversion is that it was an attempt by which he sought to fit Calvin's own imprecise testimony, as given in the Preface to *Psalms*, to the basic events of his life. Raemond, like many another author who has attempted to do this,[42] was obliged to accommodate the term "sudden conversion" used by Calvin, with the undoubtedly slow pace suggested by the completion of his formal studies and the composition of the *Institutes*, a slowness certainly indicated in all three of the documents generally used to provide insight into Calvin's religious growth and change. Even the Preface to the *Psalms*, which contains the term "sudden conversion," contains phrases which suggest a long period in which Calvin was resisting a change of heart. He noted that his obstinacy made it "very hard to draw me from that deep slough, by a sudden conversion.[43] The *Second Reply to Westphal* contained evidence that Calvin was "beginning to emerge from the darkness of the papacy" some time before the Marburg Colloquy of 1529,[44] five years or so before the first draft of his *Institutes*. A slow, painful process toward conversion is again outlined in the *Reply to Jacopo Sadoleto*. In that document, Calvin described his halting progress — punctuated with descents into "extreme terror" — toward the Word.[45]

In a sense, Raemond's own interpretation of Calvin's conversion appears at a disadvantage when compared to those of the majority of scholars who have emphasized just this gradualness, for Calvin did indeed experience an intellectual progression that led from scholasticism through humanism and on to evangelical Lutheranism before his conversion registered fully (and quite probably, suddenly) in his own mind. It may be that in the figure of Wolmar, humanism and Lutheranism were personified in a sense for Raemond. In any case, it would be rash to try and determine the rightness or wrongness of Raemond's theory in the absence of complete evidence. It is helpful to recall, as has a recent scholar of the problem, that due to the nature of Calvin's own testimony and the absence of other sources, it is very difficult to say for sure when Calvin's conversion took place, or even what kind of experience it was.[46] Raemond did hit upon some of the vital elements in that conversion experience — humanism and Lutheranism in an academic setting. His greatest error may have been that he gave too much credit to only one of Calvin's own retrospective assessments of the process, the emphasis on *"sudden conversion."*

The final picture provided by our author — a quick conversion via a human intermediary (Wolmar), followed by a long period of clandestine Protestantism and a Nicodemite's outward conformity to Rome — was one calculated to reinforce the character of Calvin as our author re-constructed it. It was that of a man both subtle and shy, a master communicator who was incapable of mastering his own ambition, a rarified spirit compared to the grossness of Luther, but ultimately one more dangerous.[47]

Calvin at Angoulême

On all Saints Day, 1533, a friend of Calvin's, Nicholas Cop, was installed as rector of the University of Paris, and in his first sermon, he gave voice to many of the essential concerns of Protestantism. Raemond did not deal with this speech at all.[48] He did take note of the stir it caused when he drily remarked that Calvin found Paris too hot for comfort under the ensuing investigation, and decided to hide out in Angoulême, where he was the guest of an old friend, Louis du Tillet, curate of Claix and canon of the cathedral of Angoulême. It is largely thanks to Raemond's description of this soujourn — from eye-witness accounts[49] — that we can reconstruct it. What Raemond believed significant was that du Tillet's house boasted a particularly well-stocked library of three to four thousand books which Calvin could use while writing his *Institutes*: "Angoulême was the forge where this new Vulcan hammered out on the anvil those strange opinions he later published; for it was there he first wove the cloth of his *Institutes*, which one may call the *Koran*, or perhaps, the *Talmud* of Heresy, being a collection of all past errors."[50] According to our author, Calvin stayed in Angoulême for three years — a manifest impossibility and an error that he might have caught himself had he been able to make final corrections of his manuscript before his death.[51] Yet for Calvin scholars, this chronological error cannot efface the value of

Raemond's account concerning Calvin's exile in Angoulême. There the reformer maintained an outward Catholic conduct while teaching Greek to his friend, du Tillet, in exchange for his room and board.[52] There, surrounded by friends such as Anthony Chaillou, prior of Bouteville, who lent his house for the purpose, the abbot of Bassac, two brothers, the *Sieur* de Torsac, and his brother Pierre de La Place, and Louis du Tillet, Calvin discussed the plan of his forthcoming *Institutes*, reading chapters aloud as he composed them. Raemond shows us a Calvin working late into the night, so absorbed in his writing that he forgot to eat proper meals.[53] Raemond was very proud of the picture he painted of Calvin at Angoulême, for he pointed out that no other historian before him had set down Calvin's activities in the *Angoumois*. His must be accounted as the only source for this particular phase of Calvin's life.

Preaching in the *Poitevin*

Between May and October 1534, it was difficult to keep pace with Calvin, whose travels took him from Noyon, in Compiègne, north of Paris, through that city to Orléans, Poitiers, and as far southwest as Angoulême. Recent historians writing of this year do not linger on Calvin's activities in Poitiers, but Raemond insisted that it was in that city and its environs that Calvin first began to offer the reformed church service, with his own adaptation of communion. This would establish, if proved, that Calvin had completed his conversion by the second half of 1534.[54]

Raemond's account of this visit in the Poitiers area is given in the eleventh chapter of Book VII. It is a brief five-page chapter, but it gives the names of several prominent people, clergymen and professors and government officials, all of whom were Calvin's protectors and converts.[55] Raemond made it clear that Calvin met with a warm reception among the learned men of the *Poitevin* region, and that shortly after his arrival there with du Tillet, he made many new friends.[56] The major theological difficulty that Calvin attempted to resolve for his followers in Poitiers was that of the Eucharist, and in particular, said Raemond, how to regard the presence of Christ in the service, whether as a corporeal substance, or as a real presence minus corporeality, or (but here Calvin would not agree) as a mere spiritual substance. Calvin was willing to concede a real presence, but not a corporeal one. He had not yet developed his ability to speak to the same degree as his ability to write, but by sheer tenacity he managed, nonetheless, to persuade his audience to his point of view. The main thing was to finish the work Luther had merely started, i.e., the destruction of the papistical mass.[57]

What emerged then from Raemond's narrative of Calvin in Poitou was the picture of an earnest, somewhat inept, but tenacious figure meeting with local savants and dignitaries already predisposed in his favor, men willing to put up with the danger and inconvenience of rendez-vous given in the caves of Saint-Benoit, Crotelles, and other natural settings, when the house on Bassestreilles street (belonging to the lieutenant-general of the area) was not deemed safe.[58] In Poitou, Calvin supervised the foundations of Calvinist administration. There the first Council was held, and there he appointed the first ministers in charge of evangelizing the countryside (they were given nicknames for safety's sake). From Poitiers was sent a minister — "The Good-Fellow" — to evangelize the University of Toulouse, because it was the one that served as a "cradle" to the finest young minds of France.[59] Raemond may be pardoned perhaps for harboring that bit of nostalgia and old school spirit.

One thing cannot help but impress the reader of this chapter: Raemond was fairly bursting with precise information about the *Poitevin* region. A glance at the map reveals that Bordeaux was at one end of the hypotenuse of a triangle formed by it, La Rochelle, and, at the other end of the hypotenuse, Poitiers. The two hundred kilometers that separated Bordeaux from Poitiers, passing through parts of Gascony, the *Angoumois*, and Poitou, was not so great a distance that Raemond would have been unable to do some independent checking on any aspect of Calvin's activity there that required it.

For a variety of reasons, not all of them clear, the story of Calvin's stay in and around Poitiers no longer attracts the attention it did in the last century and in the early twentieth century. Perhaps this is due to the fact that this particular segment of French reform is not as interesting from the viewpoint of religious theory as later decades when Calvinism had settled down into a well-defined routine defended by an articulate and precise body of doctrine. After all, Calvin did not bring reform to Poitou, he merely encouraged its growth by an appeal to those already convinced. He did not stay in the region long enough to supervise his own tentative contributions to ecclesiastical administration. It may also be true that some embarrassment is attendant on the fact that Calvin deserted his reformed brethren in France instead of remaining to suffer alongside them. Raemond, certainly, had some harsh comments regarding Calvin's exile from France. Commenting on Calvin's book about hypocritical Nicodemites, people who pretended to be Catholic while convinced of the principles of Protestantism, Raemond pointed out that Calvin, on the contrary, "safe in his refuge at Geneva, counselled his followers to be pure of heart: 'he sold other mens' skins cheaply' was the way Raemond put it."[60] Calvin scholars are fortunate that men like Raemond (and Cayet) felt that the *Poitevin* experiences were worth relating. As recent commentators have observed, Raemond, "More perceptively than many modern writers ... refused to consider Calvin's biography simply in terms of Geneva and assessed the great influence Calvin exercised from an early date throughout France."[61]

Images and Festivals

With the origins of French Reform out of the way, Raemond was free to turn his attention to Calvinism as a fully developed religious system. Before dealing with the rotten core of the apple of Calvinism, Raemond began by paring off the outward integuments, turning first to the superficial or surface differences that separated it from Catholicism, that is, images (or rather, the absence of images) and festivals. In defending images he urged a distinction between idolatry, which he believed was a specific term with historic referents, and images, a generic term, historically neutral. The former practice was an outrageous offense, common to ancient Egyptians, Babylonians, and Hebrews. With such practices the Catholic use of images had nothing in common. Raemond used logic, semantics, history, and psychology to justify the use of imagery in Catholic worship. He resented Calvinist polemic which would persuade people that Catholics could not distinguish between stone and the spiritual truth that stone merely represented: "Tell us no more that we adore wood and stone. We adore what the figure of the Crucifix represents."[62]

As for festivals, he resented Protestant unwillingness to put aside their own work in order to honor God's work, the saints, whom God wished men to honor by means of festivals. Rampant individualism, according to Raemond, was the real reason why Calvinists had reformed the church calendar. He did not mention the fact that he had himself abolished the festival of St. John in Bordeaux.

The Mass

The form of worship most divisive in the Reformation was the rite termed "The central historical issue of the Reformation," the mass.[63] Raemond accepted the differences of practice that had evolved from the days of primitive Christianity, those which reformers regarded with jaundiced eyes. That Catholics accepted such changes made Catholicism seem more liberal than Protestantism, but this liberalism was deceptive and masked Rome's self-serving defense of its own traditions. Tradition is often illiberal since it tends to be rigidly maintained and rigorously defended. Naturally Raemond was oblivious to modern concepts of liberalism and its reverse. Yet, his view of church tradition made much of one very liberal idea: the free choice of men to invent outward forms of religious worship. God, he said, gave man the Law and Commandments, but left him free fo find and to define the necessary rites. Hence, the apostles determined the forms of the mass. Having done so on Christ's command, however, they were just the right ones. Raemond thought traditions were as infallible as the pope when inspired by the Holy Spirit. Just as the apostles had devised a church service on the lines set down by Christ, so, too, in Renaissance art studios did master artists sketch the outlines of a great work, while the apprentices filled in the details from the master plan. This was not a liberal working arrangement.

Raemond wanted to establish the fact that the mass, instituted by Christ, was a sacrificial rite. He disagreed that the sacrifice had been made just once, as Calvinists and Lutherans maintained.[64] Against Calvin, Raemond pointed out that Bullinger had retained the sacrificial element: "Look at Bullinger; there you see it portrayed as it was in the time of the Apostles, just like ours."[65] Raemond erred, for Bullinger did not maintain a Catholic, sacrificial view of the Eucharist. He believed, furthermore, that all sacraments are effective only because God's grace admits man to right belief prior to his receiving them. Bullinger's gradual alignment of the Zurich church with that of Calvin's Geneva, was possible because he and Calvin agreed to reject any materialistic interpretation of the union of Christ's flesh and blood to the elements of the communion service and because they both stressed the spiritual union of God with man during the celebration of sacraments, a union made possible by grace given man beforehand.[66]

Raemond said Calvin rejected the mass because he felt it was a pagan ceremony,[67] although Calvin said it was because Christ's sacrifice cancelled the Jewish sacrifice forever. Calvin felt the mechanism of the Roman doctrine made of Christ a kind of "instant God."[68] So much that Raemond said about Calvin's faith was written in an ironic tone that one may underestimate the seriousness of his intent. The irony is amusing, but it is also seductive. Such is the case with his comments on "manducation" or eating the sacramental elements of the Lord's Supper.[69] He used the testimony of a participant to such a rite performed at Tours in 1545, and he may have remembered a similar event from his student days. His description of the service must have made fascinating reading for Catholics who had never had the opportunity (or the nerve) to view such a ceremony themselves. His description was of a self-conscious group who, with some embarrassment and not a little awkwardness, were intently performing an unfamiliar religious service, prefaced by readings from Scripture and ending with the Latin *Credo* and *Pater Noster*, a few antipapalist statements, and a pledge to secrecy.[70]

The service he described is not unconvincing or especially arresting. He had some acerbic remarks to make about Calvinists who compromised the traditional elements of communion, bread and wine, by making substitutes as it suited their convenience, such as fresh grapes for wine, or some other staple when there was no bread at hand. Raemond said that missionaries in the New World handed out substitutes because the American Indians had neither bread nor wine. He said Calvin and Bèze had given their permission since Christ's intention was to provide spiritual nourishment, faith itself, under the symbols of bread and drink.[71] Raemond was scandalized to think that the bread and wine of Scripture, as well as of tradition, might be omitted: "Then the commandment is expressly to do what the Savior did; and that commandment covers what was substantial as much as what was essential in the action of Jesus Christ ... and therefore the bread and the wine are needed to consecrate and make the sacrifice of the Sacrament."[72]

Calvin's emphasis on Word and Spirit, rather than the symbols (bread, wine) posed a distinct problem for Calvin's sacramentalist theology. Anxious to retain the forms of the Eucharistic celebration, he was yet not enthusiastic about, or perhaps confident of, the elements qua elements.[73] He tended in the early years to guard against expressions that would reduce the power of God's grace by exaggerating the symbols of it. Calvin's insistence that Christ's body never left heaven to hide under or mingle with the communion bread would have struck the Catholic reader as a slander against the very body of Christ, and so with the wine, Christ's blood. It was not really necessary, where such grave theological differences were involved, that a Catholic (or Calvinist) be an especially cunning polemicist. A straightforward presentation of the beliefs and practices of any one side was enough to gall the other. In the course of his description of the Calvinist "manducation" or communion service, Raemond drew blood. He did not do so primarily because of his ironic asides, but because he touched upon a central and unbridgeable gulf that separated Catholics from Calvinists (and other Protestants, too): how God communicates with man.

Other Points of Contention

It is not possible to rehearse all the reasons why Catholics felt Calvinism was especially deficient as a religious phenomenon, but it is useful to consider briefly such points of contention as baptism, marriage, and church government. Baptism, like the Eucharist, was the only other Calvinist sacrament. Still, Raemond did not feel it was taken seriously by Calvin, even though that reformer termed it a "sign of initiation," a promise of "the gratuitous remission of sins," and thought that it was necessary for salvation.[74] Raemond knew, of course, that despite such positive endorsements of the practice, Calvin also wrote, on the other hand, that children do not become the sons of God through baptism, but are "adopted into the fellowship of the Church" prior to it, and by virtue of a promise that God gave to all the children of the faithful.[75] He also said that if baptism is not followed by faith, it offers man no advantage whatever,[76] and that God does not condemn any man simply because he failed to receive baptism.[77] Florimond de Raemond, having carefully considered all the things Calvin had to say about this rite, concluded that Calvin was essentially a sceptic concerning baptism. His line of reasoning ran along the same kind of channel as it had in connection with the Eucharist. Because Calvin put a greater emphasis on belief and above all, upon God's grace, than upon the externals of the rite, Raemond felt the attachment to the sacrament was superficial.

The reformed, whether Lutheran or Calvinist, put a big premium on the virtues of family life. They felt Catholics were less well disposed to it because they extolled celibacy and virginity. Calvin refused to consider marriage as a sacrament, as Luther refused before him. He (Calvin) did consider it a divine institution, neither more nor less valuable than the celibate estate, but a means by which parents gave expression to the laws of God.[78] We have seen how Raemond believed celibacy and virginity were preferable to marriage.[79] We know he disapproved of divorce for spiritual or for physical incompatibility. He felt Calvin had made Geneva a regular bordello by providing easy divorces there.[80] He may not have been aware of Calvin's reasons for refusing the status of a sacrament to marriage. Calvin wrote that Catholics had misinterpreted the word "mystery" used by St. Paul (Ephesians 5:32) following his statement on marriage. Calvin thought the word "mystery" was best translated as Grace, not Sacrament. What he thought to be a metaphoric reference had been turned into a sacrament through a translator's error.[81] Raemond was shocked by Calvin's assertion that marriage was merely "an honest and approved method of living," like animal husbandry and agriculture.[82] Such rhetoric, so alien to a sacramentalist conception of matrimony, suggests how wide was the rift that separated Catholic and Calvinist conscience on this subject.

If major doctrinal differences rendered communication between faithful and reformed difficult, it is not surprising that the new practices of Calvinist church discipline could not recommend themselves either. They may have been even more disconcerting to Catholics than religious issues, since the consistories that Calvin set in place impinged subtly, and sometimes blatantly, on the civil authority as it was traditionally constituted in France. Although Raemond belittled the Calvinist ministry in a variety of ways — some of which amounted to little more than name-calling[83] — and charged that young ministers were men of little learning and subject to the whims of their flocks,[81] he was particularly irate when it came to the Calvinist consistory, or the ruling body of the reformed church. He disliked the consistory because it combined civil with religious authority[85] and because it was not an elite body, but included ordinary people like merchants, tailors, and tinsmiths in its ranks. He believed that the consistory promoted spying on people in their most private lives, that is, in their sexual and marital relationships — "the most secret activities of the bedroom."[86] As a magistrate he felt such activity to be trespassing on the judicial function. We know that he had once ruled contrary to the decisions of a local consistory, and had had his decision overruled by a higher royal court. For whatever reasons, public or private, Raemond's opposition to consistorial efforts to regulate public morality led him to very liberal postures indeed, for we find him sympathizing with Huguenots made to confess their misdeeds before such bodies, and arguing on their behalf that the public humiliation, which consistories sought to inflict, could never produce a true reform of manners and morals. He did not mention the fact that Catholics also required public displays of humility.[87]

In order to denigrate the role of consistories in the regulation of morality, Raemond rehearsed a series of stories with sexual or psychosexual overtones which his first biographer found too contemptible for comment.[88] Some were fairly innocent. He noted the attempts of ministers to regulate female attire and coiffure, and wrote that after the mid 1580s, the ministers were fighting a losing battle in this regard. Raemond had a sociologist's appreciation of the fact that singular data may be collectively significant. He thought he perceived a decline in the moral standards that Calvinists had set for themselves in those decades when they were under constant stress before the Edict of Nantes finally granted them a certain amount of social and civil parity with Catholic subjects. That document and their enhanced security may have made an exaggerated standard of purity seem less necessary. In any event, the reformed congregations may have appeared to Raemond to be relaxing their standards, and he was determined to take what polemical advantage of that situation he thought feasible.

Florimond de Raemond ended his last Book of the "History of Heresy" by conducting the Huguenots to the grave, that is, by a discussion of burial practices of many cultures both non-Christian and Christian, and of Calvinists in particular. The latter were incomprehensible to him in that they disavowed the external pomp that, he argued, even pagans had deemed appropriate to burials. The Calvinists' reluctance to indulge in ceremony was for him proof that they were irreligious. This inability of the Catholic to accept a practice so unfamiliar to his own reminds us that the division between Catholic and Protestant, involving conscience and custom, was not only profound, but also superficial, that is, the European population of the era was divided on profound issues that were expressed by relatively petty ones. Even these superficial differences were in reality also profound since they gave visible expression to the spiritual chasms that divided the two groups.

Raemond's parting comments in his great, unfinished history are directed to the "burial" of Protestantism itself. Despite a lively and often penetrating appreciation that he had for historical process, Raemond could not hide the resentment and fear that religious heterodoxy would undermine the national well-being. That fear boded ill for a heterogeneous national community and for human liberty. Raemond was a man of his times, however, and not a man ahead of them. He was born in an intolerant, narrow-minded century. He died in another.

8
History and Politics

The Historian's Politics

Three developments in sixteenth-century Europe provide the background against which one may assess the significance of Florimond de Raemond: the spread of humanist scholarship in France; the Protestant Reformation, which brought religious diversity and led to civil war; and the emergence of a critical historical sense, the product of humanist, and especially of philological, scholarship applied to the problems that heterodoxy created in government and society.

Many of the men who were moved to write about these dramatic changes in French life were *robins*, members of the *parlements*, the judiciary.[1] Raemond was one of them; others were clergymen, Catholic or Reformed. Most of the concerns of sixteenth-century French historians were common concerns of all learned men in that century. The elite educated classes shared a classical frame of reference that often included Greek, and Hebrew as well as Latin, and that left them with a certain reverence for antiquity and a curiosity concerning the origins of things, whether linguistic or political, and how modern institutions had sprung from ancient practices. Such men were privileged and well-placed members of a society devoted to French culture and to French governance. They were, by virtue of their talents and their offices, born to shape public opinion.

Of those who elected to write history, most chose secular rather than religious subjects. Theirs were the methods and insights into the past that modern historians have determined were the most advanced, or at least, the most interesting in terms of subsequent historiographical developments. Such authors specialized in the study of law and governmental institutions and were frequently French medievalists or classicists. They included men such as Guillaume Budé (d. 1540), Hellenist and philologist, who was concerned with Roman law, of whom Raemond took note;[2] Joseph

Scaliger (d. 1609), the classicist who shared with Raemond both the year of his birth and Agen, his birthplace;[3] Louis Le Roy (d. 1577), a disciple of Budé, whose major work was a comparative world history;[4] Jacques-Auguste De Thou (d. 1617), whose history of Europe in his own time spanned eighteen volumes;[5] Raemond's correspondent, Etienne Pasquier, who attempted to put French medieval history on a purely documentary basis;[6] Jean Bodin (d. 1596), whose theories of history posited a vaguely delimited absolutism to replace medieval notions of a balanced polity;[7] Pierre Pithou (d. 1596), who applied philology to studies of medieval law;[8] François Hotman (d. 1590), who attempted to reconcile royalist governmental forms of his own era with the elective forms he believed once prevailed in the early middle ages;[9] and Henri Lancelot de La Popelinière (d. 1608), who attempted to give an objective account of the civil wars, and whose book suggested that all human activity was significant if one understood its motives and causes.[10]

Even though these writers preferred secular topics rather than the religious ones that fascinated Raemond, he shared with them a lively interest in philology. He was much given to translating Greek and Latin inscriptions into French, and had rendered two of Tertullian's essays into his native language, laboring assiduously on the difficult passages. He quoted Montaigne's old friend, la Boétie: "Translating is a difficult story, The trouble's great, and there's scant glory."[11] Raemond's first biographer compared the translated essays to those of more modern writers and found his the best of the lot. Had Raemond been incompetent in the rudiments of philology, he could not have dealt so firmly with the problems posed by interpolated texts in his work on the popess. He was resolved to use his abilities to teach nonscholarly readers uncomfortable facts instead of convenient myths. He used his philological talents to promote that revival of "scientific" and erudite historiography, which had begun to emerge during the Italian Renaissance and which spread northward subsequently.[12] Following the lead given by Lorenzo Valla and others, he was able to render a more accurate history from that which was obscured by the cobwebs of legend. Criticism of myth was one of the basic functions of the new history during the Renaissance, and Raemond was one of many who were practitioners of the art. Like Pasquier, whose *Recherches* had demythologized the notion of Gaul's Trojan origins, and the founding of the French church by Saint Denis, Raemond had labored to erase the fable of a female pope. He obviously felt himself to be on the side of those authors who were in the forefront of methodological modernism, and was quick to point out to men such as Pasquier the gravity of perpetuating such errors.

At times his philological interests produced no real results, but merely served as window-dressing for modern methods, as when he engaged in a tedious squabble with Duplessis-Mornay over the meaning of the word *Lateinos* in connection with the Antichrist polemic. Raemond knew the difference in that instance between theology and cabalism. Philology was not a mere numbers game, even if he could not always resist the common temptation among sixteenth-century scholars to use number-letter relationships for predictive purposes. Florimond de Raemond found philology a tool that could be used to rebuke reformed scholarship, just as Protestants used it to establish the truth of Protestantism. Raemond was distressed by the fact that Calvinists had committed philological sin in substituting the words "minister" for "priest," and "Coene" for "Mass." If he appeared at times too ready to use philology in an interested way to support his own or his church's point of view, it must be remembered that philology itself was but a lexicographical sort of custom.[13] Catholic practice put a similarly high premium on custom (tradition). This does not mean that philologists necessarily or generally found in favor of the Catholic status quo. Experts were aware of principles of change and corruption and aware of many different factors that influenced the shape of historical experience — linguistic, legal, geo-political, and the like.[14] Learned laymen, like Raemond, who merely admired the principles of philology might have been, and often were, tempted to deduce more from the method than it could furnish. They concluded, using principles of limited utility, that these possessed a limitless significance. Misapplication of philological research was great. Sometimes Raemond appeared clumsy in availing himself of linguistic analysis, yet he was aware in a real way of his amateur qualifications, and was fairly cautious in the use to which he put such methods. We know he consulted specialists in the areas of Greek and Hebrew, though in Latin, he was more sure of himself.[15]

A second major interest of secularists among sixteenth-century historians might, for brevity's sake, be termed civic order. Under it were subsumed topics such as the state of the constitution; the nature of citizenship; the role of kings; the conception of European community versus national initiative; and last, but not for Raemond least, the proper relationship between secular and religious authority. The list of topics is almost longer than the explicit treatment given by Raemond to any item on it, and it is difficult to be more explicit regarding his views on them than he was himself. The reason for this is clear: he was not a secular historian, and did not dwell on the political history of his own times or of any prior era unless he cared to make some point concerning religious practice and spiritual authority.[16]

He had a clear idea of his own purpose, and that was to trace the progress of "heresy" or Protestantism during the Reformation and up to his own time. He looked to Cardinal Baronius as his model, though his own work was not cast in the mold of annals, as was Baronius's. He said that while he had intended to describe the growth of heresy from its inception in the early church, he had abandoned the idea because Baronius had left nothing more to accomplish than translating into French what the Cardinal wrote in Latin. His contribution to the repulse of the reformed faith would be a narrative history written in French about that new faith wherever it took hold — in Scandinavia, in eastern Europe (Bohemia, Transylvania, Hungary, Poland), as well as in France, Switzerland, and the British Isles. His book would be a popular narrative history written to fill a need, for vernacular histories were then a rarity, and only the elite could read Latin. But while his book provided information about the reform movement in his century, it was information of a limited sort, namely of religious revolution and practice. It is only through indirection that we can deduce Raemond's political philosophy from this material.

Certainly he favored a strong monarchy. He admired Jean Bodin's monumental book, *Republic* (1576), calling it "his lovely *Republic*, a work one cannot praise enough."[17] Unfortunately, he did not elaborate, but most likely it was the unrestrained sovereignty that Bodin promoted, and that one specialist has described as "an analytic truth."[18] Of Bodin's earlier book, the *Method of History* (1566), which presented a discussion of constitutional forms and change where absolutist elements were repudiated altogether, Raemond made no mention.[19] It would be unwise to assume that the theoretical aspects of constitutionalism were unimportant to our author, or that he was not concerned with the theory of law on which human history was based. He was trained as a lawyer, after all, and spent thirty-one years on the judicial bench. Yet, his conception of history was more influenced by theological frameworks than by legal ones; he could not forget that human society was subordinated to divine law.

We can, however, deduce from his treatment of ecclesiastical matters something of his ideas on secular subjects. In his discussion of the correctness of having one head of the church, he revealed his doubts on the propriety of the elective principle of government.

Cardinals might well elect popes, but for independent churches to choose their own leaders was a sure way to create "a new Anarchy."[20] He asserted the elective principle in the Lutheran church led to democracy within that institution, and in the Calvinist church, to aristocracy. Only the Catholic system agreed with the monarchical rule approved by Plato and Aristotle. Quoting Aristotle, he said, "Domination by one man alone surpasses all other governmental forms."[21] Nature approved this dictate concerning the unitary leader with inviolate power. There was but one God, one Savior, one church. Beasts recognized the Lion as king; Michael was the leader of angels. The bellwether led his flock; the bull his herd; etc. Raemond's reading of divine and natural law seemed to indicate a monarchism of the most unrestrained sort.

Because of his admiration for Francis I, the Renaissance patron of the arts *par excellence*, he refused to criticize his foreign policy, which was both pro-Protestant, and pro-Turk. Instead, he let a Venetian duke deliver to King Henry III, newly returned from Poland, a lecture on the evils of such foreign policies. Raemond (who drew this information from Monluc's *Mémoires*) obviously agreed with the duke that one might co-exist with infidels and heretics but that making offensive and defensive alliances with them ought to be taboo. To make such agreements was but tempting God to take his vengeance against the offending nation.[22] The best and highest expression of statecraft was cooperation between Catholic monarchs for the defense of the true religion.

Of course, he was inconsistent in his admiration of absolutism. He did not approve of kings who meddled with religion. He was horrified by secular rulers setting up as heads of national churches, "disposing of sacred things and holy offices according to their will and appetite."[23] A good king should protect his church's prerogatives and doctrine as the church defined it. He lamented the fact that the royal house of Navarre, Henry IV's own, had presided over the destruction of the Catholic church of Béarn: "God, what misery is comparable to theirs," he groaned.[24] He urged Henry, now safely within the Roman fold, to re-establish the church in the home of the princes of Béarn, and the counts of Foix.[25] In a burst of romantic passion, he urged Henry to join hands with other Christian princes and to go off on a crusade to the holy land to re-establish the Christianity of the middle ages. Henry IV, the "New Constantine," could restore the one true faith to the whole world, thus eradicating cultural diversity altogether.[26]

In fact, Raemond's encomiums to absolute power were marred by strong reservations of which he himself seemed to be unaware.

While subjects could not check the royal authority in any way at all, the king was not to exercise his absolute powers without the support of the church, or carry out his foreign policy without the cooperation of similarly disposed Catholic monarchs. This degree of Catholic unity, which had never existed in medieval times, but that appears to have been created out of an imagined past to serve as the ideal for a new international polity, would be obliged to await God's pleasure. God's righteous anger would first have to be mollified, and the Protestant schism completely healed before such a European community could exist. Such romantic idealism of a conservative sort, following a long period of social upheaval, would be repeated in a later age, following another long period of social and political upheaval.[27]

The perfection of the state and the defense of the true religion were for Florimond de Raemond and his contemporaries two aspects of one problem. In a letter of dedication (of his eighth Book) to the Rev. Nicolas de Villars,[28] Raemond lamented the damage that France, always a leader in piety, had sustained because of the support she had given to heresy and heretics.[29] We have seen how he looked forward, writing the last pages of his "History of Heresy" to the end of Protestantism in Europe. Shall we say of Raemond that such ideas put him beyond the pale of intellectual respectability as an author? After all, Protestantism was more than three-quarters of a century old when he was writing. Yet, when comparing Raemond's thoughts on religious diversity to those of a moderate Catholic historian of his era, whose books were praised by nearly all parties, Raemond's work appears less an anachronism than one might suspect.

Jacques-Auguste De Thou was a moderate Catholic and a passionate nationalist. As president of the *Parlement* of Paris he worked hard to make the Edict of Nantes a reality that would secure civil peace. He was termed "a peerless historian of contemporary Europe" by one modern historiographer,[30] and an upholder of the idea that law is the very essence of the national community.[31] Because De Thou did not hesitate to criticize the papacy when he felt the church in error, his works were placed on the *Index* in 1609. His books were popular in the Netherlands and in Germany during the seventeenth century.[32] Important differences mark the work of De Thou's ponderous *Universal History* (1604–1607), which he composed in Latin, and appear to separate it from Raemond's own. In his preface, De Thou said many things that echo those written by Raemond and with which he would have been in complete agreement. For example, De Thou decried compulsion in religious belief, and noted, as had Raemond, that force merely made martyrs of heretics. De Thou attributed the Lutheran schism to Catholic laziness, as did our author. He urged Henry IV to take an active, if indirect, interest in the church, as had Raemond, so that, being well-ordered the Catholic church might attract Protestants to reconciliation or readmission to its fold: "So that under their reign, the old Faith and Religion, the old customs, those of our Ancestors, the Laws of State, may be re-established: So that these Monsters of new Religions, these Religions of such late invention, all the products of idleness, which lay in wait to entrap the spirit, may be abolished: and thus Schism and divisions cease."[33] Although De Thou has established a reputation for dispassionate and enlightened history, Raemond has often been dismissed as a mere polemicist. Certainly he found it difficult to be dispassionate, although he could on occasion strike an impartial tone even when religious diversity was the issue.[34] Yet, to be fair, it must be remembered that there was more unanimity regarding the ideal state — which was never one composed of a diversity of religions — than there was controversy in Raemond's era.[35]

Even if Raemond believed that divine law regulated the affairs of men, he nevertheless devoted his own life to upholding the laws of men. It has recently been observed that during France's civil strife, sixteenth-century Frenchmen with legal and classical training were tempted to desert their civic humanist ideals that emphasized public service and to elect the quiet, individualistic pursuits of learning.[36] That was Montaigne's choice, certainly, and also that of several literary acquaintances. While Raemond regretted the loss of his poetic gifts, and may have envied his brother, Robert, the quiet life of a Jesuit priest, and though he encouraged his friend, Malvyn, to retire while young at heart, he continued to serve as a member of the *Parlement* of Bordeaux, and he continued to volunteer for community service up until the last months of his life. He wrote: "A tranquil life, without the chances which fortune brings, is like a dead sea. Still water is brackish, as the poet says. On the other hand, in the sharp furnace of adversity, virtue is put to the test, so the soul is cleansed of all salinity, and rises to divine knowledge."[37] Raemond may have been a wistful Stoic, but he was a Stoic, nonetheless. If he sometimes felt tempted by the private life, he did not give in to temptation.

In Renaissance Florence, civic-minded humanists felt that the chief task of the philosopher was to aid the ruler with wise counsel. Raemond was a civil servant, not a philosopher, and certainly not a political theorist, but he had read widely, and he, too, believed in serving the public interest. His means were first the judicial bench, and second, the bar of public opinion. In his "Epistle to Monsieur Belle-Garde, Grand Standard-Bearer," which preceded the 1599 edition of *Anti-Christ*, he begged Belle-Garde to bring his work to the attention of Henry IV.[38] Raemond may have felt that Henry was unkindly disposed toward him, since on one occasion the king had signed a writ that obliged our historian to pay to Arnaud du Faur, *Seigneur* of Pujols, and a gentleman of the royal bedchamber, an annual homage of a tuft of egret feathers. This homage bound the heirs to Suquet as well as Raemond himself.[39] If Paris had been worth a mass to his monarch, how could he protest a tuft of feathers for Suquet? His patriotic inclinations were strengthened by Henry's conversion to Rome, and he was cheered to think of the prospects of a France re-Catholicized.

It was fortunate that Raemond's patriotism did not have to stand the test of a Protestant monarch who refused to convert to the old faith. It would have been difficult for him to justify rebellion against a legitimate king, and Raemond did not join the ranks of the Catholic League, but continued to defend the laws of the realm and the sacrosanctity of legitimate monarchs.[40]

As we have noted, religious unity and governmental stability were scarcely conceived by Catholics as separable political objectives. The civil war period had produced a literature of resistance: Hotman's *Francogallia* (1573); Bèze's *Right of Magistrates* (1574); and Duplessis Mornay's *Vindiciae Contra Tyrannos* (1579). These were suspect by Catholics as having been produced by heretics for their own selfish interests and against the interests of the monarchy and the true religion. But even in resistance literature, the ability to keep separate ideas of religious uniformity and governmental authority was not common. François Hotman combined the question of religion with that of the state.[41] Furthermore, his formulation of governmental authority rested on a "dubious sense of historical relevence"[42] (popular sovereignty). His religious uniformity derived not from an hierarchical church but through the authority of Scripture. He assumed it would be interpreted in the same way by all who were exposed to it. Even those authors of resistance theory who did not combine the religious with the secular authority, nevertheless could hardly escape intimately associating the two. Calvin, for example, while anxious to establish that the realm of secular authority was "very different" from "the spiritual kingdom of Christ," was nevertheless opposed to a complete dissociation of faith and government. While the clergy did not govern Geneva, the theocratic nature of that city made for a very intimate cooperation between church and state, and Calvin would have been appalled to think that civil governors had no obligation to preserve "the pure doctrine of religion," or "defend the constitution of the church."[43]

Of course, Raemond was conservative in matters of politics and religion, but he was not exceptionally so. He can more reasonably be criticized for his imperfect historical acumen in his assumption that there was in the past a congruence of interests between royal and Roman Catholic authority, and that this congruence had resulted in the absence of war, in stable law, religious uniformity, and so on. One can attribute his "lack" of historical knowledge to his polemical purposes, but one must remember that the resistance tracts were also written by polemicists and were similarly antihistorical.[44]

It is tempting to treat political polemicists, as opposed to religious polemicists, as a superior breed of thinkers because their works are often rich in details concerning the law, geography, constitutional theory, and folk origins. Such information frequently conveys an impression of rationality that co-exists with or obscures quite passionate religious convictions.

Neither Catholics nor Protestants in this period believed in reserving to individual conscience the final say over religious affiliation and expression. It may, therefore, be somewhat startling to find that our author was able to make a rather heroic, if choleric, defense of individual liberty with regard to sexual privacy. In this area, Raemond believed that neither church nor community had the right to restrain behavior. His opinions on these matters appear to have been formed as a reaction to the interference of Calvinist consistories, in the main, but it is also possible that having upheld the restrictive views of his countrymen concerning church and state, he gave free reign to the affective side of human activity. The most rigid of political and social views had not yet produced a mere creature of institutional authority.

A Politician's History

The most progressive feature of Raemond's history was his inclusion of the story of reform in many European countries, thus qualifying as an example of comparative history. Such were also the works of Louis Le Roy, La Popelinière, d'Aubigné, and De Thou. This comparative method was valued because it minimized political and diplomatic history, emphasizing instead the customs of different social groups. In Raemond's hands, this method was a tool that was used to illustrate different religious practices among Protestant sects. He was influenced by techniques of secular historians, and adapted them for his own use.[45] He conceived of a universal history,[46] but died before he was ready to proceed to the new world where he would have been happy to trace the progress of Catholic missionary activity. The fact that he preferred to write about ecclesiastical subjects would have offended such writers of "universal" histories as Jean Bodin. Bodin had discarded theological interpretations of history altogether.[47] Of course, Raemond did not wholly exclude topics other than religious, but he preferred the latter type. His writing abounds in psychological insights gained from his own experience and wide reading. Like Bodin to some extent, Raemond felt history ought to explain human behavior with respect to geography, climate, and anthropology. He had, for example, given a geographical and climatological explanation of the differences between Lutheranism and Calvinism. Luther's religion was "material and gross," while Calvin's was "subtle and spiritual," and all because Luther was a man of the North, and Calvin a man of the South.[48] Northerners were usually given to fasting and to penitence, while southerners were despisers of both divinity and humanity and less religious than the former. Today we recognize this as mere stereotyping. It was scarcely innovative in the sixteenth century, for Plato, Tertullian, Hippocrates, and Vitruvius had put forth similar theories.[49] Raemond found his reiteration of such notions shared by authors more radical than himself, for example, by Jean Bodin and by Louis Le Roy. Whether these ideas were old or new is not so important as the fact that Raemond and other historians were aware of the need for causal factors (explanations) drawn from sources other than religious, while at the same time, they were wary of their use. In this way Raemond provided his readers with "genitures" or astrological charts of the birth of men like Luther and Calvin. They were not of his own making, but he knew that his readers were interested in them. Such interest was not limited to the poorly educated, but was promoted by scientists and even priests who sought to make astrology more natural, i.e., more scientific and reliable for prediction.[50] He was careful to associate himself with recent strictures by the papacy that discouraged reliance on the "evidence" of astrology, a possible competitor to the notion of God's providence. He continued to assert his belief in a divine first cause, and accorded a secondary causality to the stars.[51] We know he disciplined himself to refuse the predictive capabilities of the number 666, although many savants promoted cabalism as mathematical and scientific.

Raemond was typical of his learned contemporaries. He displayed some enthusiasm for pseudoscientific inquiry. To the extent that he referred to such inquiry in his writing, he revealed a consciousness of the need for expanded systems of information gathering. To the extent that he was obliged to reserve ultimate confidence in such inquiry to a traditional belief in God's providence, he revealed the limitations of pietistic men before the world of nature.

Raemond's was not a universal history because it did not devote enough space to secular activities. He admired the men who could write such history, one of whom was the *Sieur* de La Popelinière, whose *Idea of Perfect History* (1599) had appeared just as Raemond was engaged in writing his own "History of Heresy."[52] Raemond was a friend or at least an acquaintance of this writer who wished to make history comprehensive and objective, and above all, accurate. Raemond wrote: "La Popelinière, great writer of our times, told me that he was often criticized by the Protestants for having written in his history about the state of the church too frankly, and had not lied in order to make his own party look good."[53] Obviously, universal history was supposed to be objective and nonpartisan. La Popelinière's fellow Protestants thought he had let them down by writing of their failures as well as of their virtues. De Thou was similarly criticized by some Catholics for having written about his own church in a manner too frank, a fault for which his name was placed on the *Index* in 1609.[54] Raemond had criticized the misbehavior of certain anonymous Catholic clergymen prior to the Reformation, but he did not criticize any priests afterwards, or any institutions of the church.

A third writer of universal histories was Agrippa d'Aubigné, who despised Raemond, but admired La Popelinière and De Thou. Indeed, he admired the Catholic De Thou rather more than the Protestant La Popelinière. D'Aubigné listed some of the traits he thought a universal history required. It must be free of "impudent flattery ... prophetic praise ... and conceited slander."[55] There were to be unrelated asides, and accuracy was to be given the first priority. An author's passions were to be rigorously excluded from his text.[56] By such standards, Raemond's work would fail utterly the test of being considered universal history. But by such standards d'Aubigné's own work would not measure up, for it has been called "pro-Calvinist" by at least one modern critic.[57]

If the object of universal history was to make sense of the past, the task was hard enough.[58] But sixteenth-century theorists of history set themselves an even more difficult task — making sense of the past without prejudice or passion. In singling out religious from other data, Raemond gave himself a handicap that he could not overcome for he was determined not merely to explain Catholic positions, but to promote them. Prejudice and passion were handicaps in making sense out of the past.

This is not to say that he made no sense of it at all — he had brilliant insights and made legitimate analyses.[59] He also made considerable errors of fact and blatant errors of interpretation.[60] He did not hesitate to include anecdotes that were scandalous as well as amusing, even when he must have known that they were probably not true. All these factors made his "History of Heresy" a work of uneven reliability.

How can this unevenness be explained? To a limited extent it had to do with his sources. To some degree he relied on the testimony of living persons with whom he came into contact — on oral history. His sources were understandably affected by their own circumstances and beliefs. Sometimes they were officials of the state, with the prejudices of well-born people loyal to, and to varying degrees dependent on, the royal service for their livelihood, or at least, for their employment. As a magistrate, of course, he was exposed to a broad cross-section of the population of Guyenne, although, like the officials with whom he was associated, he too was protected to a degree by his own status from realistic communication with the people he served, and certainly, with those he judged. He was used to making judgments, a habit that can be useful to the historian, but which may also lead him to think that he has all the evidence he needs already at hand. Historians, like judges, sometimes forget that the evidence never admitted to the court may be the most significant evidence of all.

Occasionally, Raemond used primary sources rather than living sources of information, and he could handle primary sources with aplomb. For the most part, however, he was content with secondary courses, the histories written by his contemporaries. He checked up on them as best he could, and read the works they had read. He was very well-versed in the early writers of church history, and widely read with respect to the moderns. His favorite modern authors were generally ecclesiastical writers.[61]

Among Catholic apologists, some were dogmatists, who sought to convince readers by scholastic arguments primarily, and some irenicists, who were generally more conciliatory in tone, and who tried to persuade Protestants of their errors by referring to the Bible itself, or to the fathers of the early church.[62] Raemond's viewpoint was neither more nor less intransigent than these. He relied on the interpretations put forth by recognized Catholic commentators, by the fathers of the church, by councils, and by popes. Characteristically, he used all the techniques available — biblical, patristic, scholastic, rational, and irrational — to persuade his readership. He was an eclectic writer who used any orthodox source as best he could in order to defend his church. Like his models, he hoped to establish the validity of Roman positions by making the origins of those positions and traditions appear as ancient as possible. He had labored in the *Erreur Populaire* to show that the papal succession had never been broken, and hence was indeed a succession from St. Peter. He joined with all orthodox Catholics to demonstrate that the pope was incapable of error where doctrine was at stake.

It is the degree to which such historians and apologists clung to their notion of an infallible church that prompted one historian to say that "Catholics had no historical thesis to defend" during the sixteenth century, while Protestants made "the fullest use of historic argument".[63] It would be more fair to say that the dogmatic Catholic view was not different in principle from the dogmatic Protestant one which held that the reformed church was conformable to the divine prototype and was the one, true catholic church. This position was in fact taken by Theodore de Bèze, for whom Raemond reserved a special animus. This reformer had written a treatise on the church — on the true catholic church — that bears closer inspection if we are intent on learning more about the particular historical sense of each of these two sixteenth-century religious parties.[64]

The first thing that may be said about both Catholic and Protestant ecclesiastical historians is that they were thoroughly imbued with the notion of the duality of human history, split between the affirmative God-approved, and the negative, ungodly qualities of existence. This conception could not help but present church historians with a methodology, upholding the good and condemning the evil qualities of life, if necessary, by excluding examples or evidence pointing to disturbing conclusions.

Since the dogmatic aspects of Catholicism have already been canvassed, it is time to turn to the no less dogmatic operations of Protestant reform, at least insofar as the writings of Bèze can illustrate them. In a letter to Henry IV, which formed the long preface to the 1592 edition of his treatise, Bèze urged the king to concentrate on religious rather than on civil laws since the former were eternal aspects of human existence, and superior to fleeting civil law: "It is necessary that all things be done according to order, all the more carefully so where Religion and the Church are concerned than in civil matters pertaining only and directly to everyday things."⁶⁵ The phrase "according to order" suggests that things of spiritual import were reserved for a higher authority than the king; that this higher authority had established an order to govern such matters; and that this order was ancient and obliged all magistrates (including the king) and church leaders to preserve it: "in every well-set-up church ... God has ordained some to speak, others to listen; some to be pastors, and governors; others to be sheep and governed."⁶⁶ By insisting that the church be strictly conformable to ancient, scriptural patterns of order, Bèze was in fact reducing the scope of any prerogative authority the king might imagine he had over the church; he emerged, as it were, a governor of, rather than a law-giver to, the church. This position, as Bèze sketched it out, was strikingly akin to that which Raemond felt appropriate for a French monarch. The king, already on the point of deserting his reformed brethren, would be reduced to an enforcer of law rather than a giver of law. In this instance, the similar views of Raemond and of his *bête-noir*, Theodore de Bèze, offered a sharp contrast to those of Gallican Catholics anxious to increase the powers of the king over the church in order to break with the older tradition of papal control.

Of course, Bèze included in his preface some very conciliatory language. He conceded that in matters indifferent to faith, rather than essential to it, *adiaphora*, the magistrates could alter the government of the church. He made it clear that real doctrinal matters were not negotiable.

Fearful of change and fearful of secular control over religious principles set by higher authority, Bèze's treatise left little room for negotiation, and little for popular participation in the regulation of religion. He was as elitist in his distrust of the general Christian membership of his church as Raemond was distrustful of it;⁶⁷ as suspicious of his king; and as reluctant to risk a general examination of religious policy, structure, and doctrine.

The conservative view of both Bèze and Raemond on historical change, plus their overall commitment to a given set of religious principles and polemic, has generally excluded them from the favorable notice of twentieth-century historiographers.⁶⁸ On the other hand, their contemporary, François Hotman, whose work was ostensibly devoid of polemical religious motive, took a similarly conservative stand when he considered the nature of the Frankish constitution and concluded that the popular will had always superseded royal despotism and that kings were not permitted to tinker with or to change the constitution.⁶⁹ In a real sense, Hotman's purposes, the safeguarding of the true religion, were congruent to those of Raemond and Bèze (and Calvin), but eschewing religious topics, his work preserved an appearance of secular disinterestedness that has helped preserve his reputation as an historian.[70] Yet all three authors opposed a particular kind of custom (Frankish in Hotman's case, Catholic in Raemond's, scriptural in Bèze's) to a present that, politically speaking, appeared too free-wheeling and ultimately too threatening. All three authors betrayed a lack of confidence in historical change that approached the extreme. It is interesting, therefore, to observe that while Hotman's historical writing enters into discussions of modern preparations for changes achieved in the course of the seventeenth century (i.e., the growth of constitutional theory), the contributions of Raemond and Bèze have not.

The basic dualism that was displayed by both the Catholic and the Protestant parties made each anxious to establish his own party as that most firmly attached to the divine will and rule. Such anxiety made neither one nor the other reliable where historical objectivity was required, although the Protestant writers have generally been regarded as more successful in their efforts to treat the past as it really was, unchaining it from the bonds of Catholic tyranny and custom. Some modern scholars have indeed presented the reformed writers as more or less unencumbered by the superstitions of the past and by circumstances that they reject.[71] Yet it is difficult to see that either side was more sympathetic to history than the other. Each viewed human history as an inferior kind of truth that was at best a means for vindicating their own peculiar religious view. Now, to view human activity as an inferior truth, a position that dualism required, is at once to vitiate the prime requirement for investigating the past: the recognition of the dignity of the subject under investigation, man himself. The lack of a truly historical mentality inevitably colored the contributions of men like Raemond, Bèze, Hotman, d'Aubigné, and many other historical writers from both parties. That their handicap was not perceived by their readers goes without saying, for they shared with them the same philosophical deficiency. Raemond's own work contained much that was useful and true, mingled with some that was wrong and still more that was misleading. His was a scholarship more wide than profound, which was in transition. It was beginning to take modern methods into consideration, but had not yet achieved independence from the theology or institutions of the past. Had he been more avant-garde in his approach, more dispassionate in his assumptions, or less the spokesman for his party, it is doubtful, given the habits of his age, that he would have been as influential in molding the opinion of the Catholic majority, or perhaps it would be better to say, in fitting the pre-existent mold. While Raemond was not innovative in his conception of historical theory, or in his chosen specialty, his work was quite probably more influential because of it.

In a study of the reading choices of sixteenth-century bourgeois and legal classes in Paris, one scholar has observed that historical and controversial works were preferred over the classics and Christian humanists. The same study indicated that polemical histories were not read passively, but stimulated readers to follow through by reading opposed points of view.[72] In the generation after Raemond's death, two of his books were the subject of extensive controversy.[73] His more retrograde positions reinforced common prejudices; his more astute ones helped erase others. Polemical works stimulated more than idle controversy — they created the kind of environment where ultimately the only arms that count are those of fact and reason. Religious controversy and historical controversy in the baroque era gradually displaced religious warfare. Although such writing did not at once produce a more tolerant community, it did at least expose the more outrageous claims of religious bigots to a wider public scrutiny, and helped prepare Europeans for a more rational method of assessing history — and making it.

9
Postscript

When Philippe Tamizey De Larroque published his little essay on the life of Raemond (1867), he began with a plaintive lament over the fact that diligent historians of his own century, even those from Guyenne, had passed his subject by without so much as a nod. Raemond was a forgotten figure, and Larroque, who was a friend of one of Raemond's descendants, set about his work in order to rectify what he thought was a grave injustice.[1]

Larroque's book did much to rescue Florimond de Raemond from oblivion, and by the end of the nineteenth century his reputation had been resuscitated, as well as rescued, not only in southwestern France, but in the world of letters, for the Swiss biographer of Calvin, Émile Doumergue, had brought Raemond's testimony to the fore.[2] Twentieth-century commentary and analysis has not been abundant, but at the very least it has continued the seventeenth and early eighteenth-century critical tendency to deprecate or praise the author. It has done this, however, without taking seriously Raemond's cultural significance, which was that of an opinion molder, but even more importantly, that of a representative of his class and of his religious confession. Raemond spoke for the conservative Catholic majority of France.[3] Seventeenth-century Frenchmen understood these things very well, and as we shall presently observe, they supported Raemond's prejudices and crotchets as their own, which, indeed, they were. Those Catholics who objected to his works were far less likely to have done so because they disagreed with the assumption (of Catholic superiority) on which they were based; still less because Raemond was not primarily an archival historian or a thorough going universalist in his approach.[4] No, moderate Catholics criticized Raemond's writing for a variety of reasons that had to do less with Raemond's major themes than with his satiric, unchivalrous tone.

An example of this moderate but orthodox attitude was a caustic anecdote that the memoirist Pierre de l'Estoile (d. 1611) had included in his journal for the years 1607–1609. A visitor in Hell had reported the marriage of "Florimond Raimond" to Pope Joan, and in unmistakably journalistic style noted that the "bride" wore no crown since she was no longer a virgin; that the wedding was "à la mode," or fashionable; and that no offspring were anticipated from the union, the world being already sufficiently populous.[5] Such absurdities as this suggest that Raemond was right in saying that he had become the object of blame, scorn, and hatred because of his aggressive tone.[6] By means of ridicule, moderate Catholics appear to have made some effort to signal their distaste for a polemicist whose language was frequently insulting to the Reformed. Such signals were all the more important in the earlier century when the king and his cabinet were making considerable efforts to sound out both parties on the prospects for religious unity. Raemond's works were unquestionably an embarrassment for those Catholics who supported the unity effort.

During the last half of the century a number of events and circumstances contributed to a negative assessment of Raemond's credibility. Not until the erudite priest (*abbé*) Laurent-Josse Leclerc published a critical attack on Pierre Bayle's *Dictionary*, with its devastating treatment of Raemond's historical abilities, was there any effort made to defend Raemond against the rumors and criticisms that had been accumulating against him for nearly a century.

The first question Leclerc explored was that of Raemond's authorship of (first) *L'Anti-Christ*, and eventually of his other books as well. The question had been raised first by Pierre Matthieu, a royal historiographer to Henry IV, and, therefore, a prestigious source upon which Raemond's critics might rely. Matthieu had written in a book he published in 1606 that he believed ("je crois") a Jesuit priest named Louis Richeome of Bordeaux had been the real author of *L'Anti-Christ*.[7] Leclerc said that Matthieu was the only one who had ever given voice to such a suspicion, and he chided Matthieu (who had been dead for nearly a century) for his carelessness and lack of evidence. Leclerc objected with reason that close friends of the author's—Jean Sponde, Pierre Le Double,[8] and Louis Richeome himself—had testified to his authorship.[9] Leclerc said Matthieu had been misled by one of Raemond's disclaimers of theological expertise. It may be that Matthieu had no animus against Raemond, but it may also be that he intentionally cast suspicion on the fact of Raemond's authorship of the work on Antichrist because Raemond was out of favor at court. In any event, Matthieu's doubts were not private, but published, and were repeated by others. Among these were the Protestant ministers André Rivet and Nicolas Vignier, although both hinted that the doubt raised was itself doubtful.[10]

Such early seventeenth-century rumors, even when repeated with hesitation, could not help but roost in the pigeon holes of memory. A mid-century outbreak grew out of a line (twice repeated) in the minister David Blondel's widely read *Familier Esclaircissement*, first published in 1647. In it he said that "the *Erreur Populaire* (was published under the name of the Sr. (*Sieur*) de Raemond."[11] This statement cast some doubt on the fact of Raemond's authorship of a second work, an enlargement of the grounds for doubt. A decade later, another book on the female pope was published — this one by a Catholic priest, père Labbe.[12] In it the author said that a brand new Latin edition of Blondel's work attributed the authorship of *Erreur Populaire* to Louis Richeome.[13] Blondel had not mentioned Richeome at all, but the editor of the Latin edition had, and as it was posthumous, Blondel could not object. After this episode, things speeded up. New works appeared in the last half of the century repeating the rumors that Raemond was not the author of two works that bore his name, but that Richeome was.[14]

In the last quarter of the century, the British historian and divine, Gilbert Burnet, completed the process of denying to Raemond the authorship of his works. The rumor was speedily included in a book of plagiarisms written by the German classical scholar and bibliographer, Johann Albert Fabricius. Burnet had taken exception to a Catholic history of the Reformation written by Antoine Varillas, in which that writer relied on the sixth Book of Raemond's "History of Heresy." Of course, the sixth was wholly the work of Florimond's son, François although this did not prevent Burnet from attacking Florimond. In his criticism of Varillas, Burnet stated loosely that many people believed Richeome had written the so-called works of Raemond.[15] Pierre Bayle quoted Burnet at length in his *Dictionary*:

> People have doubted if *the works* [my italics] which appear under the name Florimond are really his. Many have said that Father Richeome, a Jesuit, was their author, and had taken the name of counsellor in the Bordeaux parliament in order to give them credibility. Perhaps it was thought necessary to set up against Mr. De Thou, whose sincerity didn't suit the Jesuits, an author of some reputation. Pierre Matthieu, in his history, says positively that people thought Father Richeome was the author of the books which appeared under the name of Florimond de Rémond. Vignier, in his *Theater of Antichrist*, and Rivet in his *Response* to the Jesuits, say the same thing; and these authors wrote

shortly after the books of Raemond were published. Blondel was of the same opinion.[16]

Leclerc had little trouble showing that Burnet had distorted the facts to prove his case against the Catholic view of the Reformation in England, against Varillas, and ultimately against Raemond, because Varillas used François's chapter as a source. Leclerc defended Raemond's status as an author by pointing to the phrases each of the authors Burnet cited (but did not quote) had in fact used to qualify their subscription to the rumors of Richeome's authorship of Raemond's books. Leclerc's scorn was directed rightfully against Burnet, and also against Bayle, for the latter had left his readers to decide for themselves the facts of the case.[17] Was this, Leclerc asked, the way Bayle fulfilled his critical responsibilities?

In fact, Pierre Bayle had all the facts before him, but failed to draw the proper conclusions in his article "Rémond."[18] Only later in his article "Papesse," which was published in a supplement, did Bayle give Raemond credit for his own work on the popess: "On the whole it is just to agree that the work of Flor. de Rémond isn't bad in its way ... and I do not think that anyone has yet given so good a refutation of the popesse story. He made many mistakes, though."[19]

By the time the eighteenth century had begun to blow away bits and pieces of the fog that enveloped religious controversy, it was too late for enlightened thinkers to do more than make an occasional reference to some fact or fantasy in Raemond's "History of Heresy." The other two works (on Joan and Antichrist) were totally forgotten. One of the last references to his history was that of Lenglet du Fresnoy, whose book on historical method appeared for the last time in 1772, and contained an endorsement of that work.[20]

If some Catholic moderates and some Protestant controversialists had cause to cold-shoulder or abuse Raemond's books, Catholic conservatives did not. Pierre Bayle noted that his books had become "a public fountain for a quantity of other authors."[21] He regretted that many of them used Raemond as a source but witheld mention of his name. He thought Raemond's writings discouraged further research. In Bayle's article on Bernardino Ochino, the general of the Observantine Franciscans who fled Italy and joined the evangelical faith in Calvin's Geneva, Bayle referred to Raemond as "the quartermaster of Catholic writers who concerned themselves with the sixteenth century reform movement." He was offended by the scurrilous, unsupported comments Raemond had made concerning the sex lives of Ochino and Peter Martyr Vermigli, another

Italian exile and evangelical convert. He was indignant to think that such inaccuracies had been copied by at least three other Catholic authors.[22]

It is true that some Catholic writers used Raemond's books in a blatantly polemical way. The worst offender was perhaps Pierre Soulier, a former tailor, who was criticized by both parties as an unlearned man.[23] Soulier had worked for the revocation of the Edict of Nantes by publishing texts composed of documents that showed Protestants in an unfavorable light.[24] Other borrowers were not quite as outrageous as Soulier, but were definitely guided by the same general interests, that is, the promotion of their own faith rather than by a strict concern for historical accuracy. One might mention Jean Baptiste Dantecourt (d. 1718), who had far better credentials than a writer like Soulier, since he was not only a theologian but the chancellor of the University of Paris as well. His arguments recall some of Raemond's. For example, he deplored the practice of letting men question religious doctrines. He denied that the reformers had good reasons for criticizing the church of Rome, yet such positions were common to most Catholics and could have come from any Catholic theologian or historian with few exceptions. Much that Raemond wrote was ancient, orthodox Catholic teaching. On the other hand, errors of fact were more likely to be his own. Such errors were easily targeted by men like Bayle and by other scholars who then discouraged many readers in the later seventeenth century and beyond from taking Raemond seriously on other subjects.

Of the Catholic polemicists who drank from Raemond's "fountain," none was better known or more successful in publishing works than the ex-Jesuit Louis Maimbourg (d. 1686), who was defrocked for having offended Pope Innocent XI (in 1681) with his extreme Gallicanism and his unusual views on the divine right of kings. Like Raemond, he felt his main purpose was not as a researcher of historical archives, but as an educator of ordinary men. In Raemond's works he found readily available material on the evils of Lutheranism and Calvinism. While Bayle, in his general criticism of Louis Maimbourg's history of Calvinism, cited Maimbourg's sources as disreputable, the information that the former Jesuit had derived from Raemond in a dozen or more citations was not exclusively polemical.[25] He used biographical information he found in the "History of Heresy" on such figures as Marguerite of Navarre, Roussel, Clément Marot, etc. He did not portray Protestants as Raemond had, however. While the latter believed they were driven by sincere but mistaken zeal, Maimbourg portrayed them as insincere, politically motivated people who loved revolution for its own sake. He did not use Raemond's text exclusively, but consulted many other authors. What Maimbourg did share with Raemond was the common conviction that Roman Catholicism was the only right religion, and that any readers who were not already within the fold ought to convert. Maimbourg was freer than Raemond to plump for intolerant positions since he served a king who was himself intolerant, and more secure in his control of France than his grandfather, Henry IV, had been. Had Raemond lived and written in the France of the Sun King, he might have adopted even more intolerant positions.

Catholic polemicists like Maimbourg and Varillas have been described as historians who labored under a "conspiracy theory."[26] Accordingly, they thought the sixteenth-century reformers had inveigled the excitable French — women especially — into perceiving Catholicism as a mere superstition, and the reformed faith as an attractive alternative. It is possible, but Maimbourg and Varillas did not derive that theory from Raemond, and it would be unwise to blame Raemond for the sins of his copiers. While Raemond failed to acknowledge that the Huguenots' resentment of the Catholic church was justified, and while he did take women to task for their irrationality and lust, he did not believe such factors accounted wholly for the Reformation. He was not a systematic theorist at all, and certainly held no conspiracy theory of religious change. He cited many factors — psychological, political, historical, cultural — that helped account for the Reformation. Rather than a conspiracy theory, he emphasized the inability of mankind to resist evil. He had great respect for the complexity of things and the difficulty of men to discover the truth.

No doubt more Catholic writers than Protestant ones looked to Raemond as a source during the seventeenth century. However, on the subject of John Calvin's early life, Raemond remained a prime source for writers of both parties. For example, Charles Drelincourt (d. 1669), a minister of Charenton and the author of a number of works defending the reformed church, undertook a life of Calvin in order to avenge that reformer against the fury of Cardinal Richelieu's treatise.[27] He used the research of Raemond to do this, and also works by Pasquier and Papire Masson, Catholics all, but of varying stamp. Of course he consulted Protestant sources such as André Rivet, too.[28] The great Bossuet (d. 1704), former tutor to the *Dauphin* and Bishop of Meaux, a brilliant controversialist, moralist, and stylist as well as historian, seems not to have scrupled to use Raemond's technique of comparing Luther to

Calvin, finding, like Raemond, that Calvin was more dignified and more virtuous.[29] On the other hand, Bossuet refrained from citing Raemond as a source, wishing to avoid the accusation of undue dependence on a polemicist of the previous century.[30]

In 1682 an impressively illustrated folio volume dedicated to the learned men of the past was published in the Catholic city of Brussels. In it appeared a reproduction of a handsome portrait of Florimond de Raemond by the engraver Nicolas de Larmessin, showing Raemond in the flower of his maturity, with a full head of hair, a mustache turned up jauntily at the ends, and a short, full beard. He appears dressed as a magistrate, with ruff, embroidered doublet, and puffy satin sleeves.[31] Although the author of this book, Isaac Bullart, said that Raemond's works had been received with "general applause," in fact, Raemond's popularity had already crested, leaving behind (as of 1682) thirty-two editions of all his published works.[32]

Just as ruffs and doublets disappeared from European courts and drawing rooms in the seventeenth century, so did outmoded styles of expression. The rational, dispassionate rhetoric of the Enlightenment began inexorably to replace the livelier prose of the Renaissance and early Baroque periods.[33] Bayle, who represented the new wave of taste as well as thought, was critical of a writer such as Maimbourg who had written history as if it were a novel in which the villainous characters are the thinly disguised critics of the author himself.[34] Maimbourg's style was not far removed from Raemond's own. Madame de Sevigné found it indelicate, lowbrow, and lamentably enthusiastic.[35] She could have said the same thing about Raemond's books if she came upon them. Enthusiasm was very nearly an infamous thing in the classical eighteenth century. The lack of enthusiasm that the elite displayed was considered a sign of superior taste. By 1695 this attitude was already in evidence. In that year a French critic named Lenfant was asked to write a preface for and to translate Frederic Spanheim's history of Pope Joan. In his preface, Lenfant decried the literary style of Catholic polemicists such as Cardinal Baronius and Père Labbe (who had written yet another book on Joan from the Catholic point of view). The noun he used to describe Labbe's work was "rodomontade," a word that reflects primarily upon the style rather than the content of a work. On the other hand, he approved of one Docteur de Launoy, another Catholic writer, whose manner (style) was not overlabored, meaning that it was courteous rather than aggressive. Lenfant, who took, with Spanheim, the erroneous view that there had really been a female pope, could forgive a Protestant, the minister Blondel, for having drawn the "wrong" conclusion about Joan because he believed Blondel's motives—like de Launoy's—were pure. What he meant by purity was not directly related to the content, but simply to the tone of the writings in question. He believed Blondel and de Launoy were interested only in the truth, and arrived at that conclusion because their style was devoid of the kind of passion that colored the writing of Raemond and of Père Labbe.[36] The age of controversy had drawn to a close.

In the eighteenth century only the critique of Bayle by Leclerc and two editions of the "History of Heresy" appeared to keep alive Raemond's memory. Of course, it is quite probable that people continued to read his work on Antichrist or on the popess, his edition of Monluc's memoirs, and his translations of Tertullian. There were thirty-seven editions in all of his works, and it would have been common enough to find some of these in the libraries of eighteenth-century people. Still, defamatory gossip and the changing taste of readers coincided with a falling off of new editions of Raemond's books after the mid-seventeenth century. New research produced alternative explanations of historical events. Even if it did not invariably render Raemond's work obsolete, enlightened readers would have found modern books satisfied their desire for historical knowledge more completely, and without the embarrassment of secular polemic.

After Larroque's biographical sketch a series of three articles by Léonce Couture on Raemond appeared in the *Revue de Gascogne* in 1868. These attempted to rescue him from historical oblivion. Couture recognized that religious prejudice and narrow judgment detracted from the work of the Bordeaux magistrate, but urged that the flaws be forgiven him in light of his genuine erudition, his competence in textual analysis, and his engaging style. The requirements of style had shifted by the mid-nineteenth century from the classical to the sentimental. Couture wished to rehabilitate Raemond for his humanistic outlook, his sincerity, and his desire to pursue truth by scholarship rather than warfare.[37] Like his predecessors in these matters, the Abbé Leclerc and Larroque, Couture believed that a son of Guyenne had been unjustly besmirched by writers such as Bishop Burnet and Pierre Bayle. He did not hold Raemond a great historian, finding his a "lesser talent," but one "quite good for all that."[38] He urged Frenchmen to find an honorable place in French letters for Florimond de Raemond.

In the twentieth century Raemond has found his way into the footnotes of various books on sixteenth-century literature and early modern historiography. Only two authors, however, have given his works enough attention and space to qualify as serious commentators.[39] The first of these is Claude-Gilbert Dubois, whose long book on sixteenth-century historiography devotes some twenty-six pages to Raemond's "History of Heresy" and the book on Antichrist.[40] Dubois finds two major differences between Catholic and Protestant conceptions of history, one methodological, the other political.

On the methodological aspect, Dubois stresses the Catholic party's reluctance to tackle the dogmatic disputes head on, turning instead to faulting their Protestant opponents on methodological grounds. In his view, Catholic controversialists were guilty of trying to avoid considering ideas that they had already decided were not debatable.[41] There is much truth in this opinion, but Dubois does not succeed in demonstrating that Protestants were less committed to certain other ideas, or less intransigent in their defense. It is debatable whether Catholics in fact clung tighter to dogma and to tradition than did Protestants to the Word and to the defense of their particular conception of church government and its administration. When Dubois faults Raemond's ideology for its "unitary" qualities — a word that he believes to be an essential expression of Raemond's approach to philosophical and governmental issues — he ignores the fact that such reverence for authority was a traditional posture of most Frenchmen.[42] In the realm of political ideology, the slogan "un roi, une loi, une foi" summarizes contemporary sentiment rather well, while the inclusion of the word "foi" (faith) reveals that early modern Frenchmen were accustomed to the idea that authority of state was inseparable from authority over the religious establishment. Raemond was no less authoritarian than the majority of Frenchmen, and that authoritarianism was shared by most Huguenot Frenchmen as well. Indeed, the Huguenot party vied with the Catholic party for the honor of having better defended the royal prerogative during the civil wars. Duplessis-Mornay, their leader, committed his religious *confrères* to the unitary ideal when he acceded to the wishes of Henry IV and drew up a report (1600) on the possibilities of achieving religious unity in France. Although Dubois emphasizes the "community spirit" and the "democratic" tendencies of Protestants and de-emphasizes or ignores their recognition of "unity" and "primacy," many Protestant leaders agreed with the Parisian minister, Daniel Du Moulin, that "it was better in any state to have a bad master, than none at all."[43] French Protestants as well as Catholics looked to a strong monarch to preserve them from civil unrest. In addition Huguenots hoped such a monarch would spare them the extension of papal authority —

and in this wish they were joined by Catholic moderates and Gallicans.

Dubois was right to characterize Raemond's *L'Anti-Christ* as a combative work in that it was designed to deflect the charge made by Protestants that the papacy was the work of Antichrist.[44] He was incorrect to say that Raemond's religious beliefs were, along with those of many other Catholics, equivalent to a renunciation of reason, while the book written by Lambert Daneau on Antichrist represents the superior reason of the Protestant faith.[45] To suggest that one variety of sixteenth- (or seventeenth)-century Christianity was more reasonable than another is to underestimate the intensity of Protestant as well as Catholic commitment to a plethora of beliefs that were something quite other than rational. A Catholic interpretation of Antichrist was no more, but no less, irrational than a Protestant one. It is all too easy—but it is also antihistorical— to confuse a moderate literary style, such as the one Daneau adopted, with the rationality of a later age. It is not the case that Daneau and other Protestants were more rational than Catholics like Raemond because they identified Antichrist with one of a number of historical popes or with certain developments in church history rather than with some future entry into the historical process. Either view is antithetical to rationalism and to rational history.

Although Dubois concedes that Raemond's "absolutism" (if one can call the kind of reverence he showed for authority absolutist, which is debatable) was softened by a provisional reluctance to eliminate Protestants, he regards "the unitary mystique" of his several works totalitarian by implication and something that led to and found completion in the revocation of the Edict of Nantes.[46] In this way, and by implication, Dubois links Raemond's desire for a strong king who could quell civil disorder and his desire for religious unity to a totalitarianism that was certainly not achieved in the France of Louis XIV. Whether such analysis is an attempt to put the cart (absolutism) before the horse (religious intolerance), or simply to discard the whole rig for a new go-cart (totalitarianism) is arguable. What is certain is that religious intolerance was an attitude more ancient in western civilization than absolute monarchy. Nor is it helpful to regard the yearning for Christian unity as a premonition of totalitarianism, which, when it appeared in the twentieth century, was not notably Christian.

Of course, Raemond was religiously intolerant and believed in strong kings. There was nothing very peculiar about such attitudes. All religious history pre-determined his lack of tolerance for alternative religious forms, while the trauma of the civil war period and a series of unstable or incompetent kings made him long for an authoritative ruler. France was far from being a unitary state in 1600, and Raemond was not a forerunner of modern fascism or communism, just as Protestant writers on religious topics were scarcely bearers of modern liberalism, a sense of community, federalism, collegiality, or democratic egalitarianism.[47] Instead of referring to Raemond as a proto-totalitarian, Dubois might have presented him as a conservative idealist, which he was. Raemond yearned for the simplicity and safety of a bygone era which he mistakenly imagined in such terms. He was indeed intolerant, but he shared his intolerance with a majority of Catholic and Protestant Frenchmen. When Protestants were in a majority, as they were in Geneva after Calvin, or in England during the seventeenth century, they were no more tolerant of religious diversity than were Catholics.[48]

The second scholarly inquiry of any length to appear prior to the present study in our own century was that of Martin Busch. It has already been mentioned in connection with Anabaptism. Busch's work, unlike that of Dubois, does not attempt to categorize Raemond's work, although it is no less comparative in approach. While recognizing Raemond's polemical purpose, Busch finds that Raemond anticipated a not inconsiderable number of recent historians who have studied Anabaptism, and Busch concludes that Raemond's approach to the study of that subject was a vision both "global and unitary."[49]

Conclusion

Popular in his own lifetime, and with many Catholic readers in the first half of the seventeenth century, Raemond's stock plummeted during the second half of that century, partly due to rumors that circulated concerning his "feigned" authorship, and partly due to Protestant resentment of his considerable influence. Philosophers such as Pierre Bayle and churchmen such as Bishop Burnet impugned not his authorship alone, but his reliability as an historian as well. Few critics of his books have been more perceptive than the nineteenth-century critic Léonce Couture, who acknowledged that Raemond was not a genius on a par with the most profound thinkers of his age, yet was by no means a despicable talent. Still, the sarcastic dictum of Bayle hangs in the air above, daring us to regard Raemond as an historian and insisting that he would have been better advised to write mere polemic and to leave history alone. Many moderns might be of the same opinion. The word polemic has so negative a connotation as to deny altogether that a work of that sort could contain any historical insight. For such critics, all polemicists are equally devoid of reason, and also of interest or value. Bayle would have had all historians possess "right conscience and perfect probity,"[50] and modern scholars have hastened to support such sentiments and to dismiss polemical historians such as Raemond as unworthy, and the time spent in reading such polemical histories unproductive.

Such opinions, however, are increasingly inappropriate and detrimental to the study of history, reflecting as they do a modern rather than historical preoccupation with values that can only be described as modern and liberal. Raemond's histories deserve the closest attention precisely because they so perfectly reflected the social and political ethics of his times, and of the next two generations of his native country and intellectual posterity. His influence and his popularity are witnesses to that fact. The neglect that is bred by a contempt for religious intolerance is quite misplaced in light of the recent professional interest in the history of *mentalités* and in the light of an exuberant but painstaking examination of every aspect of popular culture and social change. Although Raemond's books were not anticipations of scientific history writing, his concern for interesting sociological and psychological interpretation and detail lend a modern touch to the books he produced. Such interests were not common in his day, and may account for the fact that historians in more tolerant centuries continued to lift out of his histories passages that even the most sociologically minded contemporary historians of popular culture can appreciate for their rarity and persuasiveness.

Raemond's social and political values were common, and these helped him achieve considerable fame if not fortune. He had the uncommon as well as the common touch, for he was uncommonly well-informed and was uncommonly in command of his resources. Granted that his perceptions with respect to religion and society were ordinary, his achievements were not. Some of his efforts were productive of a more rational and accurate concept of the past. He was, after all, one of a number of writers who helped to expose certain mythical explanations of the past, nor did he advocate violence in the defense of his religion, preferring the pen to the sword and disapproving of torture that he believed unsuitable to the goal of religious conversion.

Although Bayle envisioned a better way to write history — without passion or distortion — most of Raemond's contemporaries wrote history through the medium of past experience: authoritarian government, religious fanaticism, and ingrained suspicion. Since Raemond's books were popular, it is fair to conclude that he sold well because he flattered popular prejudices, without offending against the norms of taste and style.

Through the systematic analysis of popular polemical histories such as those written by Florimond de Raemond, scholars of early modern European history may become more knowledgeable about the aspirations and apprehensions of ordinary people in the face of extraordinary events, and their readers may better appreciate the fearfulness and defensiveness that spiritual revolution engenders in the minds of men. By means of such study, modern historians may be able to correct the limited vision of those frustrated idealists who took up their pens to write religious history and produced historical religious polemic.

Like most of his contemporaries, Protestant as well as Catholic, Florimond de Raemond was hampered by his allegiance to an imperfect and limited vision of reality. It would be useful, and even consoling, to think that the careful attention paid such works as he wrote may shed light on the prejudices as well as the principles of sixteenth- and seventeenth-century men and women, and perhaps, by implication, on our own.

Notes

Preface

1. The latest to have done so are A. G. Dickens and John Tonkin, with Kenneth Powell, *The Reformation in Historical Thought* (Cambridge, Mass.: Harvard University Press, 1985), p. 95.

2. Such opinions, as voiced by Claude-Gilbert Dubois, *La Conception de l'histoire en France au XVIe siècle (1560–1610)* (Paris: A. G. Nizet, 1977), are carefully considered in chap. 9, and in notes 40–47.

Chapter 1. Raemond's Life in Brief

1. M. O'Gilvy, *Nobiliaire de Guienne et de Gascogne* (Paris: Éditions du Palais Royal, 1973, 1st. ed., 1856–1883) IV, p. 412, describes the Raemond arms: Quartered on the upper left on a blue field, a silver cross; on the upper right, in blue and gold, diamond shapes; on the lower left, a silver bell against a red background; on the lower right, a golden globe circled and topped in gold. The count's crown. Supports: two lions. Slogan: *Are de mou no mudera*. (See note 40 below.)

2. Ibid.

3. Ibid. p. 29.

4. Philippe Tamizey de Larroque, *Essai sur la vie et les ouvrages de Florimond de Raymond* (Paris: August Aubry, Librairie, 1867), p. 4, n.2.

5. Ibid., p. 4, n.3.

6. Raemond, *L'Histoire de la naissance, progrez et decadence de l'heresie de ce siecle*, (Rouen: P. Maille, 1647), 1st ed., 1605, p. 865. Subsequent references to this work will be to the Maille edition unless otherwise noted. It will be referred to in the text as the *History of Heresy*. In the notes, it will be abbreviated *L'Histoire*, etc.

7. Albert Dauzat, *Dictionnaire étymologique des noms de famille et prénoms de France* (Paris: Librairie Larousse, 1951), p. 507.

8. Raemond, *L'Histoire, etc.*, p. 851.

9. Ibid., p. 865. (Erroneously paginated in the 1647 ed. as 866.)

10. Ibid.

11. Ibid., p. 894.

12. Larroque, *Essai*, p. 6, n.1.

13. Raymond Darricau, "La Vie et l'Oeuvre d'un Parlémentaire Aquitaine, Florimond de Raemond," *Revue Française d'histoire du livre*, nos. 1–2, 1971, p. 110. Darricau notes that Raemond studied first at the College of Guyenne, but did not have a high opinion of it.

14. F. Jouannet, *Statistique du département de la Gironde*, II, (Paris: P. Dupon et Cie. 1843), p. 5.

15. Ibid.

16. Raemond, *L'Histoire, etc.*, p. 864. This is the statement on which Darricau (see above, note 13) based his opinion that Raemond entertained no good opinion of the College of Guyenne. Of course, when he wrote the passage Raemond was no longer the impressionable child he had once been. We do not know what he thought of the school while he was in attendance.

17. Ibid., p. 894.

18. As for the reason he was sent to Paris, Raemond said there was no alternative, since the schools of Toulouse and Poitiers had already been spoiled by reform. Otherwise, his parents would most likely have spared themselves the added expense and inconvenience of providing a Parisian education for him.

19. The *Trois Imposteurs* was purportedly a book circulating in the mid-sixteenth century, but which had entirely disappeared from circulation by the seventeenth. It was attributed to various authors, including Servetus. Its central theme was that Moses, Christ, and Mohammed had, like secular legislators (kings) of the past, tamed their people by obliging them to submit to the religious disciplines of their own (not of divine) invention. Although Bayle (*Dictionnaire historique*, art. Rémond, remark B) felt the story was of thirteenth-century origin, it may have originated as late as the latter fifteenth. It was used variously by atheists to cast doubt on all religion, and by tolerant or skeptical thinkers to demonstrate that the divine principles were few and identical. See Henri Busson, *Le Rationalisme dans la littérature Française de la Renaissance* (Paris: J. Vrin, 1957), pp. 343–51 for an excellent summary. Busson quotes Raemond at length (the expanded passage that contains the remark about Ramus holding this work in his hands indicates that one Jacques Curio, writing in 1556, had cited a Palatine sect called Lucianists who disbelieved in the sanctity of Scripture and of the inspiration of Moses. Raemond's remarks are called "troubling" by Busson (p. 349), who finds it strange that some remnant of the work has not been preserved. Larroque (*Essai*, p. 8, n.1) gives his assent to the book's having existed in the mid-sixteenth century. Whether it did or did not exist as a published work, the theme of the *Trois Imposteurs* provided for contemporaries important if divergent theses on which to debate the religious innovations of the reform period.

20. Raemond, *L'Histoire, etc.*, p. 236. Ramus (Pierre de la Ramée) was not an avowed Protestant during Raemond's attendance at Presles, but became one in 1561. However, he was sympathetic to the cause earlier, and not unlikely during Raemond's enrollment there in the 1550s. See Charles Waddington, *Ramus Sa Vie, etc.* (Paris: Charles Meyrais et Cie, 1855), p. 134.

21. Raemond, *L'Histoire, etc.*, p. 866.

22. Samuel Mours, *Le Protestantisme en France au seizième siècle*, (Paris: Librairie protestante, 1959), p. 150.

23. Between 1570 and 1598 the numbers of French reformed declined sharply, with the massacre of St. Bartholomew's Day serving as the most important event triggering this decline. See Robert Mandrou et al. *Histoire des Protestants en France*. (Toulouse, Édouard Privat, Éditeur, 1977), p. 67. Raemond's religious crisis was not the result of persecution nor was it due to any failure of nerve, but rather due to an altered perspective of religious truth.

24. Raemond, *L'Histoire, etc.*, p. 1047.

25. Larroque, *Essai*, p. 9.

26. Raemond, *L'Histoire etc.*, p. 1010.

27. There has been no little controversy on the part of Raemond's admirers as to whether or not he actually did have Protestant sympathies in his youth. That he

indeed did seems to this biographer an inescapable conclusion given the several instances in the *Anti-Christ* and in the *Histoire, etc.* in which he associates himself with the other schoolboys who were having their religious convictions and their social perceptions altered by reformed teachers, or by harsh political realities such as the martyrdoms of the reformed. The controversy over whether or not Raemond had been a Protestant is examined more narrowly in the text that follows and in note 39 below.

28. Even if the perceptive critic and Montaigne scholar, Alan Boase, could write that Piere Bayle had exaggerated a bit Raemond's ferocity toward Protestants (in "Montaigne et la Sorcellerie," *Humanisme et Renaissance*, nos. 1–2, 1934–35, p. 402), there is no doubt whatever that he was frequently ferocious. But one must object more strongly to Boase's contention that it was due to Bayle that Raemond acquired the reputation of having been one of the late sixteenth century's most formidable Catholic polemicists. Before Raemond's death he had published at least thirteen editions of his own works excluding the *Histoire, etc.*, which was first published four years after his death in 1601. Besides these he had edited two works—Monluc's *Memoirs* and Jean de Sponde's rebuttal of a theological work of Bèze. Between 1601 and 1678 some twenty-one further printings of Raemond's works including the *Histoire, etc.* appeared in several languages in Europe. Bayle did not give Raemond his reputation—his popularity as an author did. In his own lifetime, Raemond had been recognized as a Catholic Counter-Reformation polemicist by the historian Cardinal Baronius (see below chap. 3 and chap. 4), and recently, in an unpublished doctoral dissertation, Martin Busch has affirmed that his influence and political notoriety were recognized by many of his contemporaries and by most of his biographical commentators, (*Florimond de Raemond (vers 1540–1601) et l'Anabaptisme*, Université des Sciences Humaines de Strasbourg, Faculté de Théologie Protestante 1980–1981, p. 18.

29. Raemond noted that the first converts at Meaux were "really poor folk and simple: their profession bespoke their history—working men, wool carders, drapers" (*L'Histoire, etc.*, p. 847). He knew that the better sort had joined the ranks of Calvinism by mid-century, for he commented on their participation in martyrdom. Ibid., p. 864. In fact, the movement in France attracted rich and poor proportionally, according to Natalie Davis, *Society and Culture in Early Modern France* (Stanford, Stanford University press, 1977), p. 7. Some historians stress the material reasons why poor people joined the reform. See Harold Grimm, "Social Forces in the German Reformation," *Church History*, 31 (1962), while others discount such reasons. See Claus-Peter Clasen, "The Sociology of Swabian Anabaptism," *Church History*, 31 (1962). Of course, Swabian peasants as opposed to artisans had a long history of social protest over feudal dues and services, rent control, and forest laws, and were indeed attracted to Anabaptism. Raemond noted that the Moravian brothers made a positive virtue of manual labor, and would not tolerate laziness in their midst—surely the attitudes of poor folk. *L'Histoire, etc.*, p. 147.

30. Raemond told of one of the simple souls, a poor Anabaptist woman who longed to give a party for her friends but was too poor to buy refreshments for them. She believed that the Holy Spirit had instructed her to proceed with the entertainment and that food would arrive via angels. Predictably, the guests went home hungry, but wiser. The story was intended to make the sect appear ridiculous, but it does reveal that the author was aware that many poor people thought their status in this world would be improved by radical sectarian membership. Raemond was also suspicious of the reformed for emphasizing humility, modesty, and

simplicity, believing that an exterior show of virtue often cloaked inner viciousness. (*L'Histoire, etc.*, pp. 140, 864).

31. Raemond, *L'Histoire, etc.*, p. 894.
32. Ibid.
33. Darricau, *La Vie et l'oeuvre*, p. 110 says Raemond was at Toulouse along with Etienne Pasquier, Henri de Mesmes, Antoine Loisel, Pierre Pithou, and du Bartas. In the case of Pasquier, who began his law career in 1549, as in the case of Mesmes, who held a chair in law at age sixteen at Toulouse, but left in 1548, this is clearly not the case. Loisel may have met Raemond at Presles, even though he was four years older than Raemond. Both were pupils of Peter Ramus there. Darricau seems to have misread a passage of Larroque's *Essai* (p. 9) that describes the University.
34. Raemond's introduction to Calvin (Book VII, chap. 8 of *L'Histoire, etc.*) provides insight into the nature of his attitude toward learning. He admired humanist scholars, but was suspicious of their attitudes concerning religion. Philosophers, he thought, were the real patriarchs of heresy in France. They were not reliable, but had engendered Protestantism through their concerns for grammar, philosophy, and even mathematics. This was not the case with the "good" doctors of theology. Distinctions between wisdom and knowledge were many and subtle during the sixteenth century, as Eugene F. Rice, *The Renaissance Idea of Wisdom* (Cambridge, Mass., Harvard University Press, 1958) has carefully demonstrated. Although Raemond's diction recalls that of more avant-garde thinkers such as Vives, Erasmus, Budé, and Pierre Charron, his position was in reality conservative and traditional: "La Philosophie ... est une sagesse du monde; la Theologie une sagesse de Dieu," (*L' Histoire, etc.*, mp. 878.) He would not have understood or sympathized with the antitheological assumptions of Charron, whom he nonetheless admired, and even cited on occasion. (See chap. 2.)
35. Paris was not at this time a center for legal studies.
36. Raemond spelled her name Obry. See Henri Busson, *Littérature et théologie* (Paris: Presses Universitaires de France, 1962), pp. 19–23. Busson uses the Auberi exorcism and one other to contrast Montaigne's skeptical attitude with that of believers—his cousin, Del Rio, and Florimond de Raemond.
37. Busson, *op. cit.*, p. 20, says demonic possession was considered a type of illness for which the victim bore no guilt, and that such cases were believed to demonstrate the legitimacy of Catholicism to heretics. The effect on Raemond was, in the light of such opinion, classic.
38. In his *Antichrist*, p. 169, and *L'Histoire, etc.*, p. 204.
39. Raemond, *L'Histoire, etc.*, p. 204, made a statement about the state of his soul that subsequently was a matter of debate. He claimed the exorcism had snatched him from the maws of heresy: "m'a retiré de la gueule de l'Heresie." Pierre Bayle (*Dictionnaire Historique*, Desoer XII, art. Rémond p. 501), deduced from this that Raemond had thus left Protestantism. Laurent-Josse Leclerc (*Lettre Critique*, pp. 373–74), led by a desire to castigate Bayle's scholarship, denied that the statement indicated any Protestant affinity on Raemond's part. In his haste he ignored the word Raemond did use—*retiré*, which means pulled back *again from*, and wrote his opinion against Bayle's, using the quite different word *tiré*, which means simply drawn out, or preserved. Larroque supported Leclerc (in the *Essai*, p. 13), carelessly failing to observe Leclerc's error. The support of this first biographer of Raemond's for the eighteenth century prelate's mistake is all the more puzzling since Larroque recognized that Raemond had all but lost his Catholic belief before the Obry incident. And if he had lost it, he could hardly

have used the word "preserved" (*tiré*). Still later, Léonce Couture, "Florimond de Raymond," *Revue de Gascogne*, IX, (1868), p. 13, termed the phrase "m'a retiré," etc., "une phrase hyperbolique dont on a exagéré la portée." Yet the original statement is no mere hyperbole if read as it was written. Couture, nonetheless, made the best statement concerning Raemond's religious development when he observed that he had always been attracted to the "seductions du calvinisme" but had never professed it openly, and was restored to his old faith by the Auberi incident.

40. The insignia appeared on the third edition of Raemond's *Erreur populaire de la Papesse Jane*, published by Simon Millanges in 1594. Two anonymous editions (of 1587 and 1588) preceded it. When Ernest Labadie, "Additions et rectifications à la bibliographie de quelques écrivains Agenais," *Revue de l'Agenais*, 1906, pp. 22–23, examined the figure, he believed the slogan a play on the words *Rémond* (one of several alternate spellings) and *le monde*. He refused to translate. J. Momméja, "La Dévise de F. de Raymond" in the same journal of 1908, pp. 561–64, thought it meant *Arre Demoun! no mudera!* or, Get back, Demon! He will not change! My translation is derived by taking *are* to mean *lares*, the Latin word for household gods. I then rendered that into God of my Fathers, a phrase consistent with Raemond's Christian faith. The words *Du mon*, my, and *no mudera*, will not change, presented no difficulty. This translation is very similar to a statement embedded in Raemond's *Anti-Christ*: "I call God and his angels as my witness that the diversity of religion will never change the sincerity of my conscience" (p. 71).

41. Donald Frame, Montaigne's biographer, does not refer to Raemond at all in his *Montaigne, a Biography* (New York: Harcourt, Brace & World, Inc., 1965).

42. The "Lettres d'estat et office de conseiller au Parlement de Bourdeaux pour M. Florimond Raemond" are appended to Larroque, *Essai*, pp. 132–34. We must assume that the language of the letters, which mention his "sage suffizance," "litérature," "suffizance," "preudhomye," and "bonne diligence" was the product of custom rather than the result of intimate acquaintance. Most of these could be attributed to any young man who had received a university education in law.

43. The book was the *Plaintes des eglises reformées au roi sur plusieurs injustices qui leur sont faites*, (anon.). It was extensively commented upon by Élie Benoist (d. 1728) who wrote the *Histoire de l'édit de Nantes, jusques à l'édit de revocation* (Delft, 1693). The *Plaintes* may well be the source from which Bayle drew the conclusion that the kidnapping was the decisive factor in determining Raemond's subsequent actions vis-à-vis Huguenots. It is the first source of criticism of Raemond's judicial career and was undoubtedly considered by the Reformed as a damning piece of evidence that Raemond was a magistrate of mediocre ability and questionable ethical standards. (See chap. 3.)

44. Bayle, *Dictionnaire Historique*, XII, art. Rémond, remark E, p. 508.

45. Larroque, *Essai*, pp. 41–42. (See chap. 3, n.51.)

46. Raemond, *L'Histoire, etc.*, p. 1011.

47. "La nulle forme du Christianisme" was the term he used. Ibid.

48. It is significant that Raemond's treatment of the St. Bartholomew's Day Massacre was limited to this oblique reference: "the horror which befell Paris" (*L'Histoire, etc.*, p. 1056). He failed to mention that it occurred in many provincial French cities as well. As Theodore K. Rabb has noted in "Conclusion: St. Bartholomew and Historical Perspective," in Alfred Soman, ed., *The Massacre of St. Bartholomew: Reappraisals and Documents*, (The Hague: Martinus Nyjhoff,

1974), p. 255, the massacre was "a distasteful episode, easily ignored, and an embarrassment rather than a lesson" for many Catholics.

49. Guillaume de Salluste, *sieur* du Bartas's best known work was his *Commentaires et annotations sur la semaine de la création, etc.* (1583), followed by a second *Semaine, etc.* (1591). He tried to prove the existence of God and urged his readers to arrive at the knowledge of Him by contemplating the natural universe. Like Montaigne, Raemond, and Peletier, du Bartas was skeptical of reason because of the damage it seemed able to cause faith. See Henri Busson, *Le Rationalisme*, pp. 589–93, who finds du Bartas possessed "une culture assez étendue, mais superficielle" (p. 599).

50. The sonnet is fully reprinted in Larroque, *Essai*, p. 26.

51. Pierre de Brach, *sieur* de La Motte Montussan, once termed Raemond "un autre moi-mesme." He frequently praised Raemond's merits and industry. (See below, n.53.) Brach's first poems were published in 1576, an edition that contained a few examples of Raemond's own poetry. Both were very close friends of Montaigne's.

52. Jacques Peletier (1517–1582), friend of Ronsard, Rabelais, the young Theodore de Bèze, and Montaigne, had belonged to the literary coterie of Queen Marguerite of Navarre. (De Clinchamp, "Notices biographiques et littéraires. J. Peletier," *Bulletin du Bibliophile*, 1847, pp. 283–308; 439–68. Peletier says he met Raemond at Brach's home. Peletier was director of the College of Guyenne, 1573–1579, and a practicing physician in Bordeaux. He was also a *fidéiste*. See Clément Jugé, *Jacques Peletier, du Mans (1517–1582) essai sur sa vie, son oeuvre, son influence* (Paris, 1907).

53. Not all sonnets had lofty themes, Brach's ran (in part):

> Car je me crains que leur demeure
> Du disner fera passer l'heure:
> Et que mon Raimond empesché
> Soit dans son estude attaché
> Feuilletant nos lois querelleuse.
> (The entire sonnet is reprinted in
> Larroque's *Essai*, pp. 26–27.)

54. Pierre de Brach, *Oeuvres poétiques*, annotated by Reinhold Dezeimeris, II (Geneva: Auguste Aubry, Librairie, 1969) Repr., p. 5.

55. The synod of upper Guyenne and Limousin met there, for example, in 1562.

56. The incident of the capture, which occurred during a stroll on the meadow at St. Macaire, in the company of the noblewoman, Mme. de Candale, is related by Philippe Tamizey de Larroque, "L'Emprisonnement de Florimond de Raymond," *Revue de Gascogne*, XXXVI, 1895, pp. 127–128.

57. Jean de Gaufreteau, *Chronique Bordeloise*, II (Bordeaux, Charles Lefebure, 1877), p. 214. The author was the son of Jean de Gaufreteau, a colleague of Raemond's in the Bordeaux *Parlement*.

58. The name was of Basque origin and was variously spelled—*Rostegny* by Fleury Vindry, *Les Parlementaires Français au XVIe siècle*, II (Paris, 1910), Librairie Honoré Champion p. 100; *Rosteguy* by Larroque, *Essai*, who also spelled the last name *Lencre*, though it is usually spelled *Lancre*. Pierre de Lancre wrote two books in the early seventeenth century on sorcery. It is possible that Lancre drew his inspiration for these books from Raemond himself, and not

unlikely that some, if not all, of Raemond's earlier notes passed through Catharine to her brother after the death of Florimond de Raemond. See chap. 3, n.48.

59. Jules Andrieu, *Bibliographie Générale de l'Agenais* (Paris and Agen, A. Picard, 1887), p. 234.

60. Fleury Vindry, *Les Parlementaires Français*, p. 100.

61. Larroque, *Essai*, p. 38, says Jeanne Marin, but Fleury Vindry *op. cit*, p. 100, says her name was Suzanne Marin.

62. Pierre de Brach, *Oeuvres poétiques*, I, Reinhold Dezeimeris, ed. (Geneva, 1969) p. 251, wrote (sonnet) "A Monsieur de Raymond": "Ne me cherches donq point pour estre à toy semblable, À toy, Raymond, qui fus en amour variable."

63. Fleury Vindry, *op. cit*, p. 101, noted that this Florimond, born of the Marin marriage, is not to be confused with his half-cousin, also named Florimond, the son of François. François's son Florimond also became a *Conseiller* in the Bordeaux *Parlement*, and died in 1657.

64. There are three known portraits of Florimond de Raemond, according to Ernest Labadie, "Additions et Rectifications à la Bibliographie de Quelques Écrivains Agenais," *Revue de l'Agenais*, 1906, pp. 21–38. The first, and in Labadie's opinion, finest, was the work of Thomas de Leu, one of the two best engravers in late sixteenth-century France. Leu's signed engraving of Raemond appeared only on the 1601 edition of Jean-Charles de Raemond's translation into Latin of his father's *Erreur populaire* (*Fabula Joannae quae Pontificis romani sedem occupasse, etc.*), (Bordeaux, 1601). Raemond, wearing a mustache and a goatee, Is shown in an oval, the top of which is bordered by his name in Latin: *Florimondus Raemondus, Senat. Burdiga*. It is a three-quarter face pose looking to the right. A ruff shirt collar, a full-sleeved coat, and an embroidered waistcoat underneath make up his costume. The portrait appeared over a Latin quatrain (Raemond's own work?) warning the Protestants that they, who have rent the body of St. Peter, will never escape Raemond's grasp, however much they may try to flee him. Subsequently, the Leu engraving, which was made during Raemond's own lifetime, was twice copied. The first copy, by Thomas Mallery, appearing on the first (posthumous) edition of the *Histoire, etc.* (1605.) The second (and the only one of the three portraits that has Raemond facing left) was an enlargement of the 1605 portrait by Mallery—done by Nicolas Larmessin for Isaac Bullart's impressive *L'Académie des Sciences et des Arts* (Brussels, 1682).

65. The sonnet extolled her many gifts as well as her virtue. Dianne was fortunate in having more than just one literary servant among the writers of Bordeaux—Montaigne wrote for her his essay "Of the Education of Children" when she had children. Raemond's sonnet appears in Pierre de Brach's *Oeuvres poétiques*, ed. Dezeimeris, I, p. 16. The sonnet noted her illustrious family—the Foix—were descendants of medieval royalty, and though a relative of Henry of Navarre, her family were involved in the repression of Huguenots in the southwest of France.

66. Jean de Gaufreteau, *Chronique Bordeloise*, p. 85, noted that Raemond had referred to a fashion known formally as *haulseculs*. He renamed it *cache-bastards*.

67. See below, chap. 4.

68. François Lebrun, *La Vie conjugale sous l'ancien régime* (Paris, Armand Colin 1975), states simply that the opinion that chastity and celibacy were superior to the enjoyment of sexuality remained the basis of Catholic doctrine following St. Paul and especially St. Augustine, and that marriage was considered essentially a remedy for fornication (p. 85). Raemond expressly referred to St. Paul's opinion

on the superiority of the chaste state in *L'Histoire, etc.*, p. 1029. However, Janine Garrisson-Estèbe, *Protestants du Midi 1559–1598* (Paris: Édouard Privat Éditeur, 1980), p. 317, notes that shortly after the beginning of the sixteenth century, following the lead given by French Calvinist moralists, the elite among the Catholics began to copy the Protestants' apologies for the married state.

69. Erasmus of Rotterdam, when recommending Hans Holbein to his English friends, among whom was Thomas More, noted in his letter that "The arts here are freezing," quoted by E. H. Gombrich, *The Story of Art* (New York: Phaidon, 1957), p. 277. That there was more than one possible attitude of reformers toward the subject of art and its spiritual uses is a theme of Carl C. Christensen's *Art and the Reformation in Germany* (Athens, Ohio, and Detroit, Michigan: Ohio University Press, 1979). Christensen observes that while a negative attitude culminated in the preaching and writing of Carlstadt, Luther's colleague at the University of Wittenberg, Luther himself opposed an iconoclastic negativism and became the advocate of a somewhat more discriminating use of "religious imagery" within the reformed church (Christensen, pp. 13–65).

70. He had dug out of the ground many items, including a purple marble column, adorned with dancing figures, and he proceeded to have carved on this column his family crest, according to L. M. Augier (article untitled), in *L'Aquitaine semaine religieuse de l'archidiocèse de Bordeaux*, 29 April 1892, pp. 269–70.

71. His museum was situated in his garden in Bordeaux and had attracted the attention of Justus Zinzerling (Jodocus Sincerus), who was a Thuringian youth making the grand tour of France in the early seventeenth-century. He recommended that tourists in Bordeaux visit "les statues antiques des dieux et des princes dans le jardin de M. de Raimondi" in his *Voyage dans la Vieille France* (Paris, Dentu, Vanier, 1859), p. 23.

72. Arnold Hauser, *The Social History of Art*, II (New York, 1959) Vintage Books, p. 125. Raemond heaped scorn on the Calvinists, but not on Lutherans or Anglicans, who retained much of the Catholic décor in their churches. One cannot avoid the conclusion, after reading chapter 12 of Book Seven (*L'Histoire, etc.*), which concerns images and idols, that Raemond was pleading with the Calvinists to be reasonable about the use of art in church. He carefully distinguished between adoration of pagan idols and the representation of the true God. The latter was permitted by Bucer, whom Raemond quoted to the effect that reasonableness and the greater glory of God, not prohibition, should dictate the use of imagery. He included the "Minister Spangebert" (i.e., Cyriakus Spangenberg, a collaborator of Melancthon) and the Augsburg preacher-humanist Urbanus Rhegius as well as Peter Martyr among Protestants who had condoned the use of imagery in church.

73. Raemond, *L'Histoire, etc.*, p. 970: "Their eyes are not capable of judging the admirable traits one sees in antiquity."

74. Hans Baron, "The *Querelle* of the Ancients & Moderns," *Journal of the History of Ideas*, XX (1959), pp. 3–22.

75. Donald R. Kelley, *Foundations of Modern Historical Scholar-Ship* (New York, Columbia University Press, 1970), p. 80.

76. He had, for example, hung a marble slab bearing a Greek inscription near his garden gate. The inscription, translated by Raemond into French ran: "Et des grand(s) et du Feu/Il faut s'approcher peu," or, Leave great men and fire unmolested! Presumably, he enjoyed the solitude of his marble garden, or outdoor museum.

77. Léonce Couture, "Florimond de Raymond," *Revue de Gascogne*, IX (1868), p. 265.

78. Ibid. See below, chap. 4, p. 143.

79. Jean Gaufreteau, *Chronique Bordeloise*, pp. 221–22: "Florimond de Raimond, conseiller au Parlement, en estant l'autheur et directeur; et s'il fault dire ainsin, il doit avoir tout l'honneur de ce bastiment grandement commode, et pour le clergé, et le Parlement." During the French Revolution, the cathedral of St. André was damaged and the galleries were removed and never replaced.

80. Ibid.

81. Especially since much of his public service was done for the benefit of the established religion.

82. The church of the Feuillants housed the bones of Raemond and of Montaigne, until it was destroyed in 1871. (See below, chap. 3, n.92.) A lawsuit was connected with this chapel, sold by the order to the essayist's widow and brother. The sale led to the suit, initiated by Raemond's son and literary executor, François, against the Montaignes. Florimond de Raemond's death in November 1601, spared him this anguish. (Jean Gaufreteau, *Chronique Bordeloise*, p. 319.)

83. Raemond's long term of office as a *conseiller* was perhaps inconsistent with some advice he had given his friend, Geoffroy de Malvyn, when Malvyn raised the question of retiring from the Bordeaux *Parlement* himself. Raemond wrote: "I am of your opinion that one must not grow old and die in office, not even when we are happy to do it for conscience's sake. We are all too prone to get into public service too young and leave it too old" (Letter to Malvyn, 5 November 1596, in Paul Courteault, *Geoffroy de Malvyn* (Paris: Honoré Champion, 1907), p. 195; my translation.

84. Raemond was already exempted from the *taille* (though not from municipal taxes) because of his noble status.

85. His lawyer's letter requesting the reduction was dated 24 February 1590. "Projet de transactions entre Florimond de Raemond et les religieux de l'abbaye Saint-Croix de Bordeaux," in *Archives du département de la Gironde*, series H, no. 355.

86. Courteault, *Geoffroy de Malvyn*, p. 108; my translation.

87. Larroque, *Essai*, Appendix, no. 1.

88. Donald Frame, *Montaigne, a Biography* (New York, Harcourt, Brace & World, Inc. 1965), p. 305.

89. Raemond remarked (*L'Anti-Papesse*, p. 417) that the roses of poetry no longer grew among the thorns of the courthouse where the Muses had long since abandoned him.

90. Ibid.

Chapter 2. Exchange of Views: Catholics, Protestants, and Politiques

1. Raemond used the greatest deference whenever he addressed a topic Montaigne had explored in the *Essays*, as he did in the *Anti-Papesse*, when touching upon the fragility of human life. There he noted that "M. de Montagne" had so often treated of the matter that "Il faut estudier ceste lecon chez luy" (*L'Anti-Papesse*, p. 417). Raemond called Montaigne "un bel esprit de nostre France" in the "History of Heresy"; and "un des plus rares esprits de nostre aage" (*L'Anti-Christ*, p. 136). His description of Montaigne's last illness (*L'Anti-Papesse*, p. 417) notes that the essayist was still "philosophant entre les extremitez de la douleur, jusques à la mort, voire en la mort mesme." The manner of his expression

may indicate that Raemond was in attendance (as was De Brach) in Montaigne's last hours. His allusion to Montaigne's conversation as "la plus douce, enrichie de grace" (ibid.) suggests his loss was deep and personal.

2. Raemond's copy of Montaigne's *Essays* disappeared after the eighteenth century. M. de la Montagne, a counsellor in the Bordeaux *Parlement*, then transcribed from it twenty-five annotations written by Raemond. Alan Boase's study, "Montaigne Annoté par Florimond de Raemond," *Revue du seizième siècle*, XV (1928), pp. 237–78, was made from Montagne's transcription. Boase concluded that Raemond was a reliable source for the identification of people and events to which the *Essays* allude. He believed one annotation in particular proved the intimacy between the two men. In his essay "Of Moderation" Montaigne advised husbands not to encourage their wives' sexual interest. (The idea was Aristotle's, as Montaigne noted expressly is another essay on Virgil.) Raemond's comment (my translation) was: "I have often heard the author say that while he was filled with love, and of youthful ardor, and had married a beautiful and lovable wife, yet he had never toyed with her except with that respect and decency which the marriage bed requires, without ever having seen anything of her uncovered but her hands and face, not even her breast, although with other women he was extremely abandoned." Boase noted: "cette note en elle-même suffit pour établir l'intimité de Florimond de Raemond avec Montaigne" (p. 240). One must concur, since only the best of friends have the opportunity and nerve often to repeat themselves, while only a close friend would indulge in such a confidence.

3. Pierre Bonnet, "Une Nouvelle série d'annotations de Florimond de Raemond aux *Essais* de Montaigne," *Bulletin de la société des amis de Montaigne*, no. 10, April–June 1959, pp. 10–23, has termed Montaigne's reflection in his essay, "Considerations of Cicero," that he preferred the epistolary genre to that of the essay, an important insight into Montaigne's deepest self despite its "anodine" appearance. To that admission Raemond had jotted in the margins of his *Essays*: "the author certainly knew himself perfectly." Bonnet felt Raemond's remark apt and for the friends of Montaigne thought this agreement was "a capital assertion." For those interested in Raemond, it must be seen as yet another evidence of the closeness between the two writers.

4. Raemond agreed with Tertullian that the troubles in religion owed their inception to the philosophers who had book knowledge, but not true wisdom (*L'Histoire, etc.*, p. 878). Montaigne made a similar distinction between philosophy and theology in his essay "Of Prayers" when he observed that divine reason was invariably more revered when unmixed with human reasons (Montaigne, *Essays*, p. 234).

5. Raemond, *L'Anti-Christ*, p. 9.

6. For a thorough study of sixteenth- and seventeenth-century skepticism, see Richard H. Popkin, *The History of Scepticism From Erasmus to Descartes* (Assen, Van Gorcum & Comp. N.V. 1960). Popkin claims (p. 4) that Erasmus's position was a reflection of his anti-intellectualism and antirationalism where theology was concerned.

7. For the development of skepticism before the sixteenth century, see Henri Busson, *Le Rationalisme dans la litérature Française de la Renaissance* (Paris, J. Vrin 1957), who notes (pp. 413–414) that alongside speculative theology were the neoplatonic, Augustinian, and mystical traditions that looked to Dionysius (the Pseudo-Areopagite) as a guide. He names Lefèvre d'Étaples, Pico della Mirandola, and Gabriel Biel as sixteenth-century devotees of the neoplatonic strain, philos-

ophers of religion who eschewed the kinds of inquiries that sought to establish connections between spiritual and rational truths. Of course, the middle ages produced many such thinkers: Duns Scotus, St. Bonaventure, and William of Ockham, to name just a few. See also Herman Janssen, *Montaigne Fidéiste* (Nijmegen-Utrecht, J. W. van Leeuwen 1930), p. 15, where it is noted that a majority of philosophers around 1550 were fideists, skeptical of reason.

8. The hazards to Catholics were no less great when they used skeptical arguments than they were to Protestants. Popkin (*op. cit.*, p. 110) refers to this as the "crise pyrrhonienne," which threatened all positions in natural science as well as in theological matters.

9. Raemond's view of Catholic tradition is more properly considered below in connection with topics such as papal primacy, apostolic succession, and papal infallibility. In *L'Histoire, etc.* (p. 72) he referred to both Cardinal Bellarmine's and Montaigne's opinions on tradition. Their themes were his—that reason was an inappropriate tool of religious analysis, and that once directed to such matters an endless series of innovations could be expected. The following passage could have been written by either of the above authorities as well as by Raemond: "Once show a man the effrontery of scorning and examining opinions he once held in extreme reverence such as those pertaining to his salvation, and other articles of faith, and he will end by subjecting the rest of his beliefs to like incertitude; for they no longer have any basis of authority. All that he held by the authority of law and revered tradition ("l'ancien usage") shaken by this tyrannical yoke (of reform and innovation), he now undertakes to accept only those things of which he approves."

10. In his essay "Of Custom," Montaigne noted: "I am disgusted with innovation, in whatever guise, and with reason, for I have seen very harmful effects of it. The one that has been oppressing us for so many years [i.e., the Reformation] is not the sole author of our troubles, but one may say with good reason that it has accidentally produced and engendered everything, even the troubles and ruins that have been happening since without it, and against it; it has itself to blame" (*Essays*, p. 86).

11. Among those who have are Clément Sclafert, *L'Âme religieuse de Montaigne* (Paris: Éditions Latines, 1951); Herman Janssen, *Montaigne Fidéiste*; Frieda Brown, *Religious and Political Conservatism in the Essays of Montaigne* (Geneva, Librairie Droz, 1964); and Mathurin Dreano, *La Religion de Montaigne* (Paris, Librairie A. G. Nizet, 1969). It was Dreano who pointed to the similarities between Raemond's criticism of Calvinist religious practices and Montaigne's, finding that Raemond's objection to psalm-singing, lay Bible reading, and so on, were first written by Montaigne (p. 282) and borrowed by our author, whom Dreano terms a "disciple" of Montaigne, along with Montaigne's "fille d'alliance," Marie Jars de Gournay, Pierre de Brach, and the priest Pierre Charron, whom Montaigne made his protégé. Dreano observed that Raemond would never have been able to use Montaigne's prestige to uphold his own reiteration of Montaigne's ideas if Montaigne's Catholicism had been in question, which is substantially the same sentiment expressed by Frieda Brown.

12. Henri Busson casts doubt on the essayist's orthodoxy, taking Clément Sclafert (see note above) to task for insisting that Montaigne's morality was truly Christian. Busson finds it as sensual and epicurian as it was Catholic (see *Le Rationalisme dans la litérature Française de la Renaissance*, p. 473, a point made earlier in the "Conclusion" of Janssen's *Montaigne Fidéiste* as well.

13. Raemond, like Montaigne, would have preferred uniformity of religion in

France. He did recognize the political necessity of toleration, however, and on at least one occasion commented that Muslims, Jews, and Christians all recognized the one true God. The admission was made while reflecting on the *Trois Imposteurs.* (See chap. 1, p. 5, and n.20). Such religious universalism was typical of Nicholas of Cusa, Johannes Reuchlin, and Raemond's contemporary, Guillaume Postel, whom he admired immensely and believed to be orthodox (*L'Histoire, etc.,* pp. 227–28). The orthodoxy of Postel is rejected by Marion L. Kuntz (*Guillaume Postel, Prophet of the Restitution of All Things His Life and Thought* [The Hague, Martinus Nijhoff 1981], p. 49). Postel's eclecticism — what Kuntz called "Christian Judaism" — is borne out by William J. Bouwsma, *Concordia Mundi: The Career and Thought of Guillaume Postel (1510–1581),* (Cambridge, Mass., Harvard University Press 1957), pp. 61–63 and 248–49. He notes the way Postel linked the thought of Jews to the philosophy of the Greeks and how these ideas affected the Arabs. It is probable that Raemond got his universalist ideas (not prominent) from Postel, whose works he praised as he did his life in the chapter 15 of Book II of his *History of Heresy.* There he castigated antitrinitarians like Menno Simons, David George, and Michael Servetus. He ignored the fact that Postel had written an apology for Servetus. His admiration for Postel may have owed something to Postel's criticism of Calvin (Kuntz, pp. 110–11). He certainly admired his vast erudition. Another explanation of his admiration may have been his friendship with some of Postel's friends (Larroque, *Essai,* p. 111). Was it pure coincidence that Postel, who also attended the Auberi exorcism, considered it a miraculous proof of God's power in the elements of the Catholic mass and a major event of his own spiritual development? (Kuntz, pp. 143–45) and chapter 1, n.37 above).

14. Frederick Rider, *The Dialectic of Selfhood in Montaigne* (Stanford, Stanford University Press, 1973), pp. 6–7 discussed Montaigne's literary activity in terms of an impulse "to objectify himself," a kind of Renaissance demi-urge intended to relieve irreconcilable tensions in a society no longer homogeneous. Max Horkheimer, "Montaigne und die Funktion der Skepsis," *Kritische Theorie,* II (Frankfurt-am-Main, 1968), p. 205, believes that the essays resulted from an overwhelming need on the part of their author to enjoy life despite the conditions that civil war imposed on France. Raemond's writing was undertaken not for his own amusement but to serve his church and the state.

15. Raemond differed most dramatically from Montaigne on the matter of sorcery. Montaigne was a skeptic concerning witchcraft, whereas Raemond seriously considered writing a book about the subject and appears indeed to have begun collecting notes for one. For Montaigne, see Alan M. Boase, "Montaigne et la Sorcellerie," *Humanisme et Renaissance,* II (1935), pp. 417–21. For Raemond, see below, chap. 3, n.48.

16. Bèze was, like Sponde, a poet. His praise of Sponde's study of Homer was written in poetry. Bèze was later among the first of his party to describe Sponde as an unstable character — referring to Sponde's growing attraction to Catholicism. See François Ruchon and Alan Boase, *La Vie et l'oeuvre de Jean de Sponde* (Geneva, Éditions Pierre Cailler, 1949), p. 38.

17. Raemond claimed Sponde had named Du Perron as the priest responsible for saving his soul. (See "Epistre à M. Du Perron," at the beginning of La Response du Feu Sieur de Sponde ... au *Traicté des Marques de l'Église,* quoted in Ruchon-Boase, *op. cit.,* p. 56.

18. Raemond's work in progress in 1596 was *L'Anti-Christ,* which appeared the following year. In his *Response, etc.,* Sponde mentioned having read the work in manuscript form, and promised his readers that it would refute Bèze's treatise

(*Traicté des vrayes essencielles et visibles Marques de la Vraye Église Catholique* (1592).

19. See Ruchon-Boase, *op. cit.*, p. 73.
20. Raemond, *L'Histoire, etc.*, p. 966.
21. Ruchon-Boase, *op. cit.*, p. 71.
22. Raemond wrote concerning the breakdown of Calvinist discipline: "At present luxury and debauch prevails amongst them more than it does amongst ourselves" (*L'Histoire, etc.*, p. 998).
23. Sponde's aggravation can be measured by the description he gave this democratic trait of Calvinist church government: "la plus embrouillée Democratie qui fust jamais" (Ruchon-Boase, *op. cit.*, p. 73).
24. Raemond felt Calvin's rejection of a church hierarchy containing a supreme head, bishops, and priests could be traced to the fourth-century heretic Arius, who denied Christ's equality with God. Raemond was offended that a church, which claimed to be militant, had destroyed the chain of command that existed in heaven, as well as on earth. Attempting to turn the tables on Calvinists (who were very attracted to primitive Christianity), Raemond attributed their democratic errors to an inveterate hatred ("hayne mortelle") of the whole of Christian antiquity (*L'Histoire, etc.*, pp. 979–81).
25. In the *Anti-Christ*, pp. 274–75, Raemond insisted that Christ had made St. Peter foremost over the other eleven apostles, and that while they were all his (Peter's) council, he was their head. In this manner he denied the possibility of episcopal equality that was the late medieval basis for a conciliar alternative to papal monarchy.
26. Raemond, "Préface" of *La Response au traicté . . . des Marques de l'Église*. "The dying Sponde, straining to hear the words of the priest, and with eyes raised up and soul enraptured by heaven, sweetly expired, without effort nor any pain at all." Quoted in Ruchon-Boase, *op. cit.* (my trans.), p. 38. The exaggerated peace of this Catholic death was a common literary device and a polemical tool designed to impress the reader with the superior benefits of a proper (orthodox) demise.
27. Theodore Agrippa d'Aubigné (1552–1630) was a poet, Huguenot soldier, familiar of Henry of Navarre, and after Henry's conversion to Catholicism, a member of the Huguenot loyal opposition. He achieved fame for his poem *Les Tragiques* (1616) and for his *Histoire Universelle* (1616–1618). In the satire *Confession Catholique du Sieur de Sancy*, (*Oeuvres complètes*, E. Réaume and F. de Caussade, eds. (Paris, A. Lemerre 1873–1892), II, pp. 237–38), d'Aubigné reported that rumor had it that the Huguenots believed Raemond poisoned Sponde "pour avoir été reconnu en ce nouveau converti quelque trouble de conscience et sa volonté d'aller faire sa repentance à la Rochelle." Although this work was not published until 1660, other pamphlets villifying Sponde for his conversion to Rome circulated in Sponde's lifetime. Keith Cameron, *Agrippa D'Aubigné* (Boston: Twayne Publishers, 1977), pp. 104–15, notes that Sponde was a frequent object of d'Aubigné's ridicule.
28. Le Sieur de Bissouse was the financial secretary to Henry of Navarre. Raemond, "Lettre à Duplessis-Mornay," in Philippe Du Plessis-Mornay, *Mémoires et Correspondance*, VII (Geneva, Slatkine Reprints 1969), reprint ed., pp. 230–31.
29. One of a number of Raemond's spelling variations.
30. Sixteenth-century scholars exhibited an active interest in the Cabala, a mystical knowledge system once thought to be of ancient Hebrew origins, but probably no older than the twelfth or thirteenth centuries. It was based on

permutation of numbers and letter combinations. It was revived in Raemond's lifetime by Isaac Luria Ashkenazi (1534–1572), founder of modern Hebrew Cabala. Giovanni Pico della Mirandola (1463–1494) was the first Christian to use cabalistic literature to try to establish the syncretism of Hebrew Scripture with Christian belief. His work influenced humanists such as Giles of Viterbo and Johannes Reuchlin (1455–1522) to advocate systematic study of Hebrew writings. Protestants during the Reformation hoped to establish a connection between Rome and Antichrist using the cabalistic system (see chap. 5). Raemond was intrigued by the Cabala but formally disavowed its significance. He said the Cabalists "use a pack of damnable tricks in order to fool men, unlike the faithful doctors and scriptural interpreters who spoke clearly," and pointed out that when the Holy Spirit wanted to communicate, He spoke precisely, not ambiguously (*L'Anti-Christ*, p. 133).

31. Raemond, *L'Anti-Christ*, p. 129 (erroneously paginated 229 in my 1599 ed.). The Protestants, Raemond said, used *Lateinos* as a shortcut to the word Rome, and thence to papacy. They drew the conclusion that the pope was Antichrist. Raemond objected that Irenaeus (125–202) had not used either of two Greek words Duplessis-Mornay claimed incriminated the pope as Antichrist: Ἰταλικά Ἐκλησία.

32. *Traité de l'église*, 1578.

33. Raemond, *L'Anti-Christ*, p. 129.

34. John Bale (1495–1563) was an English divine and dramatist whose vitriolic pen and popular plays made him a leading Protestant polemicist. "Balee," as Raemond called him, was a frequent subject of his ire. See Herbert Barke, *Bales "Kynge Johan" und sein Verhältnis zur zeitgenossischen Geschichtschreibung* (Wurzburg, K. Triltsch 1937); Jesse W. Harris and John Bale, *A Study in the Minor Literature of the Reformation* (Urbana: The University of Illinois Press, 1940); Klaus Sperk, *Mittelalterliche Tradition und Reformatorische Polemik in den Spielen John Bales* (Heidelberg, Winter, 1973); (English summary); and Leslie Fairfield, *John Bale, Mythmaker for the English Reformation* (West Layette: Ind. Purdue University Press, 1976).

35. Matthias Flacius Illyricus (1520–1575) was born Matthias Vlachich in Istria. He studied for the priesthood, and in 1544 was made a professor of Hebrew at Wittenberg. A rigid Lutheran, he wrote a key to the Scriptures (*Clavis scripturae sacrae*, 1567) and devised the plan on which the rabidly antipapal history called the *Magdeburg Centuries* was organized. Flacius was Raemond's *bête noir* and a frequent target of his criticisms. For a bibliography on the *Centuries*, see below, chap. 6, n.5.

36. Raemond, *L'Anti-Christ*, p. 193.

37. Robert Bellarmine, cardinal and saint (canonized 1930), was a Jesuit controversialist and Raemond's principal source for his defense of Catholic dogma and tradition. His works elicited many responses from Protestants, including Duplessis-Mornay, who wrote his *Le Mystère d'iniquité*, or history of the papacy (1611) in response to the Cardinal's *De Potestate summi pontificis in rebus temporalibus* (1610), a work that attempted to establish the temporal authority of popes. His Latin *Autobiography* was published in 1675 (and in 1753), and was translated into German by Joh. Jos. Ign. v. Döllinger and Franz Heinrich Reusch as *Die Selbstbiographie des Cardinals Bellarmin* (Bonn, P. Neuser 1887). Bellarmine's works are found in *Opera Omnia* (Frankfurt, Minerva 1965). See also J. B. Couderc's *Le Venerable Cardinal Bellarmin* 2 vols., (Paris, V. Retaux et fils. 1893), and James Brodrick, *The Life and Works of Blessed Robert Francis Cardinal Bellarmine, S. J. 1542–1621*, (New York, P. J. Kennedy & Sons 1928).

38. See chap. 5, for a discussion of papal infallibility.
39. See chap. 5, for a discussion of papal primacy.
40. Raemond did not mention that the Council was also the occasion on which assembled churchmen decided to elevate the patriarch of Constantinople to a dignity equal to the bishop of Rome, although they hoped not to offend the latter by doing so. This made for ambiguity as to the authority of these two clergymen, as Geoffrey Barraclough remarked in *The Medieval Papacy* (New York, Harcourt, Brace, and World, Inc. 1968), p. 27. Raemond over-looked such ambiguity and tried to prove that Chalcedon had unequivocally established papal primacy on the firmest footing.
41. Raemond (*L'Anti-Christ*, p. 291) observed that Rome could not have given Phocas support, given the difficult situation that prevailed in seventh century Italy. He disagreed with Duplessis-Mornay's characterization of Phocas (602–610) as a cruel tyrant. Modern historians agree with the Huguenot's conception on the issue of cruelty. Speros Vryonis, *Byzantium and Europe* (New York, Harcourt, Brace, and World, Inc. 1967), p. 58, calls Phocas "brutal" and "incompetent" as well, adding that the ease with which Heraclius overthrew Phocas proves the Byzantines were sickened by his cruelties. Sir Hugh Trevor-Roper, *The Rise of Christian Europe* (New York, Harcourt, Brace, and World, Inc. 1965), p. 99, calls Phocas "the worst of emperors." He does confirm Raemond's opinion on the matter of support given him by the popes, finding in effect that the seventh-century papacy was indeed too weak to do anything but flatter and submit to the eastern emperor.
42. "Augustanian Confession," i.e., the Augsburg Confession of 1530. It was the official statement or creed of the Lutheran churches, and was written mainly by Melanchthon with Luther's endorsement, for the Diet of Augsburg, 25 June 1530. The emperor and Catholic majority rejected the Confession. Raemond's date of 1574 is explained in the ff. note.
43. Lutheran reformers wished to establish ecumenical ties with the Greek church. Twice Melanchthon's Greek translation of the Augsburg Confession was sent to the Patriarch in Constantinople (1559, 1574). The last presentation produced a series of communications between the Orthodox and the Lutherans, the latter party's rejoinders being drafted by men such as Lucas Osiander, Johannes Brenz, Jakob Andreae, etc. In all, the patriarch wrote three responses between 1576 and 1581, so Raemond was wrong to write that he had no patience for further intercourse with reform. He knew, however, that the *Confessio* presented difficulties both liturgical and philosophical for the Greeks. (See Ernst Benz, *Wittenberg und Byzanz* [Munich: Wilhelm Fink Verlag, 1971], p. 108ff.) These, together with those differences of opinion, which existed within the Lutheran party regarding the Augsburg document, seem to account for the phrase Raemond used—i.e., "thirty-three errors."
44. Raemond, *L'Anti-Christ*, p. 296, told Duplessis-Mornay: "Leave off the insults you sometimes deliver for those who know no other way of decorating their books."
45. Trained as a lawyer, Charron (1541–1603) took orders and became preacher to Queen Marguerite of Valois. Briefly a supporter of the Catholic League, Charron moved to Bordeaux in 1589, joining Montaigne's circle of friends and admirers. His work combined the essayist's skepticism with the mystic's fervent belief that God is revealed through faith, not reason. His first published work, *Trois Vérités* (1593) was a refutation of Duplessis-Mornay's use of reason to defend religion. Charron maintained, "The true knowledge of God is a perfect ignorance about Him" (*Trois Vérités*, Paris, 1595, p. 26). This point of view was

echoed by Raemond in the *Anti-Christ*, chap. 23, where he insisted that the human understanding is dimmed by difficulties presented by language. See the biography by Jean B. Sabrié, *De l'humanisme au rationalisme Pierre Charron, l'homme, l'oeuvre, l'influence* (Paris, Alcan 1913); Jean Charron, *The "Wisdom" of Pierre Charron, an Original and Orthodox Code of Morality* (Chapel Hill 1961), Eugene F. Rice, *The Renaissance Idea of Wisdom* (Cambridge, Mass. Harvard Univ. Press, 1958), chap. 7; Anthony Levi, *French Moralists* (Oxford, Clarendon Press 1964), chap. 4; René Bady, *L'Homme et son Institution de Montaigne à Berulle 1580–1625* (Paris, Société d'Edition "Les Belles Lettres" 1964), chap. 9; and Richard H. Popkin's *The History of Skepticism from Erasmus to Descartes* (Assen, Nijhoff 1960).

46. The Protestant rejection of the apostolic foundation of the papacy continues in Hans von Campenhausen, *Ecclesiastical Authority and Spiritual Power in the Church of the First Three Centuries* (J. A. Baker, Trans. (Stanford, Stanford University Press 1969), who notes (pp. 19–20) the "wrongness" of considering Peter a "first Pope," insisting that his influence was regional, and his authority was personal, neither continuable nor renewable. Jeffrey Richards, *The Popes and the Papacy in the Early Middle Ages* (Boston, Routledge & Kegan Paul 1979), stresses the political motives behind the "fanatical tenacity" of the Roman church to assert Petrine primacy, a response dictated by political competition from Constantinople (p. 9). Walter Dress, "Popes," *The Encyclopedia of the Lutheran Church* (Minneapolis, Augsburg Publishing House 1965) III, p. 1923, thinks it useless to attempt to discover the earliest claims to papal authority; "circumstances" dictated the development "at a very early date." A programmatic treatment of both Protestant as well as Catholic opinion on primacy as revealed in the document known as I Clement (first century) is given in John Fuellenbach's *Ecclesiastical Office and the Primacy of Rome* (Washington, D.C.: Catholic University of America Press, 1980), who finds that while most Catholic scholars believe Clement to have been "already a firm witness of the doctrine of apostolic succession" (p. 114), they no longer assert an explicit claim to Roman primacy before 325 A.D. Fuellenbach notes other changes in recent Catholic writing inspired by ecumenical hopes and a notable interest in collegial rather than hierarchical expressions of church office.

47. Duplessis-Mornay wrote: "C'est chose aiseé à persuader à nous, qui depuis si longtemps avons eu à les souffrir" ("Lettre de M. Duplessis à M. de Raemound, Conseiller à Bordeaux," July 1597, in *Mémoires et Correspondance* (Geneva, Slatkine Reprints IX, p. 231).

48. Ibid., p. 232.

49. Ibid.

50. Raemond, "Lettre à Duplessis" (5 Jan 1599), in Duplessis-Mornay, *Mémoires et Correspondance*, IX (Geneva, Slatkine Reprints) pp. 199–202.

51. Fronton du Duc (1558–1624) was a philologist and linguist. He was praised by Raemond (*L'Histoire, etc.*, p. 1040) as a "great man of letters, very well versed in languages" Larroque, *Essai*, p. 33, n.1, said that Duc was the object of much adulation from both Protestant and Catholic scholars. In this letter Raemond informed Duplessis-Mornay that his latest work, *De l'institution, usage et doctrine du Saint Sacrement de l'Eucharistie en l'Église Ancienne, etc.* (1598), had been refuted by a number of Bordeaux authors, one of whom was Duc. His *Inventaire des faultes, contradictions et fausses allegations du Sieur du Plessis en son livre de la Sainte Eucharistie* appeared anonymously, for want of a license from Rome. On Duc, see Carlos Sommervogel, *Bibliothèque de la College des Jésuites*, III

(Paris, Alphonse Picard 1890), pp. 233–49; and Oudin, in Nicéron, *Mémoires pour servir à l'histoire des hommes illustres de la république des lettres* (Paris, 1737), XXXVIII, p. 103.

52. Caesar Baronius (born Cesare Baronio, 1538–1607) was a disciple of Philip Neri; an industrious historian of ecclesiastical history; superior of the Oratory after Neri's death (1593); Vatican librarian, and confessor to Clement VIII. He narrowly missed being elected pope in 1605. His *Annales Ecclesiastici a Christi Nato ad Annum 1198* were honest, if biased works. His biographer, Cyriac K. Pullapilly, *Caesar Baronius Counter-Reformation Historian* (Notre Dame, University of Notre Dame Press 1975), p. 166, says Baronius had not freed himself from authority, from his conception of history as the handmaiden of dogma. Hubert Jedin, *Cardinal Caesar Baronius*, (Münster, Aschendorf 1978), p. 56, wrote that Baronius failed to give Catholic doctrine a central place in his historical writing while the Centuriators made it central to theirs, a failure on Baronius's part that Jedin views as unfortunate. He further notes that while the *Annales* were not a valid model for all times, they were an impressive foundations upon which other Catholic historians were able to build. For Baronius's praise of Raemond's book on the popess, see chap. 3, n.89.

53. Richeome's *Trois Discours*, twice cited in the *Anti-Christ*, was one of the books sent Duplessis-Mornay on this occasion. The priest was a great friend of Père Coton, the Jesuit confessor of Henry IV and of Louis XIII. Like Coton, and Raemond, too, Richeome (1544–1625) looked to Henry to revitalize Catholicism in France and to reunite a nation whose loyalties had been strained by civil war. Richeome was wrongly believed by some in the seventeenth century to have been the author of Raemond's books. See Henri Brémond, *A Literary History of Religious Thought in France* (New York, Macmillan 1928), chap. 2. In it, Richeome is described as a Christian humanist whose wit and spontaneity kept his moralistic writing from being dull.

54. Raemond, "Lettre à Duplessis-Mornay," 5 Jan 1599, in Duplessis-Mornay, *Mémoires et Correspondance*, IX, pp. 199–202.

55. Larroque, *Essai*, p. 34, n.2, says that Duc's work appeared to Duplessis-Mornay worthy of his attention. That cannot be substantiated, however, by a careful reading of the letter Duplessis-Mornay sent Raemond on 3 February 1599. Instead, "skimming" and "evasion" are the charges made by him against both the works (Duc's and Richeome's):

> Mais bien vous dirai-je que je ne tiens poinct ces deux escrits pour justes responses, qui ne font qu' escumer legerement, sans rien enfoncer; monstrans assés les aucteurs que ce n'est leur desseing ni de presser pied contre pied, ni de venir main à main, mais de tenir les champs, pour esvader plus aiséement. (*Mémoires et Correspondance*, pp. 221–22)
>
> [Well, then, I will tell you that I do not consider these two works to be thoughtful answers, for they only skim over the 1 matter lightly, without ever going deep into it, showing very well that the authors have no intention of getting on with it, nor of coming to grips with it, but only of staying in their course in order to more easily avoid confrontation.]

56. Duplessis-Mornay was not the only Protestant critic of the Cardinal's *Annales*. After an initial enthusiasm, a number of factual inaccuracies in the work (to which Baronius devoted fifty years of his life) emerged. Isaac Casaubon, the Swiss-born Son of French refugee parents and a convert to Anglicanism, turned from initial support of Baronius's "answer" to the *Magdeburg Centuries*, to vigorous criticism on the grounds that Baronius was irretrievably biased toward Rome.

57. The Huguenot authors of the *Plaintes* (1597) pp. 69–70, said that the *Parlement* of Rennes defended the burning of a Bible at the Bishop's behest, but the *Parlement* of Bordeaux had passed its own law to permit such acts. Elie Benoist, commenting on these events a century later, said that Duplessis-Mornay's book, *Traité de l'Eucharistie* (1598) had attracted papal criticism because it bore the title Privy Councillor on its title page, creating the impression that Henry IV had approved of its contents. Henry was in fact annoyed; the Bordeaux Jesuits urged that the book be burned even though the Legate preferred a refutation be written by Cardinal Bellarmine. The *Traité* was in fact burned in 1599 at the order of "quelque Justice subalterne" (Benoist, *Histoire de l'Édit de Nantes* (Delft, Adrien Beman 1693), pp. 261–63, probably by the *jurats* (municipal government) of Bordeaux.

58. Duplessis-Mornay, "Letter to Raemond. 3 Feb. 1599," *Mémoires et Correspondance*, p. 223.

59. Jacques Cujas (1522–1590) was a French jurist and scholar of Roman law, and considered by many to be the founder of the historical school of jurisprudence. He taught at several French universities, and had an international reputation for scholarship. See Berriat-Saint-Prix, *Histoire du droit Romain, suivie de l'histoire de Cujas* (1821), pp. 373–611; Ernst Spangenberg, trans., *Jacob Cujas und Seine Zeitgenossen, Mit einen Kupfer und Steindruck* (Leipzig, J. F. Harrknoch 1822).

60. Aimé-Georges Martimort, *Le Gallicanisme* (Paris, Presses Universitaires de France 1973), p. 6, notes that the origins of Gallicanism date from the reign of Philip the Fair (1285–1314).

61. Pasquier's hatred of the Jesuits rivaled Raemond's love of the order in its intensity. Pasquier had once defended (1565) the University of Paris in a successful attempt to keep the order from becoming a degree-granting institution, part of the university system.

62. The attitude of the Gallican Party toward the Tridentine legislation is treated at length in the classic work by Victor Martin, *Le Gallicanisme et la Réforme catholique éssai historique sur l'introduction en France des décrets du concile de Trente* (1563–1615), 1st ed., 1919 (Reprint ed. Geneva; Slatkine Megariotis, 1975), p. 303, my translation.

63. Speech of Henry IV to his council, May 1600. From the *Mémoires* of De Thou, quoted in Victor Martin, *op. cit.*, p. 313, my translation.

64. Publication had been forestalled since the 1570s. It had been urged by the Catholic League during the papacy of Sixtus V (1585–1590). Since the Estates General of 1614 opposed the publication, the French clergy at length voted (1615) a unilateral publication in their provincial councils. A brief, but deft, treatment is found in Aimé-Georges Martimort, *Le Gallicanisme* (Paris, 1956), and an interesting perspective relating Henry IV's assassination to absolutism and orthodoxy can be read in Roland Mousnier, *L'Assassinat d'Henri IV, 14 Mai 1610. Le Probleme du tyrannicide et l'affermissement de la monarchie absolue* (Paris, 1964).

65. Blaise de Monluc (1502–1577) was a soldier of fortune in the Italian Wars and a military leader of the Catholic cause in south-western France during the civil wars. He was detested by the Huguenot party for his cruelty. His *Commentaires* were first edited by Florimond de Raemond. (See chap. 3 above.)

66. Letter of Pasquier, undated, in *Oeuvres d'Etienne Pasquier* (Amsterdam, 1723), II, no.2, p. 519.

67. Ibid.

68. Letter of Pasquier, undated, in *Oeuvres d'Etienne Pasquier* (Amsterdam, 1723), II, no.1, p. 593.

69. Pierre Pithou (d. 1596), lawyer and writer, had argued that the word *libertés* in the phrase *libertés gallicanes* meant ancient rights common to all churches, but more adequately defended in France than in other Catholic nations.

70. Letter of Pasquier (no. 1), *Oeuvres d'Etienne Pasquier*, II, p. 593.

71. Ibid., p. 549. For Pasquier, the threat of assassinating Jesuits was amply demonstrated by the attempt in 1593 against the life of Henry IV by a Jesuit priest named Barrière, and one the following year by a man named Chatel who, though not a priest, had been educated by the order. After the Barrière episode, Pasquier wrote his famous *Catéchisme des Jésuites* (1594).

72. Letter of Pasquier (no. 1), *Oeuvres d'Etienne Pasquier*, II, p. 595, my translation.

73. In *L'Histoire, etc.*, Raemond made it clear that when France strayed from a Catholic policy internationally, domestic affairs went awry. He approved Francis I's efforts to support the Duke of Savoy against his rebellious Genevans and Henry II's constable, Montmorency's, refusal to ally with Protestant Swiss. Using Monluc as a source, he lamented Henry III's alliance with Protestant Poland. He believed it was Henry II's fault that France had launched itself on the slippery slope of Protestant alliance. That Francis I had done the same (allying with Protestants against Charles V) Raemond refused to admit. His obstinacy was compounded since Monluc's own brother, the Bishop of Valence, had spoken before the Council of Ten in Venice (1543) justifying Francis's alliance with the German Protestants. The speech was part of Monluc's *Commentaries*, edited by Raemond (1591). R. J. Knecht *Francis I* (Cambridge, Cambridge University Press 1982) makes it clear that France's aid to Protestant Germans was limited by a variety of factors, including Francis's hesitation before various policies, each with peculiar advantages and disadvantages in international politics. It was not limited by the king's reluctance to aid non-Catholics, as his Turkish alliances plainly demonstrated. The fact that Raemond could call Sleidan, the Lutheran historian, a liar for suggesting what everyone then knew for fact, demonstrates the occasional duplicity of our subject, or at least, his unwillingness to tarnish the record of his chosen heroes (Francis was one, Charles V another) by alluding to all the facts.

74. This is an oblique reference to Albert of Brandenburg, the archbishop of Mainz and Magdeburg who was to receive half the proceeds from the sale of indulgences in order to repay his debt (of 29,000 gulden) to the Fuggers for the dispensation he had purchased to allow him, when underage, to acquire his archbishopric.

75. The Pragmatic Sanction of Bourges (1438) was an agreement between France and the papacy recognizing the authority of church councils. Augustin Renaudet, *Préréforme et humanisme à Paris* (2d ed.) (Paris, Librairie d'Argences 1953), pp. 2−3 and 577, says it was the constitution of the Gallican church on paper but that long before Francis I abandoned it and obtained the Concordat of Bologna (1516), the *Pragmatique* had ceased to perform the functions for which it was designed — the safeguarding of the French church's independent selection of churchmen. Pasquier's nostalgia for the *Pragmatique*, which had by the end of the sixteenth century become the mode, was not as dominant among the parlementaires of 1516, a majority of whom went along with Francis on this matter, even while they continued to extol the *Pragmatique*. (See Renaudet, *Préréforme*, pp. 578ff. He makes the point that the parlementary majority had themselves profited greatly from an abuse of royal power — too much so to preserve a united opposition to Francis.)

76. Pasquier, Letter to Raemond, *Oeuvres d'Etienne Pasquier*, II, (no. 5), pp. 605−9, passim.

77. Nomination to consistorial benefices was one of the most important questions in the struggle between kings and popes. The Concordat of Bologna abolished capitulary elections for the office of bishop and the right to name candidates to the office was given the king, on condition that he not keep a post vacant longer than six months, or appoint unqualified candidates. The pope retained the right to invest the nominee to the office. (R. Naz, ed. *Dictionnaire de droit canonique*, III (Paris: Letouzey et Ané, 1942), p. 1387. For an exhaustive treatment of the Concordat, see Jules Thomas, *Le Concordat de 1516 ses origines son histoire au XVIe siècle* 3 vols., (Paris, A. Picard 1910). Thomas said the Concordat was widely supported in Germany, as well as in France, as a disciplinary reform, and that the most resistant body in France was the University of Paris's Faculty of Theology (p. 412).

78. Pasquier, Letter to Raemond, *Oeuvres d'Etienne Pasquier*, II (no. 5), p. 610.

79. Raemond, *L'Histoire, etc.* p. 51.

80. Ibid.

81. Raemond, *L'Histoire, etc.*, p. 50.

82. The last lines of his *Histoire, etc.* revealed Raemond's hope that uniformity of religion would be established in France. "Someone else, living in a happier century after me, will conduct heresy to its grave, where it will sink into Hell" (p. 1064).

83. He urged the "soldiers of Jesus Christ" (i.e., Jesuits) to persevere until everyone recognized their merits, to pursue their victories until "the spoils of the enemy" (Protestants) are yours, and the battle field too." The Jesuits were, he said, "the very stuff of heresy's ruin" (*L'Histoire, etc.*, p. 540).

84. According to Jean-Guy Vaillancourt, *Papal Power A Study of Vatican Control over Lay Catholic Elites* (Berkeley, University of California Press 1980), p. 34, the alliances of national states with the papacy probably account for much of the anticlericalism and laicism during the last decades of the *Ancien Régime* (and after) in France and in other European countries.

85. One recalls that despite the determination of the crown to eradicate nonorthodox approaches to Catholicism, both Jansenism and Quietism persisted into the eighteenth century. Protestantism survived "in the desert," i.e., underground, until the brink of revolution. A Protestant named Rabaut St. Etienne claimed to speak for two million French Protestants when in August 1789, he demanded liberty rather than toleration for them. John T. McNeill, *The History and Character of Calvinism* (New York: Oxford University Press 1954), pp. 369; 416.

Chapter 3. Pen and *Parlement*

1. Unless otherwise indicated, my references are to the 1599 edition. (See chap. 4, n.1 below.)

2. He wrote in the *Anti-Christ*, p. 4: "Do not hope to find any profound Theology, or anything nearly like that which the dignity of the subject requires. It is a science that I have only glanced at from a distance, to which I have devoted but little time—whatever I could spare from the demand of other studies, and from my judicial duties."

3. The *Erreur Populaire* (later, *L'Anti-Papesse*) had gone through five French editions and one Latin edition by 1601. The *Anti-Christ* had appeared twice. Raemond's editions of Blaise Monluc's *Commentaires* and Jean de Sponde's reply

to Bèze were printed one time each during his lifetime and so were his translations of Tertullian's two essays.

4. Pope Clement VIII was "disconsolate" over the Edict because he felt "liberty of conscience ... the worst thing in the world." Quoted in John T. McNeill, *The History and Character of Calvinism* (New York, Oxford University Press 1954), p. 250. But see George D. Balsama, *The Decomposition and Rebirth of Post-Reformation France* (Dubuque, Hunt Publishing Company, 1974), p. 85, who observes that Clement, along with other French churchmen, began to view the Edict as a protection against the expansion of Protestantism in France. That the issue of ascendance of either Catholicism or Protestantism was not clear-cut or immediately apparent, even to contemporaries, may be judged by the fact that the Catholic cult was not reestablished in Béarn until 1621. Protestants and Catholics eyed each other with mutual and lively apprehension for two decades after the Edict went into effect.

5. Florimond's son, François, in his "Note to the Reader" (*L'Histoire*, etc.) advised that his father, working for the French and in favor of France, had chosen to write in the vernacular, a language to which he was most attached ("infinement jaloux").

6. The hostility of the *politiques* or royalist Catholics to the League was nearly as strong as that of the Huguenots. See Frederic J. Baumgartner, *Radical Reactionaries: The Political Thought of the French Catholic League* (Geneva: Librairie Droz 1975), p. 20. Baumgartner notes the self-serving interests of the League to preserve aristocratic privileges threatened by Henry III (p. 56), and feels the ultra-montanism of the League has been exaggerated—that it was more Gallican than is generally appreciated. This point of view is corroborated by Robin Briggs, *Early Modern France 1560−1715* (Oxford: Oxford University Press, 1977), p. 27, who claims that the extreme papalism of Sixtus V embarrassed the League. However, moderate *politique* and Gallican Catholic tendencies did not attract widespread attention among Leaguers until the 1590s, when these groups made headway against ultra-Catholic, ultra-papalist leadership, according to Hubert Méthivier, *L'Ancien régime en France* (Paris: Presses Universitaires de France, 1981), pp. 156−57.

7. It would have been impossible for him to do so since the last French edition of *L'Histoire, etc.* appeared in 1648, and the last Latin edition, plus *L'Erreur Populaire* (in Dutch) as late as 1691.

8. Daniel Ligou, *Le Protestantisme en France de 1598 à 1715* (Paris: Société d' Édition d' Enseignement Supérieur 1968), p. 49, calls the effort by Henry IV to grant both parties some (but not all) of what each wanted a policy "ondoyante et diverse," the object of which was balance.

9. Robert Mandrou, *Introduction to Modern France 1500−1640* (New York, Holmes & Meier 1976), p. 129, terms Henry's a "policy of vacillation which did not conciliate the malcontents of either party."

10. During the reign of Henry IV, when conciliation was the main object of government. Raemond's book sold only two editions: 1605 and 1610. In the following reign (Louis XIII, 1610−1643), when a perceptible change in policy was in effect and the leadership of the Huguenot party was seriously divided, *L'Histoire, etc.*, with its strong hint of Protestantism's imminent demise, sold briskly, with new printings emerging in 1611, 1614, 1623, 1624, and 1629 (all in French). During this period three foreign language editions (Dutch, German, Latin) were printed, all in 1614.

11. This edition also contained the French translations of two essays by Tertullian,

the second–third century Roman apologist for Christianity: *De la couronne du soldat* (*Corona Militis*), and *Aux martyrs* (*Ad Martyres*).

12. "L'Imprimeur au lecteur," in *Erreur Populaire* (Bordeaux, 1587). The printer, Simon Millanges, observed that many people thought that one reason France had been plunged into civil war was the laxity among French Catholic clergymen, which had persisted ever since the "reign" of Pope Joan, thereby testifying not only to the widespread credence even Catholics gave her, but also to the seriousness with which they viewed such laxness. The 1587 edition containing Millanges's observations is anonymous and very rare. A copy may be viewed in the *Bibliothèque Municipale* of Bordeaux, where I saw it.

13. Léonce Couture, "Florimond de Raymond," *Revue de Gascogne*, IX, 1868, p. 267, n.1, observed that Raemond did R. T. too much honor in both printing as well as refuting his pamphlet on the *Erreur Populaire*.

14. "Mon desseing n'a jamais esté de me mettre en crédit par ces petits avortons qui sortent de chez moy (ce seroit vouloir sur le sable bastire une gloire solide)" in *Erreur Populaire*, p. 303.

15. The other was Jean de Sponde's *Response au traité des vrayes essencielles et visibles marques de la vraye église* (1595).

16. Jean Giono, in the Preface to *Commentaires de Blaise De Monluc*, Paul Courteault, ed. (Paris, A. J. Picard 1964), pp xix–xx.

17. Refer to chap. 2, n.73.

18. In his essay "Of the Arms of the Parthians," Montaigne said: "It is a vicious practice of the nobility of our time, and full of softness, to put on armor only on the point of extreme need and to take it off as soon as there is the slightest appearance that the danger has gone" (*The Complete Essays of Montaigne*), Donald M. Frame, ed. and trans. (Stanford: Stanford University Press, 1965), p. 293.

19. Raemond, "Addresse à la Noblesse de Gascongne," in Blaise de Monluc, *Commentaires*, Alphonse De Ruble, ed. (Paris: Madame V. Renouard, 1864–1872), p. 351.

20. Ibid.

21. "Cy dessou reposent les os De Monluc, qui n'eust onc repos." (Ibid.)

22. Paul Courteault, Monluc's third editor (after Raemond and De Ruble) explained that as Monluc aged, he came to believe that only tolerance could alleviate the suffering of France. (See Introduction to Monluc's *Commentaires*, Paul Courteault, ed., with Preface by Jean Giono (Paris, A. J. Picard 1964), p. xxv.

23. Henry claimed that Monluc's work was "the soldier's Bible," a remark that reveals the admiration of the military caste for the bold strategy of the man, even when, as in Henry's case, his own family and former religious party had been Monluc's target.

24. Raemond, "Lettre à Monseigneur le Duc D'Espernon, Paer et colonel de France," in Monluc, *Commentaires* (De Ruble), pp. 352–54.

25. Ibid.

26. Ibid.

27. Raemond was well aware of the blemishes in his completed work, and promised to bring to completion a revised second edition of the *Commentaires*, one "sans aucune ride." He never got around to it. "Avis au Lecteur," *Commentaires de Blaise de Monluc* (De Ruble), p. viii.

28. Ibid., pp. viii–ix.

29. In *L'Anti-Christ*, p. 39, Raemond followed a detailed account of atrocities

which had occurred during the civil wars with this exhortation: "Let us not accuse only the so-called reformed party; they have made the Catholics masters of the fine art of cruelty so that each side can destroy the other, to the great shame and ignominy of the name Christian, and even of that of Frenchman, malodorous now the world over, dishonored because of this event." His comment echoed that of his friend Montaigne, who speculated that no hostility excelled Christian hostility when led on by zeal. (See his *Apology for Raymond Sebond* in *The Complete Essays* of Montaigne, Donald M. Frame, ed. and trans. (Stanford: Stanford University Press, 1965), p. 324.

30. Alphonse De Ruble, *Commentaires de Blaise de Monluc*, "Introduction," p. ix

31. Ibid., p. xiv.

32. See n.22 above.

33. Monluc's *Commentaires*, Paul Courteault, ed., p. xxv.

34. Ibid., p. xxvi.

35. Ibid.

36. Ibid.

37. The *robins* were upper level office holders, a new legal nobility as compared to the old nobility with its military orientation and ancient lineage. Raemond was a member of the former by virtue of his seat in the *Parlement* of Bordeaux; he was also a member of the old nobility. His loyalties were with each group, and there is no evidence that he felt any stress due to conflicting interests.

38. Monluc's *Commentaires*, p. xxix.

39. For the most popular rebuttals of Protestant works on Antichrist, see chap. 5, n.20.

40. On Daneau, see chap. 5, n.91.

41. The popularity of the *Erreur Populaire* is best attested by its commercial success. (See n.3 above.) In addition, Raemond had received letters of congratulation from scholars with European reputations. Justus Lipsius, the Belgian savant and a former Calvinist, wrote to thank Raemond for a copy he had sent him in 1593, lauding its clarity of style and the wisdom of having written in the vernacular. Shortly thereafter, Cardinal Baronius complimented the book. (See chap. 4, n.33.) After the publication of *L'Anti-Christ*, he received a letter (11 March 1599) from Pope Clement VIII giving him permission, at the request of Cardinal Joyeuse, to read books on the *Index* in order to pursue his "History of Heresy." The letter, in Latin, referred to his earlier works as "luculenter scripti," a phrase that revealed the kind of reputation Raemond had been building for himself throughout the 1590s within Catholic circles. "Clemens pp. VIII Dilecto Filio Florimondo Raemondo, etc." (*L'Histoire, etc.*, pp. 400–403). Lipsius wrote a second letter to Raemond in November, 1600, repeating the pleasure he had derived from reading the *Erreur Populaire*.

42. On Malvyn, see Paul Courteault, *Geoffroy de Malvyn Magistrat et humaniste bordelais 1545(?)–1617* (Paris: Bibliothèque Littéraire de la Renaissance, 1907). The Malvyns were styled *seigneurs de Cessac*, Geoffrey being the second member of his family (his father Charles was the first) to serve as a member of the *Parlement* of Bordeaux. They were *robins* rather than of the ancient nobility, Charles rendered thanks to the king for his noble house and the *seigneurie* of Cessac only in 1564. Charles achieved considerable prestige in his parlementary role, having been made *Premier President* of that body (Larroque, *Essai*, p. 68, n.2). He was an author as well, and had published works on the origins of the Franks. Geoffrey had less serious literary gifts, but his poetry, like Raemond's,

found its way into the published poetry of Pierre de Brach, and some of it was published by Raemond as well in the *Commentaires* of Monluc and in Sponde's answer to Bèze's treatise. (Larroque, *Essai*, p. 69 note.) The Malvyns were cousins to the Montaignes.

43. The dedication was definitely to Geoffrey, and not to Charles, as Darricau (*La Vie et l'oeuvre d'un parlementaire Aquitain Florimond de Raemond*, (Bordeaux, 1971), p. 114, mistakenly wrote. Charles de Malvyn died in 1581.

44. Raemond to Malvyn, Letter of 5 November 1596, reprinted in Paul Courteault, *Geoffroy de Malvyn*, p. 194.

45. Darricau, *op. cit.*, p. 121, lists this as the first edition of the *Anti-Christ*, published at Lyon by J. Pillehotte, 1597. In 12^0, it was 893 pages long, excluding the table of contents, and included verses entitled: "in V. L. Fl. Raemundi ... Anti-Christum," signed Petrus Le Double; also some by Louis de Bernard. Only one other edition was printed in Raemond's lifetime, under the title *L'Anti-Christ et L'Anti-Papesse*, with the two Tertullian essays in trans. by Abel L'Angelier, which is the copy I use throughout as reference. The two subsequent editions appeared in 1607 and 1613.

46. On 5 November 1596, Raemond wrote Geoffrey de Malvyn that he was trembling with fear while awaiting the publication of the *Anti-Christ*, but seeing that it was already too late for second thoughts, he was determined to stand up to all the insults that envy and calumny could hurl his way. (Letter reprinted in Paul Courteault, *Geoffroy de Malvyn*, p. 194).

47. He brought out the revised and expanded third edition of *Erreur Populaire* in this year and the translations of the Tertullian essays.

48. Raemond said several times that he intended to write, and had begun to collect materials on, a work to be called *Arrests célèbres*, or *Famous Decisions*. He mentioned it first in his *Anti-Christ*, p. 41, while reproving Bèze for underestimating the Bordeaux *Parlement*'s zeal in prosecuting witches. On another occasion, in a letter to Malvyn (5 Nov. 1596), he promised the book would contain a sketch of Malvyn drawn with a "craion d'honneur" and that it would serve as a textbook for young magistrates. (Letter reprinted in Paul Courteault, *Geoffroy de Malvyn*, p. 195.) Larroque (*Essai*, p. 87, n.1) regretted the loss of these notes, but see chap. 1, n.58. A second book, which Raemond was hoping to write but abandoned, was to have been called *Princes of the Church*, similar he said to those of Platina, Panvinius, and Papire Masson (*Anti-Christ*, p. 220). In it he promised to deal at greater length with the concept of papal infallibility. He lost heart, however, seeing how thoroughly Cardinal Baronius's *Annales Ecclesiastici* had treated such history. (Letter to Duplessis-Mornay, 5 January 1599, in Duplessis-Mornay, *Mémoires et Correspondance* IX, pp. 199–202.)

49. "Je dis que j'en ay veu un autre dans Witemberg" (*L'Anti-Papesse*, p. 366). The date of this journey to Germany is not known, and this is the only reference to it in Raemond's writing. The trip was certainly made after the last previous edition of the *Erreur Populaire* (1595) and the first publication of this edition (renamed *L'Anti-Papesse* [1599].)

50. The pamphlet was the *Plaintes des eglises, etc.* (for the complete title, see chap. 1, n.43). It is henceforth referred to as the *Plaintes*.

51. There is no evidence that Raemond did, as one of the *Plaintes* three charges against him purported (*Plaintes*, p. 132), attempt to revenge himself on the Huguenots as a party in order to recoup the ransom money (one thousand *livres*) paid for his release in 1572. (The authors of the pamphlet claimed he had collected four thousand écus by 1597. An écu was worth three *livres*, so the

authors claimed he had extorted twelve times the ransom money—vengeance indeed!) One must concur with Raemond's first biographer in dismissing the charge as a fabrication, not merely (as Larroque observed) because Raemond was friendly with certain Protestants (du Bartas), or again because Duplessis-Mornay respected him (*Essai*, p. 16), but because only two other charges were raised against him. Two complaints lodged against a man whose twenty-five years of judicial service spanned much of the civil war period are insufficient evidence on which to base a *prima facie* case of systematic discrimination and malpractice.

52. The other two complaints (grievances) in the *Plaintes* concern a murder case in which Raemond participated and in which he and his colleagues sent the wrong man to his execution (p. 116); and the disinterment of a young Protestant girl from a Catholic cemetery. (Ibid., pp. 153–54.)

53. That Raemond was not a conscientious judge, that he was in fact a corrupt one, was first denied by the Catholic abbé, Laurent-Josse Leclerc, in his *Lettre critique sur le dictionnaire de Bayle* (The Hague, 1732). The statement (*Judicat*, etc.) derived from a tripartite *bon mot*, which had circulated in the Bordeaux region around the middle of the seventeenth century, long after Raemond's death in 1601. It had charged him with having grown old without greying, with having written from ignorance, and with having spent money on building projects in a profligate manner. The original saying did *not* include any charge that he was an unprincipled judge. Leclerc believed Gilbert Burnet (later Bishop of Salisbury) was the source for the statement that Raemond was a corrupt magistrate, having substituted the charge for one of the original three of the *bon mot* in his *History of the Reformation in England*. (Leclerc, *Critique*, pp. 382f.) Leclerc combined a defense of Raemond generally with a condemnation of Protestant attitudes toward Catholicism and ecclesiastical history.

54. Jacqueline Thibaut-Payen, *Les Morts, l'église et l'état* (Paris: Éditions Lanore, 1977), p. 160, says that the violence that made itself manifest on such occasions was often led by curates rather than by parishioners, and that their aggressive spirit was the same as that of the magistrates. Élie Benoist, *Histoire de l'édit de Nantes Jusques a l'édit de révocation* (Delft, 1693), Book V, p. 217, refers to the frequent complaints made by the reformed that their funerals were marred by outrages of all kinds.

55. Both these groups were called *ordres* of French society by the authors of the *Plaintes*. Besides the magistrates and clergy, the authors of the *Plaintes* named *des Peuples, la Noblesse*, and *du Conseil* as *ordres* that had caused them difficulty, obviously eager to distribute as widely as possible the blame for their suffering. But clergy, they called their mortal enemies: "Les Prestres, les Moines, en un mot tous ceux qui en l'Eglise Romains s'appellent Ecclesiastiques, sont nos ennemis mortels, & en font profession ouverte" (p. 18), while, "les Magistrats flattent les passions des Prestres, fomentent ces seditions du Peuple, applaudissent aux violences de la Noblesse" and in sum, let their decisions be guided by popular prejudice (p. 20).

56. There were four principal ones: (1) a new edict, for they deemed that of 1577 too vague as to details; (2) the free exercise of their faith; (3) a more secure living for Protestant ministers; (4) more security for Protestant towns. (Benoist, *Histoire de l'édit de Nantes*, Book V, p. 218ff., and especially p. 226.)

57. These were the famous *Chambres mi-partis*, courts of the *parlements* composed half of Protestant, half of Catholic magistrates. The edict of 30 June 1598 contained seven articles (nos. 60–67) that provided for the administration of justice to the effect that, wherever a Protestant was involved in a civil or in a

criminal case, the Catholic judge was obliged to call upon a Protestant one to help him arrive at an objective decision. (Daniel Ligou, *Le Protestantisme en France de 1598 à 1715*) p. 14.

58. Term given civil and criminal courts judging in the first instance and established under Henry II in 1551. The incident in Bergerac was described in the *Plaintes*, p. 100.

59. "Quant aux charges plus honorables, de tous costez nous en somme forclos" (*Plaintes*, p. 99.) In Orleans, the mayor refused to grant the title *Eschevin* (municipal magistrate before 1789) to any Huguenot or even to any former Huguenot, whatever his merit; the Lieutenant General of Aix had ordered all Huguenots refused institution to any public office whatsoever on pain of confiscation of goods, etc. (*Plaintes*, p. 104.)

60. Élie Benoist, *Histoire de l'édit de Nantes*, Book V, p. 215.

61. See note 63 below.

62. The Bordeaux body was not the only judicial authority to demand the disinterment of Protestants. The *Plaintes* named such action occurring in Provence, Normandy, Anjou, Dauphiné, Touraine, Maine, etc., but the authors singled out the *Parlement* of Bordeaux as the most determined to aid the enemies of the reformed party. (*Plaintes*, pp. 151–52.) Raemond mentioned similar laws having been passed by the *Parlements* of Paris and Toulouse, (*L'Histoire, etc.*, p. 217.)

63. "Un arrest auparavent tous ces excez ja mentionnez, prononcé en pleine audience par Florimond de Remond President lors comme plus ancien Conseiller, pour rendre solennelles ces desnaturées passions, les rendre, s'il estoit possible, naturelles aux François. Il s'agissoit d'un enfant enterré au cimetière d'Ozillac en Xainctonge. Il fut ordonné, de mesme main, que tous les corps de ceux de la Religion qui depuis dix ans auroyent eu terre en quelque cimetière, seroyent arrachez de leurs tombeaux" (*Plaintes*, pp. 153–54.)

64. Raemond, *L'Histoire, etc.*, p. 1061. The pamphlet has since disappeared.

65. Michel Vovelle, *Mourir Autrefois* (Paris, Editions Gallimard/Juilliard 1974), p. 10.

66. Chap. 18, Book VIIII.

67. Raemond, *L'Histoire, etc.*, p. 1056.

68. Geoffrey Rowell, *The Liturgy of Christian Burial* (London, Alcuin Club/S. P. C. K. 1977), p. 81, says that Calvin felt burial rites were useful as well as godly, and when he drew up regulations for burials in Geneva in 1541, urged that decent rites be afforded. Calvin also believed in leaving the form of such rites to be determined by the assembled bereaved. He himself was buried without pomp of any kind in a site no longer identifiable with certainty.

69. Ibid.

70. Ibid

71. Vovelle, *Mourir Autrefois*, p. 10. Rowell, *The Liturgy*, p. 83, says that despite the preference of such Calvinist ministers in England as Walter Travers, who disapproved of graveside prayers for English Calvinists, the pre-Reformation practice persisted.

72. Raemond, *L'Histoire, etc.*, p. 1063.

73. The edict of Amboise of 1563 expressly provided for common use of parish graveyards at night (for reasons of safety, of course). Huguenots were frequently obliged for the same reason to make do without a funeral cortège. (Thibaut-Payen, *Les Morts*, pp. 158–59).

74. The unwillingness of Catholics to permit Protestants the use of Catholic burial facilities resulted in the separate facilities clause of the edict of Nantes,

such to be purchased through equitable public taxation. A secret article (no. 45) provided, however, that no more exhumations of Protestants buried in Catholic cemeteries would be permitted in the future. (Thibaut-Payen, *Les Morts*, p. 161.) That the article was secret suggests that Raemond's justification for disinterring Protestants (i.e., Catholic jealousy of their exclusive rights to parish cemeteries) was one with which his society was quite familiar.

75. He wrote, "In the consecration of cemeteries, the secular power is totally excluded" (*L'Histoire, etc.*, p. 1061).

76. His reasoning ran thus: "And for this cause all the laws which have been relative to this matter (of burial) have been papal, and all addressed to bishops or other ecclesiastics—never to secular persons who have nothing to do with religious matters, or those connected to them. And although people turn frequently to secular judges, it is only for protection against the violence of those who oppose the bishops' laws" (ibid).

77. *L'Histoire, etc.*, p. 1062.

78. Ibid.

79. Ibid., p. 1063.

80. Ibid.

81. See chap. 2, n.82.

82. The *Plaintes*, p. 116, noted: "Le mesme Parlement (Bordeaux) en Decembre xcv (1595) fit executer à mort un nommé Bourron de Castelmoron, pursuivy pour meurtre. Les parens ont depuis faict telle pursuite contre les faux tesmoins & si advantageusement verifié la calomnie, que les Juges et le sieur de Remond mesme qui avoit esté Rapporteur du proces, ont esté contraint de confesser, que vrayment en avoit fait mourir cest homme à tort. Et toutefois on n'a jamais sceu en avoir justice contre ces faux tesmoins, non pas mesme obtenir main-levée des biens confisqués." It appears that Raemond did not have sole responsibility for the unfortunate decision, for the other judges likewise confessed their error. The fact that the condemned man's property was confiscated and may not have been returned to his lawful heirs does seem to suggest the studied indifference to Protestant rights, which helped produce the *Plaintes* and which resulted in the new Edict of Nantes.

83. The Abbé Leclerc, commenting on this case, raised several objections. He pointed out that there is no proof to the effect that it was Raemond who let the real murderer go free. (One might add that there is also none that indicates that the identity of the real murderer was known.) Leclerc rather fatuously added that it is also not known whether or not the homicide was committed in cold blood—the implication being that there might have been extenuating circumstances (such as passion) for allowing the real culprit to go free. However, the objection would presumably have held as true for a Calvinist suspect as for a Catholic one—and the Calvinist was executed. (Leclerc, *Lettre Critique Sur le Dictionnaire de Bayle* (1732), pp. 396–97.) Larroque (*Essai*, p. 42) called the decision "un malheur, un grand malheur" but pointed out that even the most enlightened and honest of judges is prone to err occasionally. He put a great value on Raemond's having owned up to error.

84. Raemond noted wryly: "The whole reformed party of France just then in good standing ... rose up, taking the Governor's part and complained to the king, saying that the Court of the *Parlement* wanted to regulate and police their religion, and got the case revoked to the Privy Council, where the Consistory brothers did everything in their power and finally wore down all resistance to their demands" (*L'Histoire, etc.*, p. 1001.)

85. François de Raemond commented on his father's impatience to get into the French material of the *Histoire, etc.* in "Au Lecteur" (precedes Book I, unpaged).
86. Raemond, *L'Histoire, etc.*, p. 945.
87. Ibid. He claimed that besides harassments and interruptions, the long road he had taken through foreign resource material was one few others had trod, and that he found an infinity of thorns and difficulties along his route.
88. Raemond, "Voeu de L'Autheur" (unpaged), *L'Histoire, etc.*
89. Raemond called the Cardinal "le Caesar des Escrivains de son aage" (*L'Histoire, etc.*, p. 393). Baronius praised Raemond in the *Annales Ecclesiastici* (for the year 853, no. 62) as he was in the process of considering the Pope Joan legend and having first mentioned the contributions made to her exposé by Papire Masson: "Sed prae caeteris commendandus, qui magno pietatis zelo succensus, veritatis singulari amore flagrans, exaestuansque ejus elucidandae immenso mentis ardore, locupletius ista pertractans, singula quaeque curiosius pervestigans, nihil indiscussum relinquens, fama nobilis Florimundus de Remundo, regius consiliarius in Parlamento Burdegalensi, vir cum primis illustris ac pius, et doctrina insignis, cujus lucubrationes de antichristo adversus novatores magnopere celebrantur" (Caesar Baronius, *Annales Ecclesiastici*, XIV, Augustino Theiner, Ed., (Rome: Barri-Duci & L. Guerin, 1868, p. 407).
90. For modern scholarly evaluation of the *Magdeburg Centuries*, see below, chap. 6, n.6 and of Baronius, see chap. 2, n.52.
91. The Registers described him as "conseiller en la Cour, et très grand personnage."
92. This church also contained the body of Montaigne, who was buried in a *cave* or hollowed out place in front of the main altar, but moved and reburied in a new chapel of this church in 1614, when the enlargement of the church left Montaigne's remains far from the main altar. (Donald Frame, *Montaigne*, pp. 306−7.) These facts are mentioned because Raemond was buried beside Montaigne in 1601. (Raymond Darricau, *La Vie et l'Oeuvre*, p. 113.) The two friends did not rest long beside each other, for there is no evidence that Raemond's remains were shifted after the enlargement of the church. The bodies of the two men were, however, housed in the same church until 1871, when a fire destroyed most of the church. Montaigne's remains were then salvaged, and reburied in the Faculty of Letters and Science building of the University of Bordeaux, which was new in 1886, and which, according to Frame, was but a few yards from the site of the former Feuillants's church. Raemond's remains, according to Darricau, remained in their old location until 1887, when the last vestiges of the damaged church were demolished. A city council decision of 6 December 1887, ordered the remains of all the bodies buried in the old church to the cemetery of the Chartreuse, which lies today on the edge of the massive urban renewal of downtown Bordeaux (called Meriadeck). There, in the cemetery of the Chartreuse is found the Tomb of the Feuillants, 23rd series, no. 204. The cemetery office possesses a faded pasteboard card with the names of a dozen or so people of mixed gender whose remains are in an urn under this tomb, a small marble rectangle, whitish-yellow of color. The list does not state that the remains of Raemond are contained in the urn. The question of precisely where his ashes are appears moot.
93. The efforts of Cardinal Sourdis on Raemond's funeral sermon are in part preserved in a manuscript *Life* (of Sourdis) by his biographer, de Bertheau. The latter observed that Sourdis felt the deepest grief at the passing of "ce puissant genie," although a nineteenth-century reader found Sourdis's oration to have been "ridiculement déclamatoire" (E. A., "Un Document inédit sur Florimond de Raymond," *Revue Catholique de Bordeaux*, 1892, p. 704).

94. François de Raemond, "A monseigneur l'illustrissime et reverendissime Cardinal de Joyeuse" (before Book I, *L'Histoire, etc.*) (unpaginated).

95. Brach wrote in a letter to their common friend and correspondent, Justus Lipsius, the sage of Louvain, that with both Montaigne and Raemond gone—his two closest friends—his heart was heavy indeed. Letter to "Monsieur Lipse, A Louvain" in Pierre de Brach, *Oeuvres poétiques*, III, Appendix, CV, Reinhold Dezeimeris, ed. (reprint) (Geneva: Slatkine Reprints, 1969).

96. François published at least one original work after laboring to complete his father's *Histoire, etc.* It was entitled *Les Impostures inventées contre les papes, rapportées suivant la verité aux ministres de Calvin pour monstrer par leurs propers passages qu'ils sont les vrays precurseurs de la beste* (Bordeaux, 1616). (Jules Andrieu, *Bibliographie Generale de l'Agenais*, Paris, 1887, p. 234).

97. Jean-Charles de Raemond, abbé de la Frénade, Florimond's second son, translated the *Erreur Populaire* (*Fabulae Jeannae Quae Pontifici Romani Sedem Occupasse Falso Credita Est*, Bordeaux, 1601: Reimpr. *Error Popularis, Seu Fabula Jeannae Papistae*, etc. (Cologne, 1614), performed at the request of Cardinal Baronius. His other works include *Les Triomphes du roy* (Henry IV), (Paris, 1609); *La Couronne Royale* (Paris, 1610); *Regrets Funèbres sur la mort de Henri IV*, (Paris, 1610); *Le Sacre et couronnement du Roy Loys XIII* (Paris, 1620); and *La Response aux injustes plainctes des ministres de Charenton; ensemble l'arrest du privé conseil donné sur le subject de leur livre intitule: defense de la confession des églises prétendues de France*, etc., (Paris, 1622). (Ibid.) From a consideration of their titles, it is at once apparent that neither son was as productive as their father in the service of their church, although each produced one work of a purely polemical nature.

98. "It would be as great a crime in me not to recognize your piety as it would be ungrateful not to acknowledge the kindness with which you have honored the departed, and the funerary honors which you have accorded him" ("A monseigneur l'illustrissime et Reverendissime Cardinal de Sourdis," precedes Book III of *L'Histoire, etc.*).

Chapter 4. Pope Joan

1. The first edition was entitled *Erreur populaire de la Papesse Jane* (Bordeaux, S. Millanges, 1587). After 1599 it was frequently entitled *L'Anti-Papesse ou l'erreur populaire de la Papesse Jane*, having appeared in the same edition with Raemond's second original work, *L'Anti-Christ* (1st ed. 1597). All references are to (*AP*) *L'Anti-Papesse* in the combined edition, *L'Anti-Christ et L'Anti-Papesse* (Paris, Abel l'Angelier, 1599).

2. Despite her birthplace, her nickname was frequently given as John the Englishman (Jean l'Anglois). Said Raemond, "these people cannot agree where in fact she came from" *AP*, p. 363.

3. Charles Homer Haskins, *The Rise of Universities* (New York, Henry Holt & Co. 1923), p. 4.

4. Panvinius (1520–1568), a Vatican librarian, had as his ambition the rewriting of all Roman and Christian antiquity from reliable sources. His work ran to sixty-eight volumes, seventeen on the history of the papacy. *The New Catholic Encyclopedia*, New York: X, pp. 950–51. McGraw-Hill).

5. Kenneth Scott Latourette, *A History of Christianity*, (New York: Harper & Row, 1975), I, p. 466. Raemond, *AP*, pp. 429–30.

6. August Potthast, *Bibliotheca Historica Medii Aevi* (Berlin: W. Weber 1896), I, p. 241. Mailly's work was the *Chronica Universalis*.

7. Mailly put her reign between Urban II (d. 1099) and Paschall II (1099–1118); Stephen of Bourbon (1262), after Sergius III (d. 911) and before Anastasius III, who succeeded immediately. Some versions of Polonus lodged Joan after Leo IV (d. 855), and before Benedict III. In fact, there was no interval between these two, but 855–57 became the most-cited dates for Joan.

8. Margaret King, "Book Lined Cells," in *Beyond Their Sex*, Patricia Labalme, ed. (New York: New York University Press, 1980), pp. 79–80.

9. Frantisek Palacky, *Documenta Mag. Joannis Hus Vitam, etc.*, (Osnabrück, 1966, Biblio-Verlag pp. 59–61).

10. "Neque certa historia est . . ." was Aeneas's phrase. (Rudolf Wolkan, ed., *Der Briefwechsel des Eneas Silvius Piccolomini* (Vienna, A. Hölder 1918), 68, p. 40.

11. On Gerhard, see Robert D. Preus, *The Theology of Post-Reformation Lutheranism* (Saint Louis, No: Concordia Publishing House 1970), pp. 52–53. Preus calls him "the third preeminent Lutheran theologian after Luther and Chemnitz." He was a professor at Jena from 1616 until his death, (1637), and was known for his orthodoxy. His reference was to what he imagined to have been Aeneas's work rather than Schedel's: "Aeneas Sylvius, Pontifex ipsemet tandem factus, hanc Historiam exscripsit in sexta mundi aetate p. 170. operis Historici [sic] impressi Norinberg. anno 1493. per Kobergerum." (Gerhard, *Locorum Theologicorum*, Jena, 1620 V, p. 1004). It is on that very page p. 170) in the *Nuremberg Chronicle* that one reads the major facts of Joan's story and sees her figured as John VII, a female figure, crowned, holding an infant. On Schedel see Adrian Wilson, *The Making of the Nuremberg Chronicle* (Amsterdam, Nico Israel 1976), pp. 20, 28. Foresti (p. 168) numbered Joan (Johannes) VIII; Platina gave Joan a VII (Johannes VII). Schedel followed Platina's enumeration.

12. Quoted in Denis Hay, *The Italian Renaissance in its Historical Background* (Cambridge: Cambridge University Press, 1970), p. 143, n.2.

13. In Platina's book Joan's number is VII (John VII), a number very rarely assigned her. Since Schedel numbered his Joan VII, too, Schedel may have been following Platina's example.

14. This test was "performed" by a young cleric probing beneath the hole in the chair to determine if the newly elected pope had male genitalia.

15. Natalie Zemon Davis, *Society and Culture in Early Modern France*, (Stanford: Stanford University Press, 1965), pp. 72–73, finds that many women in the late Renaissance were still illiterate, with well-born women literate in the vernacular rather than in classical languages. She notes (p. 134) that Pope Joan had "limited potential" for criticism of the hierarchical social structure because her arrogance had caused her to sin.

16. Raemond, *AP*, p. 367.

17. Martin Luther, *WA, Tr*, no. 6447, p. 667. "Item: Zu Rom Hab ich gesehen in einer grossen Gassen, so stradks nach S. Peters Münster Gehet, offentlich in einen Stein gehauen einen Papst, wie ein Weib mit einem Scepter, päbstlichen Mantel, trägt ein Kind an arme; durch dieselbe Gasse zeucht kein Papst, dass er solch Bilde nicht darf sehen." After this Luther related quickly how this Mainz-Born whore had been brought low by the Devil, adding: "Es nimmt mich Wunder, dass die Päpste solch Bilde leiden können; aber Gott blendet sie, dass man sehe, was Papstthum sei: eitel Betrug und Teufelswerk."

18. "Verum his omissis, Joannam papissam transsiliant oportet, si continuare suam ab apostolisseriem volent" from "Vera Christianae Pacificationis et Ecclesiae Reformandae Ratio" (1549), in *Joannis Calvini Opera Quae Supersunt Omnia*, VII (Brunswick: C. A. Schwetschke, 1868), p. 633.

19. Raemond's son, Jean-Charles, made the first Latin translation in 1601. The first Dutch edition appeared in 1614.

20. Pierre Pithou (1539–1596), respected legist and historian, published works from original manuscript sources.

21. Onofrio Panvinio, *Annotationi*, appended to *Battista (sic) Platina Cremonese Delle Vite De' Pontefici*, (Venice, 1650), p. 228. The first edition of Panvinius's correction of Platina appeared in 1562.

22. Ludwig Bethman, "*Sigiberti Gemblacensis Chronigraphia*," in *Mon. Germ. Hist.* Script. (Hanover: Impensis Bibliopolii Aulici Hahniani, 1844), VI, p. 340, said that a monk altered Sigebert to contain the popess tale.

23. Raemond, *AP*, p. 387.

24. Ibid., p. 378.

25. Andreas Burckhardt, *Johannes Basilius Herold*, (Basel: Helbing & Lichtenhahn, 1967), p. 126ff. pp 134–140.

26. Raemond, *AP*, p. 367, charged Herold with having "adjusted" Polonus, but Joh. Jos. Ign. v. Döllinger, *Die Papst-Fabeln des Mittelalters* (München, J. G. Cotta 1863), p. 9, said Polonus was altered several years after his death (1278) to include this myth.

27. Ludwig Weiland, "Martini Oppaviensis Chronicon Pontificum et Imperatorem," in *Mon. Germ. Hist. Script.*, XXII (Hanover: Weidmannsche Verlagsbuchhandlung, 1872), p. 386, said that the first useful edition of Polinus dates from 1616.

28. Georg Waitz, "Mariani Scotti Chronicon," in *Mon. Germ. Hist. Script.*, V, p. 493, found that while Herold's *Scotus* was a flawed work, Herold was not guilty of classification; and in *Patrologia Latina* (Migne, ed., Paris: J. P. Migne, 1879), CXLII, cols. 619–20.

29. Josef Benzing, *Die Buckdrucker des 16. und 17. Jahrhunderts Im Deutschen Sprachgebiet* (Wiesbaden: Harrassowitz, 1963), p. 36; Martin Steinmann, *Johannes Oporinus*, (Basel, Helbing & Lichtenhahn 1967), p. 2 n.15.

30. "Typographical fixity" is a term used by Elizabeth Eisenstein, "The Advent of Printing and the Protestant Revolt," in Robert M. Kingdon, ed., *Transition and Revolution* (Minneapolis; Burgess Publishing Company, 1974), p. 244. However valid in other contexts such fixity did not prevent the permutation of the popess myth in the post-print era. Raemond took umbrage at Protestant authors—John Bale, Johann Turmair (Aventinus), Benedict Marti (Aretius), Johann Funck (Funcius), and four Centuriators (M. Flacius Illyricus, J. Wigand, M. Judex, J. Faber)—who had produced innovations on the popess story. All these were either reformed Christians or Lutherans.

31. Raemond's own Roman art collection was a regular garden museum. A young German tourist urged traveler's in 1627 to visit it. Justus Zinzerling, *Voyage dans la vieille France*, T. Bernard, trans. (Paris: Dentu, Vanier, etc. 1859), p. 23 (1st ed., 1627).

32. A picture of this statue (now in the Vatican Museum) appears in Cesare D'Onofrio, *Mille Anni di Leggenda Una Donna Sul Trono di Pietro* (Rome: Romana Società editrice, 1978)—the best book on the popess legend.

33. Baronius described Raemond as a pious, learned man whose book on Joan

left the Protestants defenseless. (*Annales Ecclesiastici* Augustus Theiner, ed. (Rome: Typographia Tiberina, 1868), XIV, p. 407.

34. D'Onofrio, *op. cit.*, p. 82, and fig. 60.
35. Bartolomeo de' Sacchi (Platina), *Hystoria de Vitis Pontificum Periucunda* (Venice, 1504), p. lvii.
36. D'Onofrio, *op. cit.*, pp. 138–44. Illustrations of the *sella*.
37. Ibid., p. 215, n.45.
38. Raemond, *AP*, p. 411.
39. Ibid., p. 373.
40. Etienne Pasquier, *Oeuvres* (Amsterdam, 1723), II, p. 354.
41. Joan was often called John VIII, although more circumspect writers omitted the VIII.
42. Raemond, *AP*, p. 383.
43. Kenneth Scott Latourette, *op. cit.*, p. 302.
44. Ibid., p. 304.
45. Raemond, *AP*, p. 409: "A German can no more leave women alone than he can wine."
46. Ibid., p. 407.
47. Robert Bellarmine, "Coelibatum jure Apostolico rectissime annexum ordinibus sacris," *Opera Omnia* (Frankfurt: Minerva; 1965), II, pp. 454–60.
48. *Super Coelibatu Monachatu. etc.*, (1521).
49. *On Monastic Vows* (1521); *On the Married Life* (1522).
50. These men (see n.30 above) helped write the *Magdeburg Centuries*, printed in Oporinus's shop 1559–1574. Raemond despised them.
51. Raemond, *AP*, p. 409: "a letter falsely published under the name Hildaric" was his exact phrase.
52. Raemond, *L'Histoire de la naissance, progrèz et décadence de l'hérésie de ce Siècle* (Paris, 1605). Subsequently printed twenty times between 1605 and 1746 in Latin, German, and Dutch translations.
53. See Joan Morris, *The Lady Was a Bishop* (New York: Macmillan, 1973).
54. Emile Telle, *L'Oeuvre de Marguerite d'Angoulême reine de Navarre et la querelle des femmes* (Geneva, 1960), p. 39.
55. Maité Albistur and Daniel Armogathe, *Histoire du Feminisme Français du Moyen Age à nos jours* (Paris, 1977), ch. 4.
56. Marguerite's book *Le Miroir de l'âme pécheresse* (1531) was condemned by the faculty of theology of the university of Paris for subversive ideas. Francis got this condemnation lifted.
57. Sherrin M. Wyntjes, "Women in the Reformation Era," in *Becoming Visible: Women in European History*, R. Bridenthal and C. Koonz, eds. (Boston: Houghton Mifflin, 1977).
58. Retha M. Warnicke, *Women in the English Renaissance & Reformation* (Westport, Conn.: Greenwood Press, 1983) has upset the traditional view, which accords more credit to Protestantism in this regard.
59. See Merry E. Wiesner, *Women in Sixteenth Century Europe: A Bibliography* (St. Louis: Center for Reformation Research, 1983).
60. Roland Bainton's *Women of the Reformation in Germany and Italy*, (Minneapolis: Augsburg Publishing House, 1971); *Women of the Reformation in France and England* (1973); *Women of the Reformation From Spain to Scandinavia* (1977); and Nancy Lyman Roelker, "The Appeal of Calvinism to French Noblewomen in the Sixteenth Century," *The Journal of Interdisciplinary History* 2 (1971/72): pp. 391–418 and "The Role of Noblewomen in the French Re-

formation," *Archiv für Reformationsgeschichte* 63 (1972), pp. 168–95, are examples of such research.

61. Raemond, *AP*, p. 397.

62. Joan was a repugnant symbol to Protestants and to Catholics alike, and could hardly have been a role model for women. The scope which the sixteenth century did offer women in religious life is reviewed in Joyce Irwin's "Society and the Sexes," a bibliographical essay of broad scope in Steven Ozment, ed., *Reformation Europe: A Guide to Research* (St. Louis: Center for Reformation Research, 1982), pp. 343–359. However, Irwin notes that at the end of the sixteenth century marked a rigidity vis-à-vis the role of women set in (p. 345).

63. An example of one female, Marie de Gournay, author of a work (1622) on the quality of men and women, deserves mention here. Marie was the protégé of Raemond's dear friend, Montaigne. She was known by Raemond and must, as an associate of Raemond's literary circle, have read his book on the popess. Nevertheless, neither its misogynist message nor Montaigne's own reticence on the subject of female education discouraged her from taking an aggressive stance on the nature of women.

64. Pierre Bayle, *Dictionnaire Historique et Critique* (Paris: Desoer, 1820), XI, art. "Papesse," remark F, p. 370. A few Twentieth-century writers have clung to the belief that Joan was historical. See in this connection Clement Wood, *The Woman Who Was Pope* (New York: W. Faro, Inc., 1931). Wood, writing from a rabidly anti-Catholic point of view, concludes that "Joan was as historical as Charlemagne" (p. 56).

65. Pierre Bayle, *op. cit.*, p. 373.

66. Blondel was a Protestant clergyman whose book, *Familier esclaircissement de la question si une femme a esté assise au siège papal de Rome entre Leon IV, & Benoist III* (Amsterdam: Jean Blaev, 1647), was a vindication of Raemond's conclusion that the popess was imaginary.

Chapter 5. The Antichrist

1. The term appeared first in I John 2:18 and 22.
2. II Thess. 2:3.
3. Richard Kenneth Emmerson, *Antichrist in the Middle Ages* (Seattle: University of Washington Press, 1981), p. 5.
4. John M. Headley, *Luther's View of Church History* (New Haven: Yale University Press, 1963), p. 247, refers to Luther's association of the Turk and papacy with Antichrist, attributes to Luther this "double abomination of the last time," and notes that subsequently, Protestants distinguished two Antichrists. See also Rudolf Mau, "Luthers Stellung zu den Türken" in *Leben und Werk Martin Luthers von 1526 bis 1546*, Helmar Junghans, ed. (Göttingen: Vandenhoeck & Ruprecht, 1983), pp. 647–662, which clarifies the reformer's intellectual development in the light of political as well as spiritual pressures. See n.64 below.
5. It is found as Part II, art. IV "de Papatu," parag. 10 ff. of the Schmalkald Articles that Luther wrote himself.
6. The most important passages in *Daniel* concerning the monster are in chaps. 7, 8, 11, and 12.
7. *Daniel*, 8:8–12.
8. John Chrysostom, "Epistolam secundam ad Thessalonicenses," 4, in

Patrologiae cursus completus. Series Graeca, 62 (a Brepols-Turnhout reprint of J. P. Migne's ed. of 1844. Chrysostom wrote: "Nero typus Antichristi. Cur Deus permissurus sit Antichristam venire. Ideo neque ita, neque cito futurum dixit, quamquam semper idem dicit: Sed quid? Ut reveletur, inquit, ipse in suo tempore. Nam mysterium jam operatur iniquitatis. Neronem hic dicit, ut qui sit typus Antichristi: ille enim volebat existimari deus" (p. 486).

9. Matthew Spinka, *John Hus's Concept of the Church* (Princeton: Princeton University Press, 1966), p. 125.

10. Christopher Hill, *Antichrist in Seventeenth Century England* (London: Oxford University Press, 1966), p. 7.

11. Luther's suspicions that the pope was Antichrist grew out of a long founded dissatisfaction with papal authority. The first allusion Luther made to the pope as Antichrist was in December 1518, when he observed that the pope and bishops of the church were less servants of God than antichrists in his temple. See Scott H. Hendrix, *Luther and the Papacy* (Philadelphia: Fortress Press, 1981), p. 75. The comment was made in a letter to Wenceslaus Link. Headley (*op. cit.*, p. 59) says Luther's equating of the Roman tyranny with the Antichrist was a "gradual recognition" that developed between 1518 and 1521. This conviction has been called a "complex", which controlled his later life and all his writings by August Franzen, in *Kleine Kirchengeschichte* (Freiburg, 1965) as noted by Remigius Bäumer, *Martin Luther und der Papst* (Münster: Aschendorff, 1979), p. 56, n.14. Ulrich von Hutten's German edition (1526) of Valla's *De Donatione* was of critical importance for Luther's identification of the papacy and Antichrist.

12. In Luther's last tract, "Against the Roman Papacy, an Institution of the Devil," in *Luther's Works*, Eric W. Gritsch, ed., 41, p. 292, Luther wrote: "Boniface III was elected after him [i.e., Gregory the Great]. This is when God's wrath began. This Boniface persuaded the regicide Phocas that he should be pope, or chief of all the bishops in the whole world. The bell was cast then, and the Roman horror accepted with joy. ... For this is what several of his predecessors had sought and pined for, but had not been able to attain, because St. Gregory and several devout bishops, his predecessors, had not tolerated it." Luther's perception of the onset of Antichrist's influence over the papacy was subject to change. See n.83 below.

13. "And he shall speak great words against the Most High, and think to change times and laws: and they shall be given into his hand, until a time and times and the dividing of time" (*Daniel* 7:25).

14. Emmerson, *op. cit.*, p. 7.

15. In Luther's reproof of Emser, 1521, "Concerning the Answer of the Goat in Leipzig," in *Luther's Works*, Eric W. Gritsch, ed., 39, pp. 133–34, Luther said that Hus's preaching and that of Jerome of Prague, his disciple, were the kind that, because of their truthfulness, do disturb; but that such disturbance was produced by God's word, and was thus blessed. Though Emser warned Luther to refrain from making similar disturbance, Luther regarded his predecessors as honorable men: "I would rather share Hus's disgrace than Aristotle's honor," he said.

16. Luther's treatise "On the Papacy in Rome" (1520) in *Luther's Works*, Eric W. Gritsch, ed., 39, p. 75, stated: "But Rome or papal power are not signs of Christendom, for this kind of power does not make a Christian, as baptism and the gospel do. That is why it does not belong to true Christendom either and is a human order." He contrasted the real spiritual church with that which was made simply to instill order. The latter was typical of the papal church.

17. The dominion of Antichrist was equated in sixteenth-century polemics to

temporal authority of the pope. The revelation by Lorenzo Valla, written in 1439, and republished by Ulrich von Hutten in Germany early in 1520, exposed the papal claim to rule central Italy as fraudulent. Luther translated Valla's work in 1535 under the title *Einer aus den hohen Artikeln des Allerheiligesten Bepstlichen Glaubens genant Donatio Constantini, Durch D. Martin Luther Verdeutscht, ihn das auffgeschobene Concilium von Mantua* (Wittenberg, 1537). Even before this Luther had referred to Valla, notably in his *Responsio Lutheriana Ad Condemnationem Doctrinalem per Magistros Nostros Lovaniensis et Colonienses factam* (1520), saying: "At nunc Laurentius is est et quottidie magis fit, cui nec Italia nec universa Ecclesia multis seculis similem habuit, non modo in omni disciplinarum genere ... sed et constantia et zelo fidei Christianae non ficto. Quid hic promovit non modo doctrinalium damnation, nisi quod sese irrisit et hunc magis glorificavit?" in *WA*. Bd. 6, p. 183. John Calvin viewed the abuse of temporal authority as a cause of the neglect of spiritual duties. He deplored Pope Zacharias's crowning of Pepin, and Pope Leo's of Charlemagne as shady deals performed for additional temporal authority. See *Institutes*, John Allen, trans. (Philadelphia: Presbyterian Board of Christian Education, undated) II, Bk. IV, chap. 7, p. 402. Like Luther, Calvin believed Rome had become the "seat of Antichrist" (ibid., p. 410).

18. In August 1519, Luther observed: "Denn Luzifer wollte nur Gott gleich sein, mit dieser Behauptung aber würde sich der Papst über Gottes Wort und damit über Gott selbst stellen. Das aber sei nach 2 Thess. 2:2ff. das Kennzeichen des Antichristen." (Quoted in Remigius Baümer *op. cit.*, p. 54.) In 1541 Luther said of the popes that they had become Antichrist and antigod and had set themselves up "even above God" in "Against Hanswurst" (i.e., Heinrich of Braunschweig/Wolfenbüttel, a fierce opponent of reform), in *Luther's Works* Eric W. Gritsch, ed., 41, p. 205.

19. In the early phase of reform, the pope/Antichrist theme was fed by sermons and tracts of reformers who followed in Luther's wake: Zwingli, Bullinger, Calvin, etc. Simple, heavily illustrated brochures and broadsides were aimed at the broad public. See R. W. Scribner, *For the Sake of Simple Folk* (Cambridge: Cambridge University Press, 1981) pp. 148ff. *et passim*. Also popular were the works of poetasters and playwrights. Of the latter, John Bale was most significant. Raemond believed Bale ("Balee") had generated a host of imitators. See Emmerson, *op. cit.*, pp. 229ff. Only later in the sixteenth century came monographs on the subject. Of these the most important work was Lambert Daneau's *Tractatis de Antichristo ... in quo antichristiani, regni locus, tempus, forma, ministri, fulcimenta, progressio, etc.* (1576). It was translated into French the next year (1577) in Geneva (*Traité de l'Antéchrist*) and appeared again in 1579. Two more Latin editions from Geneva (1582 and 1583) were followed by a Dutch edition (1583) and an English edition (*A Treatise Touching Antichrist, etc.*, London, 1589).

20. Both Sander's *40 demonstrationes quod Papa non est Antichristus, etc.*, 1583, and Cardinal Bellarmine's "Ubi de Antichristo," Bk. III of *De Summo Pontifice*, 1583–1593 were frequently cited by Raemond in his own work.

21. Robert Bellarmine, "De Potestate Spirituali," Bk. IV of *De Summo Pontifice*, Justinus Fèvre, ed. (Frankfurt: Minerva G. M. B. H., 1965), p. 77: "Demonstravimus hac genus, pro ingenii nostri tenuitate, Romanum Episcopum totious Ecclesiae Catholicae summum Pastorem esse a Christo institutum, nec in Antichristum degenerasse unquam, aut aliquo alio modo summam hanc dignitatem perdidisse."

22. He directed readers to consult the eighth through fifteenth chaps. of Book IV of Bellarmine's first volume. *L'Anti-Christ*, p. 220.

23. Luther said in *The Table Talk*, William Hazlitt, ed. (London: George Bell

and Sons, 1902), p. 244: "That Caiaphas, Pilate and St. Peter came to Rome and appeared before the emperor is mere fable; the histories touching that point do not accord." But see n.24 below.

24. Pontien Polman, *L'Élément historique dans la controverse religieuse du XVIe siècle* (Gembloux: J. Duculot, Éditeur, 1932), pp. 471–72, says that the twenty-five year stay dates only from the fourth century. Luther felt that claim was "grosse Lügen." See *WA*, Bd. 7, p. 671. Luther did not, however, reject the possibility that Peter had visited the city: "Wie wol aber ichs halt, S. Peter seh zu Rom gewesen, und noch, wolt ich dennoch nit drauff sterben als auff ein artickel des glaubens" p. 673. Calvin similarly doubted the authenticity of Peter's twenty-five year stay in Rome, but felt that the exact length of his stay definitely required further proof. He did add: "I will not dispute his having died at Rome; but that he was bishop there, especially for any considerable time, is what I cannot be persuaded to believe" (*Institutes*, Bk. IV, chap. 6, p. 380–81).

25. Ibid., p. 473.

26. *L'Anti-Christ*, p. 277. Raemond thought St. Mark had the evangelical message straight from Peter's mouth, having heard Peter preach in Rome. Nowhere in Mark is any mention made that he had listened to Peter preaching at Rome.

27. Ibid., p. 275.

28. Tertullian wrote that Peter had been distinguished by Christ "quod primus agnisto Christus," and also, "ob vigorem fidei." Tertullian, *Liber de praescriptionibus Adversus haereticos, in Patrologiae Cursus Completus Omnium SS. Patrum, Doctorum Scriptorumque ecclesiasticorum*, J. P. Migne, ed., I (Brepols-Turnhout 1980 reprint of the Migne ed. of 1844 (Amboise), pp. 34 and 387. He also wrote that his (Peter's) authority derived from him through all the bishops, as his derived from Christ, and Christ's from God. (Ibid., p. 33.) Such interpretations were heretical, as C. Dodgson, in his commentaries on Tertullian, recognized. See Dodgson's *Tertullian*, I, in *A Library of Fathers of the Holy Catholic Church* (Oxford: Parker, 1842), p. 492. Dodgson names Saints Cyprian, Gregory Nazianzen, and a number of other fathers who interpreted the position of Peter as purely personal rather than hereditary.

29. Martin Luther, "Against the Roman Papacy, an Institution of the Devil," in *Luther's Works*, Eric W. Gritsch, ed., 41, p. 314: "Now the Lord wants to say You are Peter, that is, a man of rock. For you have recognized and named the right Man, who is the true rock, as Scripture names him, Christ. On this rock, that is, on me, Christ, I will build all of my Christendom." On p. 315: "whoever believes in Christ is built on this rock and will attain salvation."

30. Martin Luther, "Address to the Christian Nobility," in *Luther's Works*, James Atkinson, ed. (Philadelphia: Fortress Press, 1966), XLIV, p. 135.

31. Ibid., pp. 138–39.

32. John Calvin, *Institutes*, J. Allen, trans., II, chap. 6, section 4, p. 371: "Since it is the doctrine of the gospel that opens heaven to us, it is beautifully expressed by the metaphorical appellation of *keys*. There is no other way in which men are *bound* and *loosed*, than when some are reconciled to God by faith, and others are more firmly bound by their unbelief."

33. Ibid., p. 279.

34. Ibid., p. 372. "That in the person of one man God gave the keys to them all."

35. Rudolf Pesch, "The Position and Significance of Peter in the Church of the New Testament: A Survey of Current Research," in *Papal Ministry in the Church*, Hans Küng, ed. (New York: Herder and Herder, 1971), p. 21. Pesch points out that the so-called Petrine office as stated in Matt. xvi:18–19 cannot be said to

persist throughout that book, but varied between the notion that doctrinal authority is Peter's and the notion that disciplinary powers are the community's.

36. The fourth and fifth centuries were periods of great uncertainty concerning primacy. Walter Ullmann, *The Growth of Papal Government in the Middle Ages* (London: Methuen & Co. Ltd., 1955), p. 4, notes that while the bishop of Rome from earliest times exercised monarchic powers, "the theoretical exposition of his authoritative function followed considerably later." The Council of Constantinople (311) ruled that the bishop of that city would have primacy of honor *next* after Rome's, and the Roman See retained its prime position regarding honor at Chalcedon, even though parallel jurisdiction of the bishops of both Rome and Constantinople was set forth then (451) as policy. Pope Leo I nevertheless rejected the canons pertaining to parallel jurisdiction, and they were never accepted in the West. In the generation following Chalcedon, the patriarch of Constantinople claimed for his title "prince of the whole church." An appreciation of the fluidity of conceptions regarding papal primacy and the development of notions of "plenitudo potestatis" at the hands of Innocent III (d. 1216) can be had by reading Kenneth Pennington, *Pope and Bishops* (University of Pennsylvania Press, 1984), chap. 2. Pennington reveals the ingenuity of Innocent III in handling gospel texts in order to enhance his own powers over that of the other bishops.

37. *L'Anti-Christ*, p. 289.

38. Martin Luther, "Address to the Christian Nobility," in *Luther's Works*, James Atkinson, ed., p. 160.

39. For the older view, see Konrad Algermissen, *Christian Denominations*, J. W. Grundner, trans. (St. Louis: B. Herder Book Co., 1946), p. 354. For the newer interpretation, see August Bernhard Hasler, *How the Pope Became Infallible*, Peter Heinegg, trans. (New York: Doubleday & Company, 1981), and Brian Tierney, *Origins of Papal Infallibility 1150–1350, A Study on the Concepts of Infallibility, Sovereignty and Tradition in the Middle Ages* (Leiden: E. J. Brill, 1972), pp. 115ff.

40. Infallibility was disavowed by Pope John XXII in 1324 as the work of the devil. Hasler, *op. cit.*, p. 37, points out that this disavowal was made because infallibility was perceived as a limitation on the freedom of subsequent popes.

41. Leopold Willaert, *La Restauration Catholique* (Namur: Secrétariat des Publications, 1960), p. 306, argues that the Spanish Inquisitor, Torquemada (d. 1468) was the first to assert papal infallibility in a formal way.

42. Bellarmine had created a furor by denying that popes could err either in faith or morals. The Renaissance public was not unaware of the irregularity of the private lives of its popes, and Raemond's treatment of infallibility was less assertive than Bellarmine's.

43. That legislation was never registered by France.

44. Williston Walker, *A History of the Christian Church* (New York: Charles Scribner's Sons, 1959), p. 70, describes Zephyrinus as thoroughly confused about doctrinal issues, and ultimately influenced by his successor, Calixtus.

45. Raemond said, "si le corps eust failly, l'ame pourtant estoit demeurée pure & nette" (*L'Anti-Christ*, p. 215).

46. Ibid., p. 216.

47. Ibid., p. 218. The tombstone was uncovered under the altar of a Roman church and was inscribed: "Hic jacet corpus sancti Foelicis Papae et Martyris, qui Constantium damnavit." Why Felix would have condemned his patron, Constantius, is neither clear nor plausible. Joh. von Döllinger, *Die Papst Fabeln des Mittelalters* (Frankfurt am-Main: Minerva, 1962. 1st. ed., 1863), (Munich: 1863), p. 121, notes of this inscription that it was "ein unachtes Machwerk aus später Zeit,"

which was nevertheless accepted as evidence by the Catholic historian, Baronius, and by his church, as proof of Felix's orthodoxy.

48. John XXII preached two sermons on the beatific vision between 1331 and 1332, causing great scandal because they were contradictory to the church's traditional teaching that the souls of saints went immediately to paradise and received the full vision of God. This traditional teaching was not yet defined as dogma when John stated that the vision was postponed for saints (as was punishment for sinners) until the day of judgment. John put this forth as his personal opinion only, but recanted on his deathbed.

49. *L'Anti-Christ*, p. 218.

50. Martin Luther, *Table Talk*, William Hazlitt, ed. (London: George Bell and Sons, 1902), p. 217: "But I say the pope is an arch heretic (heresiarch) for he is an adversary to my blessed Saviour Christ: and so am I to the pope, because he makes new laws and ordinances according to his own will and pleasure, and so directly denies the everlasting priesthood of Christ."

51. Nicolas Vignier, in *Le Theâtre de l'Antichrist* (1610), accused the pope of sheltering ancient heresies "comme en un abbregé." Quoted in Thérèse Moyne, "L'imagerie de Controverse Catholique Dans Les Livres Illustrés à Lyon, etc.," in Philippe Joutard, ed., *Historiographie de la Réforme* (Paris: Delachaux & Niestle, S.A., 1977), p. 18.

52. *L'Anti-Christ*, p. 89.

53. The term was applied by Raemond to Protestants because he felt they refused to believe that God died upon the cross and denied good works. (*L'Anti-Christ*, p. 31). Protestants regarded Catholic preoccupation with works and superfluous sacraments as a reflection on the liberty given man in the gospel or new covenant. They contrasted the last with the first Law and found the Catholics still behaving as if under the latter.

54. *L'Anti-Christ*, p. 95: "Or ce peuple vivant ainsi parmy nous, ou plustost mourant & remourant mille fois le jour sert de lustre au nom Christien. Tant s'en faut qu'il luy soit contraire, que tout au rebours il le fortifie & le confirme."

55. Emmerson, *Antichrist in the Middle Ages*, p. 41.

56. *L'Anti-Christ*, p. 326. Raemond noted disdainfully that "ce second Elie" was, like the first Elias, once saved from destruction, in Luther's case, by lightning. Luther compared himself on at least one occasion to Elias: "Indeed, we are even people like Moses, Joshua, Elijah (Elias) and all the other saints, for we have the same word of God and (the same) spirit which they had. And we are preachers, ministers, and officials of the same God that they were, although they (served Him) more grandly than we." Quoted in Mark U. Edwards, *Luther's Last Battles* (Ithaca: Cornell University Press, 1983), p. 104.

57. *L'Anti-Christ*, p. 327.

58. Antichrist was always associated with the last times. Jewish apocalyptic tradition ruled out his arrival during the period of Roman imperial authority. See Wilhelm Bousset, *Der Antichrist in der Überlieferung des Judentums des Neuen Testaments und der Alten Kirche. Ein Beitrag zur Auslegung der Apokalypse* (Göttingen: Vandenhoeck und Ruprecht, 1895), p. 85. Joachimite interpretation stressed that the pope/Antichrist would cause the destruction of the Roman Empire.

59. Christopher Hill, *Antichrist in Seventeenth Century England*, p. 179.

60. Bellarmine devoted most of his twelfth chapter of *Ubi De Antichristo* to the subject: "Jam vero quod Antichristus sit futurus Judaeus, et circumcisus, certum est, et deducitur primum ex dictis. Nam Judaei nunquam reciperent hominem non

Judaeum, a aut incircumcisum pro suo Messia. Imo etiam quia Judaei expectant Messium ex familia David, et tribu Juda; sine dubio Antichristus licet vere sit de tribu Dan . . . Deinde omnes Veteres clarissime docent Antichristum fore Judaeum" in *Opera Omnia*, II, Justinus Fèvre, ed., p. 33.

61. Aside from Mau, *op. cit.*, an excellent treatment of Luther on the Turks can be found in Mark U. Edwards, *Luther's Last Battles*, chap, 5, pp. 97–114.

62. The identification was first made by Alvarus of Cordoba in the eighth century.

63. John Headley, *Luther's View of Church History*, p. 246.

64. Martin Luther, "Against the Roman Papacy, an Institution of the Devil" in *Luther's Works*, 41, p. 339: "The Turk leads the world astray too, but he does not sit in the temple of God, nor does he use the names of Christ, St. Peter, or Holy Scripture; instead, he attacks Christendom from the outside and boasts of being its enemy. But this inward destroyer claims to be a friend, wants to be called father, and is twice as bad as the Turk."

65. Melanchthon's comparison of the papacy as Antichrist with the virtue of Christ appeared as the booklet of woodcut drawings by Lucas Cranach, for which Melanchthon furnished the texts. It was entitled *Passional Christi und Antichristi* and appeared in 1521 at Wittenberg. (John Headley, *op. cit.*, p. 247).

66. Daneau's work was titled *D. Aurelii Hipponensis episcopi liber de Heresibus ad Quodvultdeum, a quo eodem additae sunt haereses ab orbe condito ad constitutum Papismum et Mahuumetismum* . . . (Geneva, 1576).

67. John Calvin, *Commentaries on the Book of the Prophet Daniel*, Thomas Meyers, trans. (Grand Rapids, Mich.: Wm. B. Eerdmans Publishing Co., 1949), reprint ed., II, p. 26.

68. Martin Luther, *The Table Talk*, William Hazlitt, trans. and ed., (London: George Bell and Sons, 1902), p. 359: "My fear is, that the papists will unite with the Turks to exterminate us."

69. *L'Anti-Christ*, p. 101.

70. James repeated the Protestant argument that Gog in Hebrew means hid; the implication was always that the pope was a hypocrite in hiding within the church. See James's *A Fruitfull Meditation . . . of the vii–x Verses of the Second Chapter of the Revelation*, in *The Works of the Most High and Mightie Prince, James*, etc. (London: Robert Barker and John Bill, 1616, p. 75.

71. The king who died (from drowning) while retreating from Suleiman I was Louis II of Hungary. John Zapolya, governor of Transylvania, was given his crown by the Turks for refusing to join the struggle of Christians against Suleiman. These events occurred in 1526.

72. France signed treaties with the Turks in 1569, 1581, and 1604.

73. *L'Anti-Christ*, p. 88.

74. John Headley, *op. cit.*, pp. 247–48, speaks of a crisis in Luther's perception of the Turk coming in 1529 as a result of the Turkish assault on Vienna. During this time Luther adopted a prophetic tone of warning that the "Turk was the Germans' schoolmaster" and that they would have to learn to lead more upright lives. Even before this the conclusion that evangelicals could participate in an imperial (though not a religious) war for defense had been reached by the reformer. Mark Edwards (*op. cit.*, pp. 112–13) notes that Luther's view of warfare against the Turk changed as his perception of the reform movement itself changed from an earlier, ideological expression to a less spiritual, more political, and even more "prudent" and materialistic phase.

75. Rev. 14:9.

76. *L'Anti-Christ*, p. 309.
77. Ibid., p. 310.
78. Matthew Spinka, *Advocates of Reform from Wyclif to Erasmus* (London: SCM Press, 1953), p. 336.
79. John Calvin, *Commentaries on the Book of the Prophet Daniel*, Thomas Meyers, Trans. (Grand Rapids: Wm. B. Eerdmans Publishing Co., 1949), pp. 124 and 135.
80. *L'Anti-Christ*, p. 307.
81. Daniel, 8:11: "Yea, he magnified himself even to the prince of the host, and by him the daily sacrifice was taken away, and the place of his sanctuary was cast down."
82. *L'Anti-Christ*, pp. 117−21.
83. The reformers abandoned the medieval view of the imminent coming of Antichrist and tried to find instead the date of his coming. Luther held various opinions as to which pope first ushered in his reign before settling on Gregory VII late in his career. (See Headley, *op. cit.*, p. 196.) Bullinger, in *A Hundred Sermons upon the Apocalipse, etc.* (London: John Daye, 1573), chose the year 763 by adding 666 to 97, the year he believed *Revelation* was published, obtaining thereby a most uneventful year. For this reason, he settled on 756 instead, the year Pepin donated the Exarchate of Ravenna to the papacy, thereby extending the temporal jurisdiction of the popes. (Bullinger, sermon LXI, p. 198.) John Bale thought the number 666 would do, for it was then Pope Vitalian set the mass to music, an invidious practice according to reformed opinion. Leslie P. Fairfield, *John Bale, Mythmaker for the English Reformation* (Purdue: Purdue University Press, 1967), p. 95. Lambert Daneau believed the year 666 signaled the birth of the Antichrist, equating birth with coming.
84. Raemond's refusal to set a date for Antichrist's coming was motivated by his desire to defend the papacy.
85. *L'Anti-Christ*, p. 128. Irenaeus was apparently the first to attempt to name Antichrist by the use of numbers.
86. Bullinger, *A Hundred Sermons upon the Apocalipse, etc.* He insisted that the naming of the "beast" was easy for men of faith and industry.
87. For a discussion of Mornay's work and Raemond's criticism of it, see above, chap. 2.
88. *L'Anti-Christ*, p. 132.
89. Ibid., pp. 133−134.
90. The point is made by Alan Boase in *The Fortunes of Montaigne* (London: Methuen & Co. Ltd., 1935), pp. 32−34.
91. See Claude-Gilbert Dubois, *La Conception de l'histoire en France au XVIe siècle* (Paris: A. G. Nizet, 1977), pp. 517, 549. Dubois is impressed by their rational procedures, but see Paul de Felice, *Lambert Daneau* (Geneva, 1882; reissued by Slatkine Reprints, 1971), p. 171. Felice noted that "Daneau partageait, au sujet de l'Antichrist ... les idées de son temps." Needless to say, those were not primarily rational where Antichrist was concerned. On Vignier, see Bernard Dompnier, "L'Histoire religieuse chez les controversistes réformés du début du XVIIe siècle" in Philippe Joutard, *Historiographie de la Réforme* (Paris: Delachaux & Niestle S.A., 1977), pp. 19−20, who, far from characterizing Vignier's *Le Theâtre de L'Antichrist* (1610) rational, finds it "peu coherent" and irrational.
92. François Laplanche, *L'Écriture, le sacré, et L'histoire; érudits et politiques*

protestants devant la Bible en France au XVIIe siècle (Amsterdam: APA-Holland University Press, 1986), p. 166, notes that "Henri IV fit interdire l'impression du nouvel article de foi." He gives an excellent recapitulation of the Antichrist controversy in France during the seventcenth century (pp. 163–77).

93. John Quick, *Synodicon in Gallia Reformata: Or, the Acts, Decisions, Decrees, and Canons of Those Famous National Councils of the Reformed Churches in France* (London, 1692) I, p. 227.

94. William Martin, "Waiting for the End," *The Atlantic Monthly*, vol. 249, no. 6 (June 1982): 31–37.

Chapter 6. Luther and Lutheranism

1. Raemond, *L'Histoire, etc.*, p. 394.
2. Ibid.
3. Ibid., "Voeu de l'Auther" (unpaged preface).
4. See Donald R. Kelley, *The Beginning of Ideology Consciousness and Society in the French Reformation* (Cambridge, Cambridge University Press 1981), p. 5. He observes that ideology is historical, not sociological or philosophical and a dynamic force that can either change or maintain the status quo. Counter-Reformation Catholicism was ideological in this sense. Raemond used it to challenge the Protestant view of religious history and to undermine the status quo of the toleratïon guaranteed by the Edict of Nantes.
5. The *Centuries* have often been viewed as Protestant polemic even if written from documentary sources on lines prescribed by earlier Renaissance historians. See A. G. Dickens and John Tonkin, *The Reformation in Historical Thought* (Cambridge, Mass.: Harvard University Press, 1985), who note that the work was "tainted by propagandist aims"; not free of "tiresome calumnies" (i.e., the Pope Joan story); and altogether a "backward-looking survey" (pp. 28–29). However, Simon L. Verheus, *Zeugnis Und Gericht*, (Nieuwkoop, B. De Graaf 1971) finds merit in the fact that the Centuriators put Christ and his doctrine at the center of the historical process (p. 33). Joachim Massner, *Kirchliche Überlieferung und Autorität im Flaciuskreis* (Berlin, Lutherisches Verlaghaus, 1964) p. 33 makes a useful distinction between Flacius and Catholic historians, finding that the former did not reject tradition per se, but only such traditions as could not be demonstrated to be scriptural.
6. On Sleidan, see text below and notes 27 and 28.
7. Raemond, *L'Histoire, etc.*, pp. 871–72. Raemond's was an elitist point of view which associated the lower classes with unwanted social disturbance.
8. *Ibid.*, p. 23. Raemond rehearsed the areas of the world where Catholicism had advanced at the expense of the idolators: "... la mission de nos Prestres aux mondes nouveaux, a esté l'accroissement de la grandeur du nom Chrestien, qui se doit estendre jusques aux derniers bouts de la terre, avant qu'arrive le dernier jour qui doit clorre le monde: Ainsi en toutes les oeuvres de Dieu, il faut remarquer les pas de sa sagesse."
9. Ibid., p. 20.
10. For the political background of the Huguenot decline, see Nancy Lyman Roelker, "Family, Faith, and Fortuna: The Chatillon Brothers in the French

Reformation," chap. 9 of *Leaders of the Reformation*, Richard L. DeMolen, ed. (London, Susquehanna University Press 1984).

11. The last page (p. 1056) of the history makes it clear that Raemond hoped "heresy" would be eliminated at some point in the future: "Quelque autre qui vivra en un Siecle plus heureux apres moy, conduira l'Heresie entiere dans le sepulchre, pour aller faire sa descente aux Enfers."

12. See, for example, his treatment of the "prophetic" indulgence critic, Frère Thomas (Thomas Illyricus), whom he thought an exemplary cleric. (Also see, Larroque, *op. cit.*, p. 105ff, who notes that Joseph Scaliger thought Thomas was bent on obtaining a cardinal's hat by means of ill-gotten monies (Raemond, *L'Histoire, etc.*, pp. 48–49); as well as his portrait (ibid., pp. 178–87) of Philip Melanchthon, as a sweet-souled, neurotic who remained uncertain about major doctrinal issues; his admiration of Guillaume Postel (ibid., pp. 227–28; p. 94) defended against charges that he was a necromancer or an anti-Trinitarian; his inclusion of the letter sent him in 1599 by Pope Clement VIII, permitting him to read banned books for research purposes, and after it his defense against the possible charge that he included it out of sheer vanity—he claimed his innocence was his best defense (ibid., pp. 400–3); his tribute to Père Edmond Augier, a Jesuit priest often described as the instigator of the St. Bartholomew massacres in Bordeaux, (1572)—Raemond hailed him as a great theologian and philosopher (ibid., p. 531–32); the importance of psalm-singing in the spread of Calvinism in France (ibid., pp. 1031–44); his occasional chats with court officials about public affairs—with the "Chevalier de Lansac" (Catherine De Medicis's ambassador to the Council of Trent) concerning Lansac's reception in Geneva by Theodore de Bèze (ibid., p. 946); his talk with the de Noailles brothers (François and Gilles, former ambassadors to the Porte) concerning the lack of religious liberty in Christian lands like France (ibid., p. 462), etc.

13. Raemond, *L'Histoire, etc.*, p. 28, used an astrological chart prepared by a famous astrologer ("Ionctin") who mistakenly used 22 October 1483, for Luther's birthdate instead of November 10. The year 1483 has traditionally been given for the reformer's birth year. Recently, the reexamination of a manuscript outline of the major events of Luther's life, now viewed as certainly penned and signed by the reformer, challenges the year 1483 and points to 1484 as the correct birth year. See Reinhart Staats, "Luther's Geburtsjahr und Das Geburtsjahr der Evangelischen Kirche 1519," in *Bibliothek und Wissenschaft*, 18 (1984), pp. 61ff.

14. This material came from Cochlaeus's *Commentaria, etc.*

15. This was also one of Cochlaeus's themes.

16. Raemond, *L'Histoire, etc.*, pp. 31–32.

17. Ibid., pp. 101–2. "Comme un bon Machiaveliste," Luther knew his reform would be accepted more readily if he preserved the appearance of catholicity— hence the ceremonies, sumptuous churches, images, and exterior devotions of Rome were retained.

18. That the Reformation drew upon ancient and condemned ideas was a standard of Catholic controversy.

19. Raemond, *L'Histoire, etc.*, p. 101, said that Luther read Wycliffe and Hus and drew from them the largest part of his ideas. The link between Hus and Luther is reviewed by Jaroslav Pelikan, *Obedient Rebels* (New York: Harper & Row Publishers, 1964), chap. 7, who finds that from early childhood on, it is likely Luther learned to sympathize with the Hussites. Cultural exposure to Hussite ideas may also have been strengthened by experiences within his Augustinian order. Both Pelikan and A. G. Dickens, *The German Nation and*

Martin Luther (New York: Harper & Row Publishers, 1974), p. 94, agree that the Hus-Luther relationship was forced on Luther ultimately by Dr. Eck at Leipzig. Raemond's statement suggests a more deliberate process of absorption on Luther's part, and makes no mention of the pressure exerted by Eck. Dickens finds "little direct knowledge" of Wycliffe by Luther, who lacked ready access to his works, while "Luther's revolt of 1517–18 was in no way inspired by the example of Hus." (p. 94).

20. The Vaudois position had been explored by Cochlaeus, who drew his information from a very old source.

21. Raemond, *L'Histoire, etc.*, p. 102. These two ideas Raemond saw reflected in Luther's concept of the invisible church. In his *Sermon on the Power of Excommunication* (1518) the reformer made a distinction between the internal church, which one entered by divine call, and the external, regulated by men. He would have rejected the Donatist concept that only the sinless are in the church, since for him the communion of faithful was not dependent on human decision. Raemond was correct, however, in seeing a similarity between the Donatists' spiritual emphasis and Luther's notion of an invisible church. See Wilhelm Pauck, *The Heritage of the Reformation* (Oxford, 1950), pp. 36–38.

22. Raemond, *L'Histoire, etc.*, p. 103. Luther began to advocate the practice in 1519 on the grounds that the giving of both bread and wine to the laity was initiated by Christ. Three years later, to offset the radicalism of Andreas Karlstadt, who said that giving communion in one kind only was sinful, Luther recommended patience and the willingness to continue with the bread only (as in the Roman church) in order to avoid giving offence.

23. *Catalogus testium veritatis* was the Latin for these lists.

24. None of the men on this list had actually been declared to be heretics.

25. Raemond, *L'Histoire, etc.*, p. 46. He said that Brother Thomas, a well-known friar in southwestern France, also protested the excessive claims made for indulgences, but from within the church.

26. Ibid., p. 47.

27. Ibid., p. 48. A. G. Dickens, "Johannes Sleidan and Reformation History," in *Reformation Conformity and Dissent* (London: Epworth Press, 1977), pp. 17–43, says that despite Sleidan's oft-repeated statements of impartiality, "His selections and rejections create a strongly anti-papal and anti-prelatical atmosphere throughout the book" (p. 32). In fact, Dr. Eck was widely regarded the victor of the debates.

28. Raemond, *L'Histoire, etc.*, p. 55, included what he thought was Luther's abjuration in his own text since, he said, Sleidan had purposely left it out of his: "le frère Martin Luther de l'Ordre de S. Augustin, proteste que je revere & suy la sainte Eglise Romaine, en tous mes faits & mes dits, presens, passez & avenir: que s'il m'est eschappé & si j'ay dit quelque chose contraire, je veux et suplie estre reputé pour non dit."

29. Raemond had chosen a passage (see n.28 above), registered before a notary and witnesses, of a letter Luther sent to Leo X on 16 October 1518, when Cajetan was in the process of examining him for his statements concerning indulgences. In the letter, Luther said the doctrine of indulgences was unclear, that he subjected his opinions to the church, and to those more instructed than he, especially to Leo himself. He added, however (and Raemond did not mention), that he had not recanted because Cajetan had not been able to point out where he erred. See Erwin Iserloh, Joseph Glazik, and Hubert Jedin, *Reformation and Counter Reformation*, V, *History of the Church*, Hubert Jedin and John Dolan

(New York: The Seabury Press, 1980), Part One, "The Protestant Reformation," (Iserloh) p. 58.

30. *Historia vom Ursprung, auff-und abnemmen der Ketzereyen und was sie seyter Anno 1500 . . . in Teutschland, Boheim, Ungern, Sibenburgen, Poln, Dennemarcken, Schweden, Norwegen, Engellandt, Frankreich, für wunderbarleche Veranderungen . . . verursacht Acht Teil begreiffendt. Anfangs durch Herrn Florimondum de Remond*, (München, 1614). This translation was by Gilles Aubertin.

31. The extensive treatment given by Raemond to this radical movement in Germany and Switzerland in Book II of *L'Histoire, etc.* is the subject of an unpublished dissertation by Martin Busch entitled *Florimond de Raemond et L'Anabaptisme*, University of Strasbourg, 1980–1981. Busch concludes that Raemond's analysis is still supported by recent scholarship into Anabaptism, especially with regard to its link with the early views of Zwingli; somewhat less so for the Lutheran link, although even here, the link is defended—less through the Müntzer-Luther connection than through the Carlstadt-Luther one (*pace* Karl Holl). (Busch, pp. 231–32.)

32. Raemond, *L'Histoire, etc.*, p. 127, remarked on Zwingli's irresolution and traced Balthasar Hübmaier's rejection of pedobaptism to his earlier views. John Christian Wenger, *Even Unto Death: The Heroic Witness of the Sixteenth-Century Anabaptists* (Richmond, Va., John Knox Press 1961) does the same for Conrad Grebel (p. 18). That Zwingli's position was moderate is the view of Robert C. Walton, *Zwingli's Theocracy* (Toronto, University of Toronto Press 1967), p. 171. G. R. Potter, *Zwingli* (Cambridge, Cambridge University Press 1976), p. 191, records the difficulty Zwingli had finding biblical precedent for the practice, and his resort to analogy (circumcision), negative arguments from silence, and incidental remarks in Scripture. He also explains very cogently that Zwingli's ultimate acceptance of infant baptism was dictated by the political requirements of the Swiss reformation as well as by the religious.

33. Raemond, *L'Histoire, etc.*, pp. 125–26, insisted that this statement was inspired by Luther's treatise on the *Freedom of a Christian* (1520) in which Luther distinguished between faith and works and quoted Christ (Mark 16:16): "He who believes and is baptised will be saved; but he who does not believe will be condemned." The Catholics pursued a logical opposition between faith and reason, forgetting that Scripture was more important a guide for Luther than logic. Not even Anabaptists dispensed with baptism, and Luther persisted to retain it as a sacrament, and to insist that the promise (faith) instilled at baptism lasted a lifetime. See "The Babylonian captivity of the Church," translated by A. T. W. Steinhauser and revised by Frederick C. Ahrens and Abdel Ross Wentz, in *Luther's Works, Word and Sacrament II*, Vol. 36 (Philadelphia: Muhlenberg Press, 1959), p. 3–126.

34. Robert C. Walton, *op. cit.*, p. 208, notes that Zwingli's break with such radicals as Conrad Grebel and his friends was dictated by a realistic assessment of the times, i.e., his realization that the church needed support from the magistrates to survive.

35. See Harry Loewen, *Luther and the Radicals* (Waterloo, Ont.: Wilfrid Laurier University, 1974), p. 73, who shows that after a period of relative patience, Luther took a firm stand against Anabaptists and began to associate the more radical revolutionary figures of Carlstadt and Müntzer with the former group.

36. The precise relationship between major reformers and the Anabaptists is a much debated question. Raemond's view was that the major reformers' doctrine took on different flavors as it flowed from them to the radicals. (*L'Histoire, etc.*,

p. 124.) Ernst Troeltsch, *The Social Teaching of the Christian Churches* (London, Geo. Allen & Unwin, Ltd., 1931), II, pp. 694–99, found that "the great reformers," especially Luther, had indeed given rise to Anabaptist ideals (the "sect-idea"), but subsequently abandoned earlier individualistic idealism. He never ruled out the probable influence of late medieval heresies (Waldensians) on Anabaptists, and noted as well that humanism and biblicism were important influences on the radicals. Troeltsch's view is more or less reflected in Émile G. Léonard's *Histoire Générale du Protestantisme* (Paris, Presses Universitaires de France, 1961), I, p. 89, who notes that Anabaptism did have much in common with early Lutheranism, but that Luther went on to develop distinct views on man, sacraments, the state, and society. Such views as Troeltsch's and Léonard's are not very satisfying because they suggest more differences between the radicals and the major reformers than similarities or constants. Some interesting observations on the nature of the difficulties, which persist in the attempt to link the reformers to the radicals, are made by John Oyer, "The Influence of Jacob Strauss on the Anabaptists," in Marc Lienhard, ed., *The Origins and Characteristics of Anabaptism* (The Hague, Nijhoff, 1977), pp. 62–82. Oyer warns against the distortion that results from trying to push too exclusively the derivation of Anabaptism (itself not a monolithic movement) from a "text-only" analysis. He argues for a greater attention being paid to the context of the sixteenth-century "socio-religious world," even if this means having to deal with relationships between men and movements, not always easily demonstrated.

37. Raemond, *L'Histoire, etc.*, "Les Anabaptistes ne veulent autre livre que la Bible sacrée, tout-fut jetté au feu à leur entree. Fut-ce pas des premieres opinions de Luther, écrivant l'an 1520 à la Noblesse d'Alemagne? qu'il falloit bannir des Universitez les Aristotes & Platon, etc." p. 126.

38. Ibid., p. 127.

39 Martin Luther, *Luther's Works*, vol. 36, p. 59.

40. It was the sacramental nature of baptism which Catholics felt was threatened by the suggestion that faith was necessary before the baptism could be effective.

41. See Loewen, *op. cit.*, pp. 84–85, who points out that in combatting the Anabaptist position, Luther was driven increasingly to defend the sacramental nature of baptism, stating (1535) that it had three requirements for a sacrament— an external element, (water), the Word of God, and the command of Christ. Thus, whether or not faith was present, the rite would still be valid.

42. The word was applied by Luther to all who believed that sacraments have only a symbolic significance, i.e., that they do not convey the corporeal presence of Christ. He applied it first to Zwinglians.

43. Raemond, *L'Histoire, etc.*, p. 178, explained that the Confessionistes who subscribed to Melanchthon's Augsburg Confession, were Luther's work because "Philippe" was "le fidele Achate" of Luther. (Achates was a friend of Aeneas; his fidelity was so exemplary that *Fidus Achates* became a proverb.)

44. See Martin Busch, *op. cit.*, pp. 233–34. Busch notes that Raemond's position on Thomas Müntzer as a principal promoter of Anabaptism is highly debatable, though even here he says great care must be exercised, since Müntzer was involved with the movement. On the other hand, he believes that Raemond's vision that narrow ties existed between the major reformers (Luther, Zwingli) and Anabaptism "aux nivaux de ses origines et de ses caractéristiques constamment démontré par De Raemond, bien que par motivation polémique, reste fort plausible." Busch cites with approval the work of John Yoder, who pleads for an exploration of Anabaptist origins, which is connected to the "official" reformers.

See John H. Yoder, "Introduction," *The Origins and Characteristics of Anabaptism*, p. 8. Busch and Yoder support the approach used by Raemond and the need to trace the streams (of radical Anabaptism) back to their source.

45. Raemond, *L'Histoire, etc.*, pp. 396–97.
46. Ibid., p. 152. "father of all the Sacramentarians of our time" was his judgment against Karlstadt.
47. Ibid., pp. 154–55.
48. See George Huntston Williams, *The Radical Reformation* (Philadelphia, The Westminster Press 1962), pp. 42–43, who stresses the "virtual agreement" between Luther and Carlstadt on Eucharistic theology up until their split in 1523. Likewise noting the similarities between Carlstadt's theology and Luther's is Ronald J. Sider, "Karlstadt and Luther's Doctorate," in *Journal of Theological Studies* 22 (1971), pp. 168–69. See also his book *Andreas Bodenstein Von Karlstadt: The Development of His Thought 1517–1525* (Leiden, E. J. Brill 1974) in which he states that Carlstadt's thought was shaped by "the interplay of Augustinian, Lutheran, and mystical theological concepts" (p. 6). Differences that set Carlstadt apart from Luther are stressed by Calvin A. Pater, *Karlstadt as the Father of the Baptist Movements: The Emergence of Lay Protestantism* (Toronto: University of Toronto Press, 1984), who says that Carlstadt's concepts of sacraments "devolved into signs" (p. 64), without details as to what it devolved from. It is the prior relationship that concerned Raemond, since it was that which he hoped to establish as evidence for his major thesis, i.e., that Luther inspired the Spiritualists just as he had the Anabaptists and Sacramentarians. Like Pater, Mark Lienhard, *Martin Luther Un Temps, Une Vie, Un Message* (Paris: Le Centurion, 1983), stresses the cleavage between the two men without trying to explain why it occurred so late (1524–1526) in their relationship.
49. Williams, *op. cit.*, p. 109.
50. Raemond, *L'Histoire, etc.*, p. 243.
51. See Paul Maier, *Caspar Schwenckfeld on the Person and Work of Christ* (Assen, Royal Van Gorcum Ltd. 1959), pp. 18–19 and n.4. Raemond was well advised not to take Luther's word for Schwenckfeld's Zwinglian interpretation of the Lord's Supper. Like Maier, Raemond thought him a Spiritualist. See also R. Emmet McLaughlin, *Caspar Schwenckfeld Reluctant Radical* (New Haven, Yale University Press, 1986), who emphasizes the christological impulse (p. 86) in Schwenckfeld's interpretation of the Eucharist, a view that accords well with the Spiritualist interpretation of Schwenckfeld held by Raemond.
52. Raemond, *L'Histoire, etc.*, p. 244.
53. Ibid., p. 591.
54. Martin Luther, *Luther's Works, The Christian in Society*, Vol. 45, p. 18, *The Estate of Marriage* (1522).
55. Raemond, *L'Histoire, etc.*, p. 302.
56. Luther, *The Estate of Marriage*, p. 18.
57. Raemond, *L'Histoire, etc.*, p. 299.
58. Ibid., p. 304. Raemond feared that divorce would mushroom and social stability perish. He particularly disliked the fact that Luther permitted divorced partners (even the adulterous one) to remarry, he reported.
59. Martin Luther, *The Estate of Marriage*, p. 30, said that while Christ allowed the injured party (nonadulterous spouse) to re-marry after divorce, he (Luther) would permit the guilty to do so as well, provided he took himself "to a far country." He said he did this because the government was lax in punishing adulterers, and because he felt their remarriage would discourage them from a worse evil—fornication. (Ibid., pp. 32–33).

60. The wide basis was provided by Luther's fourth ground for divorce (after impotence, adultery, sexual incompatibility); "where husband and wife cannot get along together for some reason other than the Matter of the conjugal duty" (*The Estate of Marriage*, p. 34). In such cases, neither spouse was to be permitted remarriage.

61. Ibid., pp. 35ff.

62. Raemond, *L'Histoire, etc.*, pp. 304–5. He called the vow of chastity "le plus noble de tous," citing Saints Augustine, Ambrose, and Gregory for support.

63. Ibid., pp. 302–4. Raemond called Luther many names reflecting the incontinence that preoccupied our author. Among these were "ce bon père Luther Epicure"; "S. Père de la chasteté" (wryly); and "l'Evangile de la Liberté au monde."

64. Ibid., p. 303. Raemond quoted Luther's use of the proverb (Catholics did not refer to it as a proverb, however) in Latin and translated it: *Si non vult uxor, veniat ancilla* — "Si la femme ne veut, vienne la chambrière." When a Lutheran apologist sought to exculpate Luther by suggesting that the verbs were more approximately rendered in different tense: *Si non velit uxor, ancillam venire debere ac oportere*, Frederick Staphylus, a Catholic university (Ingolstadt) inspector, denied that any alternate rendering could change the immoral intention of the writer. Raemond sided with Staphylus.

65. Martin Luther, *The Estate of Marriage*, pp. 18–19.

66. Ibid., pp. 46–47.

67. Raemond, *L'Histoire, etc.*, p. 301.

68. Ibid., p. 305.

69. Martin Luther, *The Estate of Marriage*, p. 49.

70. Raemond, *L'Histoire, etc.*, pp. 584–85.

71. Raemond was sensible of the sacramentalist aspects of Luther's system, but it was the nonsacramental (and nonauthoritarian) aspects that he sensed formed the bond between Luther and the rest of Protestantism.

72. "Provisional Spiritualist" was a term used by George Huntston Williams, *op. cit.*, p. 43. The comparison of Luther to the fanatics (i.e., the radicals) and also to Zwingli and to Erasmus, in whom spiritualism was also prominent, was made by Erwin Iserloh, *op. cit.*, p. 189.

73. Joseph Lortz, *The Reformation a Problem for Today* (Westminster: The Newman Press, 1964), p. 1061. Lortz's book *The Reformation in Germany* (New York, 1968), 1st ed., 1939, pioneered a more sympathetic understanding by Catholics of Luther the man, and to a somewhat lesser degree, of Luther the theologian. Lortz admitted later that he had failed to grasp Luther's significance as a theologian and conceded that his theology was closer to Thomas Aquinas's than one might think. He insisted also that Luther's doctrine of justification does not separate Catholics from Protestants. See Jared Wicks, ed., *Catholic Scholars Dialogue with Luther* (Chicago, Loyola University Press 1970), p. 32. Peter Manns, Lortz's successor at the Institut für Europäische Geschichte in Mainz, has proceeded from Lortz's position to investigate the theological problems involved. He concludes that Luther was for Catholics as well as Protestants a "Father in the Faith." In his "Luther und die Heiligen" in Remigius Bäumer, ed., *Reformatio Ecclesiae, Beiträge zu kirchlichen Reformbemühungen von der alten Kirche bis zur Neuzeit. Festgabe für Erwin Iserloh* (Paderborn: Schöningh, 1980), pp. 535–80, Manns attempts to de-polemicize Luther's pronouncements on faith as opposed to works, and suggests that Luther did accord more of a place to works and charity than polemical considerations made it then possible to state. A deep understanding of and agreement with Luther is apparent in Otto H. Pesch's "Die Theologie

der Rechtfertigung bei Martin Luther und Thomas von Aquin. Versuch eines systematisch-theologischen Dialogs," in *Walberger Studien, Theol. Reihe*, IV (Mainz: Matthias-Grünewald-Verlag, 1967). A recent survey of these matters and others is Gottfried Maron, *Das Katholische Lutherbild der Gegenwart* (Göttingen: Vanen Hoeck and Ruprecht, 1982).

74. Raemond, *L'Histoire, etc.*, p. 77.
75. Ibid., pp. 584–85.

Chapter 7. Calvin and Calvinism

1. Raemond, *L'Histoire, etc.*, p. 838, took the Rhine to task for having failed to keep reform from France. To Strasbourg (Argentine) he addressed this reproach: "Ce fut dans ton Argentine, qu'ils appelloient la nouvelle Jerusalem, ... ou l'heresie a plusieurs testes dressa son Arsenal & recuillit une partie de ses forces pour la venir assaillir." For Strasbourg's importance as a publishing center (arsenal) for pamphlets destined for sale in France, see W. G. Moore, *La Réforme Allemande et la littérature Française* (Strasbourg: Publications de la Faculté des Lettres de l'Université de Strasbourg. 1930), p. 101; here Moore cites Raemond's passage for support.

2. Hubert Méthivier, *L'Ancien régime en France* (Paris: Presses Universitaires de France, 1981), pp. 90–91.

3. Lefèvre d'Étaples (1460–1536) was a humanist whose first books concerned philosophy and mathematics. In 1508 he accepted the patronage of his former pupil, Guillaume Briçonnet, who housed him in his abbey of Saint-Germain-des-Prés. Called by Briçonnet to Meaux, Lefèvre worked on his translation of the New Testament and was a leader of the Meaux Circle. He spent his last years at Marguerite's court at Nérac. See De La Tour, Pierre Imbart, *Les Origines de la Réforme*. vol. 2, (Paris: Librairie Hachette et cie, 1944) 2d. ed., pp. 488–523, and vol. 3 (Paris, 1914), pp. 109–153 and 288–303. Also, Guy Bedouelle, *Lefèvre D'Étaples et l'intelligence des Écritures* (Geneva: Librairie Droz, 1976).

4. Farel (1489–1565) was also one of Lefèvre's students. More iconoclastic than many of his Meaux peers, Farel fled France (1523) for Switzerland where he eventually joined forces with Calvin. See Edouard Urech, *Guillaume Farel* (La Chaux-de-Fonds: Éditions G. Saint-Clair, 1965).

5. Arande was Marguerite of Navarre's almoner and later, Bishop of Saint-Paul-des-Trois-Chateaux in Dauphiné.

6. Roussel (1480–1555) began his collaboration with Lefèvre in 1501. His earliest works were a commentary on Boethius's *Arithmetic* (1521) and a translation of Aristotle's *Magna Moralia* (1522). Also a refugee (1525) at Strasbourg, Roussel returned to France in 1526 and ever after served Queen Marguerite. He was her almoner and received the bishopric of Oléron due to her patronage. He was murdered while preaching in his own pulpit by a Catholic fanatic. See Charles Schmidt, *Gérard Roussel, prédicateur de la Reine Marguerite de Navarre* (Strasbourg: A. Cherbulier et cie, 1845).

7. Raemond, *L'Histoire, etc.*, p. 847.

8. Ibid., pp. 845–56. Guillaume Briçonnet (1470–1534) entered upon a clerical career in 1507, having first served as a royal financial officer. A pluralist (like his two brothers), he enjoyed the bishoprics of Lodève and of Meaux and the abbey of Saint-Germain des-Prés in Paris. A parish reformer, he paid for parish preachers for his diocese out of his own (ample) resources. Briçonnet, like his mentor

Lefèvre, was imbued with a mystical piety and a deep devotion to the Virgin, which, according to L. Cristiani, *L'Eglise à l'époque du Concile de Trente* (Paris, Bloud Gay, 1948), sharply distinguished him and other followers of Lefèvre from the nascent Protestantism of their milieu. (Christiani, p. 365.)

9. Raemond, *L'Histoire, etc.*, pp. 846−47.
10. Ibid., pp. 850−51.
11. Samuel Mours, *Le Protestantisme en France au XVIe Siècle*, (Paris: Librairie Protestante, 1959), p. 78, says that Guyenne's Agenais region was the first won for reform as a direct result of proximity to Marguerite's evangelical preachers in Nérac. Raemond (*L'Histoire, etc.*, p. 851) lamented that Guyenne would also be the last region to give up "heresy," for its neighbor, Béarn, was only with great difficulty being re-catholicized while he was writing his history.
12. Calvin wrote to Roussel from Ferrara (1536) berating him for having accepted a bishopric that made, he pointed out acerbically, following the Evangile impossible. The letter is quoted by Schmidt, *op. cit.*, pp. 114−17.
13. Schmidt, *op. cit.*, p. 160, concluded that Roussel's doctrine was principally Protestant and Calvinist, with little if anything at all identifiable as Catholic. Schmidt referred to Raemond's interview with the old man from Clairac (present at Roussel's deathbed), who claimed Roussel reproached himself at the end for his cowardly retention of the mass. Schmidt, like Calvin, remarked that Roussel regarded the Mass as idolatrous. The interview is related by Raemond, *L'Histoire, etc.*, p. 851.
14. Raemond, *L'Histoire, etc.*, p. 856, said that he had spoken with Gilles Caillau, "bon religieux Cordelier," who had given the last rites of the Roman church to Queen Marguerite.
15. See J. H. Merle D'Aubigné, *History of the Great Reformation* (New York, Robert Carter 1843), III, pp. 356−57, in which Lefèvre is described sometime before 1512 as turning from conventional, Roman Catholic piety to the word of God: "a new era opened in France, and the Reformation commenced its course." See also Émile Doumergue, *Jean Calvin Les hommes et les choses de son temps* (Lausanne, Georges Bridel et cie. 1899), I, p. 101. Here, the support given Lefèvre for his translation and publication of the *New Testament* by the French court is "proof" that "la Réforme française a été nationale et biblique."
16. Two early twentieth-century examples: (1) Pierre Imbart De La Tour, *Les Origines de la Reforme* (Paris, Librairie Hachette et cie, 1914), III, p. 428, who observed that Lefèvre's approach did not lead to schism and that Luther's acts preceded Lefèvre's and surpassed them; and (2) Augustin Renaudet, *Pré-Réforme et humanisme à Paris* (Paris, Librairie D'Argences 1953, 1st ed., 1916), p. xiii. Here the author noted that native elements of French reform were not wholly lost, although Lutheran ones took precedence. (What remained was Fabrisian sensitivity and Erasmian intelligence according to this source.) A provocative analysis by Robert Mandrou, "Pourquoi se réformer?" in *Histoire des Protestants en France* (Toulouse, Edward Privat 1977), suggests three alternatives to Luther's approach were available on the eve of Reformation. The best essay on the problem of origins remains Lucien Febvre's "Une Question mal posée les origines de la Réforme Française et le problème général des causes de la Réforme" (1929), reprinted in *Au Coeur religieux du XVIe siècle* (Paris, Sevpen 1957), pp. 3−70.
17. The recognition of a need for a wider diffusion of a vulgarized Bible was already apparent in France during the last third of the fifteenth century. Although the greatest number of Bibles between 1475 and 1517 were printed in Latin, the

first French edition of the Bible was published in 1487, the work of Charles VIII's confessor, Jean de Rély, a friend of Lefèvre. (See Pierre Imbart De La Tour, *op. cit.*, II, pp. 544–46.) De La Tour says the Bible remained primarily the book of the Latin-reading minority, rather than of the artisan or bourgeois classes into the sixteenth century, and that France was slower by far than Germany in its effort to make the Bible readily available to the lower classes.

18. Raemond, *L'Histoire* etc., p. 874, ignored the fact that Lefèvre's edition of the New Testament (1523) and of the whole Bible (1534) preceded the work of Olivétan, who revised Lefèvre's translation and published it, 1536–1539. (See Émile Doumergue, *op. cit.*, pp. 99–101.) If Raemond had mentioned Lefèvre's work, and pointed out that it was in many respects a revision of Rély's earlier effort, his foreign influence theme would have suffered.

19. Raemond, *L'Histoire, etc.*, pp. 879–80.

20. Émile Doumergue, *op. cit.*, I, p. 451, n.1 noted: "On sait que Fl. de Raemond ne se pique pas d'une minutieuse exactitude chronologique." One might add, neither did Calvin. In fact, chronological exactitude had not become the norm in sixteenth-century scholarship as it did in subsequent generations.

21. Raemond, *L'Histoire, etc.*, p. 879.

22. Doumergue, *op. cit.*, I, p. 433 says Reginaldus was one of a group of Jesuits who helped spread Bolsec's distortions of Calvin.

23. Cochlaeus's biography of Luther and Bolsec's of Calvin were the two most infamous biographies written in the sixteenth century. Raemond used both, along with more respectable sources.

24. Pontien Polman, *L'Élément historique*, p. 132.

25. Bèze wrote two biographies of Calvin. The first, in French, was a preface to Calvin's *Joshua* (1564). The following year, his name appeared on another biography, also prefaced to *Joshua*. This was in reality the work of Nicholas Colladon. Bèze's second life of Calvin appeared in Latin as *Joannis Calvini Vita*, and was included in his edition of Calvin's letters, *Calvini Epistolae et Responsa* (1575).

26. Bèze contributed to and helped to prepare the *Histoire ecclésiastique des églises réformées* (1580) for press.

27. Bèze and Colladon claimed that Olivétan began to initiate his cousin into the "pure religion" and to dissuade him from "papal superstitions." Upholders of this idea included Abel Lefranc, *La Jeunesse de Calvin* (Paris, Librairie Fischbacher 1888), p. 39; the editor of Calvin's correspondence, A. L. Herminjard; Émile Doumergue, *op. cit.*, pp. 116–17; T. H. L. Parker, *John Calvin: A Biography* (London, J. M. Dent & Sons Ltd. 1975), p. 18. These authors assert different dates for the coming to fruition of this influence with a time span as wide as eight years. The major problem with such speculation is that no definite documentation exists to prove it.

28. Félix Bungener, *Calvin: Sa vie son oeuvre et ses écrits* (Paris: J. Cherbuliez, 1862), sagely noted (p. 34) that neither Olivétan's nor Wolmar's influence were crucial factors in Calvin's conversion because they merely added to his knowledge of, but not to the resolution of, his personal doubts about Catholicism. Similarly, François Wendel, *Calvin: The Origins and Development of His Religious Thought*, Philip Mairet, trans. (London: Collins, 1963), p. 20, claims that Olivétan "left no immediate traces" on Calvin, not ruling out efforts by the older cousin to convert the younger one to reform. The strongest disavowal of the significance of Olivétan's efforts is found in Alexandre Ganoczy, *Le Jeune Calvin: Genèse et évolution de sa vocation réformatrice* (Wiesbaden, Franz Steiner Verlag GMBH 1966), pp.

40–46, who sees Calvin's education at the orthodox College of Montaigue (1523–1527) as that of an obedient, respectful student ready to register his cousin's ideas, but not to adopt them.

29. A simple discussion of the documents (*Reply to Jacopo Sadoleto* [1539]; *Commentary on the Psalms* [1557]; and *Second Reply to Westphal* [1556], occurs in Williston Walker, *John Calvin The Organiser of Reformed Protestantism 1509–1564* (New York, 1969; Schocken Books, 1st ed., 1906), pp. 70ff. A sophisticated theological analysis of Calvin's conversion is in Ganoczy, *op. cit.*, pp. 287ff. In it, he analyses the phrase "subita conversio" on a plane he calls "theologicoprophetic" rather than simply "historical." He concludes that Calvin held a penitential notion of conversion, not the idea of rupture stressed by most authors. Ganoczy does not believe the Sadoleto reply fits the facts of Calvin's life (p. 294). More recently, Harro Höpfl, *The Christian Polity of John Calvin* (London, Cambridge University Press 1982), Appendix I, notes the striking difference between the description by Calvin of his conversion in the *Reply to Sadoleto* as opposed to that in the preface to *Psalms*, the former involving "protracted struggle" against Sorbonne philosophy and theology; the latter a sudden conversion by God's direct action on the "stubborn" and "superstitious" young Calvin. William J. Bouwsma, *John Calvin: A Sixteenth Century Portrait*, (New York Oxford University Press 1988), p. 10, follows the rejection of a sudden conversion in agreement with Ganoczy, and not with commentators who, like Raemond, have attempted to account for Calvin's use of the phrase "subita conversio."

30. Raemond, *L'Histoire, etc.*., p. 882, wrote that Wolmar had encouraged Calvin to jettison the study of law for theology, had opened up to him "quelques secrets" of Lutheranism, and (p. 883) had been the first to instill "le venin de l'heresie dans l'ame de ce jeune homme." Bouwsma, *op. cit.*, pp. 10–11, treats the so-called "conversion" as "only a shift and quickening of his interests," insists that these were not "incompatible with the evangelical humanism of a whole generation of students at Paris," and not specifically Protestant. Significantly, his only mention of Wolmar (p. 12) is to affirm that Calvin studied Greek with him and dedicated a commentary (on Second Corinthians) to him. Among historians who take Raemond's belief that Wolmar was the decisive person in Calvin's conversion was Émile Doumergue, *op. cit.*, who thought it inconceivable that Wolmar, using the New Testament as his Greek text, had made no commentaries of a Lutheran or evangelical sort on it. T. L. Parker, *op. cit.*, p. 18, and Wendel, *op. cit.*, p. 23, have echoed Doumergue, as have Höpfl, *op. cit.*, p. 286, n.47, and A. G. Dickens and John Tonkin, *The Reformation in Historical Thought* (Cambridge, Mass., Harvard University Press 1985), p. 95.

31. Some historians believe Calvin met Wolmar at Orléans, others, like Raemond himself, think they met at Bourges.

32. Lefranc (*op. cit.*, pp. 81–82) rejected the Wolmar influence with regard to religious initiation, but admitted that it was of literary import and helped him arrive at a later date at his conversion. Some injustice to Lefranc's position is done by Ganoczy (*op. cit.*, pp. 49–50), who makes it appear that Lefranc did believe Wolmar caused Calvin to become a Lutheran. Ganoczy lists some historians who similarly reject the Wolmar influence. He notes that these authors simply refuse to go further than did Bèze in seeing Wolmar only as a Greek instructor, one who made no change in Calvin's religious perception. (Ganoczy, *op. cit.*, p. 50, n.212.)

33. See Williston Walker, *op. cit.*, pp. 79–80.
34. I have used the English translation provided in Williston Walker, *op. cit.*, pp. 71–72.
35. Calvin's words were: "I was so obstinately addicted to the superstitions of the papacy" (Walker, p. 72).
36. Calvin remarked with regard to his legal studies: "I yet devoted myself to them more indifferently" (Walker, p. 72).
37. Calvin made a point of stressing his love for quiet and tranquillity, "being by nature shy and timid" (Walker, p. 72).
38. Calvin noted his astonishment that "before a year passed, (but he doesn't say what year!), all those who had some desire for pure doctrine betook themselves to me in order to learn, although I myself had done little more than begin" (Walker, p. 72).
39. Ganoczy says (*op. cit.*, p. 55) that Calvin was studying "humanités classiques" in Paris.
40. Raemond, *L'Histoire, etc.*, p. 883: "Wolmar ne cessa de l'accourager par ses lettres, & toutefois lors que Calvin parle de sa vocation, il n'en dit mot; Dieu, dit-il, par sa providence secrete, me fit tourner d'austre costé."
41. Raemond claimed that the "encouragement" sent by Wolmar to Calvin for the "grandeur of his enterprise" (*L'Histoire, etc.*, p. 883) came in the form of letters written after Wolmar had gone back to Germany, which he did in 1535. That was after Calvin had composed the *Institutes*, and after he had penned his famous apologetic letter to Francis I (August 1535), which formed the *Dedication* to the first (1536) edition. Since many historians consider the *Institutes* to have proven Calvin's conversion, the conclusion that Raemond was manipulative is really inescapable. The grand enterprise was not his conversion.
42. Varying widely, the results of such efforts include Jacques Pannier, *Recherches sur l'évolution de Calvin* (Strasbourg: Istra, 1924), p. 43, who thought there was a slow breaking away and that the "subita conversio" was either a "rapid progression" or "an involontary exagerration" on Calvin's part; John Viénot, *Histoire de la réforme Française* (Paris: Librairie Fischbacher, 1926), mentioned "the slow evolution under the pressure of thought and facts" and the reluctance of a timid Calvin to make a definite break with Rome (see pp. 189–90); John T. McNeill, *The History and Character of Calvinism* (New York: Oxford University Press, 1954), pp. 114–15, finds Calvin's conversion was a "cumulative pressure within his soul," which followed his exposure to different reform and orthodox controversies. He thinks that the interview with Lefèvre in Nérac (1534) may have produced Calvin's break with Rome. Jean Rilliet, *Calvin* (Paris Arthème Fayard, 1963), p. 31, finds that conversion came at the end of a long resistance, but does not dwell on the problem of how quick conversion was; Ganoczy, *op. cit.*, p. 363, sees it as something consistent with the reformer's never having abandoned Catholicism at all, and is unusual in that he does not attempt to fit the documents he feels are autobiographical into the usual historical-chronological format. (See pp. 300–301.) A very sudden conversion is seen by Pierre Couthial, "The Golden Age of Calvinism in France; 1533–1633," in W. Stanford Reid, ed., *John Calvin: His Influence in the Western World* (Grand Rapids: Zondervan Publishing House, 1982), who believes it occurred when Calvin began to write the *Institutes*.
43. Walker, *op. cit.*, p. 72.
44. Ibid., p. 76.

45. *Reply to Sadolet*, in J. K. S. Reid, *Calvin: Theological Treatises*, XXII, p. 251.

46. Höpfl, *op. cit.*, p. 226, believes it difficult even to say what conversion meant for Calvin. Bouwsma (*op. cit.*, pp. 10–11) by stressing the academic, humanist, and evangelical background of Calvin's university days, does in this instance align himself with an important element of Florimond de Raemond's own analysis, without, however, alluding to Raemond's history.

47. Raemond, *L'Histoire, etc.*, Book VII, chap. 10, passim.

48. See Wendel, *op. cit.*, pp. 40–41, who notes that while it was once thought that Calvin had written Cop's discourse, historians now have evidence to the contrary; but see Bouwsma, *op. cit.*, p. 15, who thinks it probably was the case that Calvin "collaborated" on Cop's sermon.

49. Raemond, *L'Histoire, etc.*, p. 885: "J'ay apris de ceux qui l'ont veu & practiqué de ce temps là."

50. Raemond, *L'Histoire, etc.*, p. 883. This statement has been widely accepted by historians until recently. See for example, Doumergue, *op. cit.*, I, p. 372, and Wendel, *op. cit.*, p. 42. Recently, Ganoczy (*op. cit.*, p. 88) has stated that the entire composition (but not its preparation) was done in Basel (1535–1536). See, however, Ford Lewis Battles, Introduction to *Institution of the Christian Religion* (Atlanta, John Knox Press 1975), p. xxviii, where he says that while Calvin wrote the "first fruits" of his theological studies in Basel, it is not possible to say how much he may already have written while in France.

51. Ganoczy (*op. cit.*, pp. 72–4) indicates that Calvin was in Angoulême about three months, from the end of 1533 to April 1534, when he went to Nérac to visit Lefèvre. After that he moved rapidly around France and at the end of the year fled, with du Tillet, to Strasbourg.

52. "Calvin sejourna quelques années dans la ville d'Angoulesme, portant toujours par l'exterieur le masque d'un Catholique, se trouvant à l'Eglise, mais le plus rarement qu'il pouvoit. Il fut employé par le Chapitre, pour prononcer les oraisons Latins, selon la coustume, lors que le Synode s'assemble, qu'on apelle la Cène: ce qu'il fit deux ou trois fois dans l'Eglise S. Pierre. Pendant le temps qu'il sejourna dans Angoulesme, il ne fit aucun exercice de Religion contraire à la Catholique, ny exhortation, ny priere. Il n'en avoit pas encor l'usage" (Raemond, *L'Histoire, etc.*, p. 889).

53. Ibid., p. 884. Of this group, Bouteville, nicknamed the Lutheran Pope, and Pierre de la Place, whom Raemond did not mention, but who later revealed his membership in the group when in Angoulême, were committed Protestants. La Place perished in the St. Bartholomew Day Massacre. Du Tillet eventually abandoned Protestantism and was reconciled to Rome.

54. Doumergue, *op. cit.*, I, pp. 458–64 and Appendix I and XI, relied heavily on Raemond's account of Poitiers. He defended him against critics such as Bayle and Herminjard, in part because Doumergue believed Raemond's principal source, the former Calvinist minister of Poitiers, Palma Cayet, a man close to the Huguenot Captain François de La Noue and to Jeanne d'Albret, mother of Henry IV, had no reason to hide the facts. Cayet's *Remonstrance Chrétienne et très utile à Messieurs ... de la noblesse françoyse, etc.* (Paris, 1596) was the source Raemond relied on for much of what he wrote concerning Poitiers.

55. They included the prior of Trois Moustiers, François Fouquer, Calvin's host in Poitiers; Charles Le Sage, a professor; the Lt.-General of the district (Raemond named Renier, but should have named his successor, François Doyneau,

Seigneur de Sainte-Soline, a man of letters as well as military skill); Antoine de la Duguie, who was made a professor in 1542; Philip Véron, the *Procureur* (public prosecutor) at Poitiers; Albert Babinot, a minister, and Jean Vernon, another minister, native of Poitiers; and Jean Boisseau, Sieur de la Borderie, a prominent lawyer who lived to be seventy-eight years old, and died in 1591, a Catholic. These men were the core of Calvin's elite group of followers.

56. Raemond, *L'Histoire, etc.*, p. 891. The fact that du Tillet, for many years Calvin's close friend and follower, would later (1538) leave both Calvin and Calvinism and write his former friend reproachfully for having lacked the courage of his convictions (i.e., failing while in France to preach to any but a small group of committed followers) was regarded as evidence that substantiated the picture Raemond painted of Calvin in Poitiers—a clandestine figure who let prudence be his guide. (Daumergue, *op. cit.*, I, pp. 525–26)

57. Raemond, *L'Histoire, etc.*, p. 891, seethed as he described Calvin's concern to eliminate the "impious" aspects of the Catholic (and Lutheran) mass, and render his "Coene" as pure as it had been in its original form during the days of the primitive church.

58. Ibid., p. 892.

59. Ibid., pp. 893–94. This "Bon-Homme" ("Good-Fellow") is identified by Doumergue, *op. cit.*, I, p. 462, who notes that (Albert) Babinot had to give up a chair in law in order to become one of Calvin's ministers. The information on the early organization of the church came from Palma Cayet.

60. Raemond. *L'Histoire, etc.*, pp. 914–15.

61. A. G. Dickens and John Tonkin, *op. cit.*, p. 95.

62. Raemond, *L'Histoire, etc.*, p. 899.

63. Donald R. Kelley, *Foundations of Modern Historical Scholarship* (New York, Columbia University Press 1970), p. 152.

64. John Calvin, *Institution of the Christian Religion*, Ford Lewis Battles, ed. (Atlanta, 1975), p. 141, lines 5–7. Calvin reiterated the notion that man cannot by his own ritual guarantee a promise given by God.

65. Raemond, *L'Histoire, etc.*, p. 908.

66. That agreement was the *Consensus Tigurinus* (1549).

67. Raemond, *L'Histoire, etc.*, pp. 973–74.

68. Kilian McDonnell, *John Calvin, the Church, and the Eucharist* (Princeton, Princeton University Press 1967), p. 328. See Calvin, *Institutes*, IV, xviii, 5. Calvin rejected the real presence of Christ in the bread because it contradicted the finality of his resurrection, and the real presence of Christ at each communion service (ubiquitarianism), which conflicted with the notion of his humanity. See Benjamin Charles Milner, *Calvin's Doctrine of the Church* (Leiden, E. J. Brill 1970), pp. 126–28. Ronald S. Wallace, *Calvin's Doctrine of the Word and Sacrament*, (London, 1953), pp. 218–25, points out that Calvin wished to preserve the mystery of the sacrament without offending against morality, Christian practice, or reason.

69. Raemond, *L'Histoire, etc.*, Book VII, chap. 15.

70. Ibid., pp. 910–11.

71. Ibid., p. 912.

72. Ibid., p. 913.

73. Calvin said that "the authority of God ... the mark of distinction by which sacraments excel, and have their weight and dignity, and whatever men mingle

with them is frivolous." (Commentary on Ezekiel 4:1), quoted by Ronald S. Wallace, *op. cit.*, p. 134. See also Ganoczy, Calvin, *Théologien de L'église et du ministère* (Paris, Les Éditions du Cerf 1964), pp. 124–25. He notes the difficulties involved in Calvin's sacramentalist theology, while conceding that in later life Calvin tended to depart somewhat from his early (Zwinglian) spiritualism and adopted a more materialistic (*réaliste*) or Lutheran point of view toward the sacraments.

74. John Calvin, *Institutes* (ed., Warfield), II, pp. 583, 587.

75. John Calvin, "Articles Agreed upon by the Faculty of Sacred Theology of Paris in Reference to Matters of Faith at Present Controverted; With the Antidote," in *Tracts and Treatises* (Grand Rapids, William B. Eerdmans Publishing Company, 1958), I, p. 74.

76. John Calvin, *Institutes*, II, p. 596.

77. Ibid., II, p. 629.

78. François Lebrun, *La Vie conjugale sous l'ancien régime* (Paris, 1975), p. 14.

79. Raemond, *L'Histoire, etc.*, p. 1029.

80. Ibid.

81. John Calvin, "The True Method of Giving Peace," in *Tracts and Treatises*, III, pp. 300–1.

82. Ibid.

83. He claimed that the very word "minister" was an unwise choice because the original meaning of the term was a man who prepared animals for sacrifice, or a lowly assistant to a priest. (*L'Histoire, etc.*, p. 983.)

84. Raemond, *L'Histoire, etc.*, p. 986. The point about the education of these ministers has been a debatable one. Samuel Mours, *Le Protestantisme en France au XVIe siècle* (Paris, Librairie Protestante 1959), pp. 224–25, says that in 1561–1562 many pastors were coming from Geneva and Lausanne with only a course in theology taught by Calvin before the Church of St. Pierre in a public lecture, nor were the French academies all prepared to provide the numbers of pastors requested. Mours adds that the ordination of candidates was lax before France had time to perfect its provincial synods. But see Janine Garrison-Estèbe, "Vers une autre religion et une autre église (1536–1598)", *Histoire des Protestantes en France* (Toulouse: Édouard Privat, 1977), pp. 76–77, who cites Robert M. Kingdon's study of eighty-eight ministers of churches around Geneva and Lausanne, and her own study of 125 ministers of the Midi and concludes: "Les livres de raison, les écrits, les publications diverses ... renforcent cette impression d'une très grande culture."

85. Höpfl, *op. cit.*, p. 95, remarks that indeed "the substance of *auctoritas* was slipping away to the ministers" at Geneva and that the civil authority was in a weak bargaining position vis-à-vis the consistories. Bouwsma, *op. cit.*, p. 210, concurs, noting a tendency for the political and ministerial functions to "blur."

86. Raemond, *L'Histoire, etc.*, p. 995.

87. The "amende honorable" or act of contrition that required lapsed Catholics to make a public act of contrition before readmission to the life of their church was, after all, not so different from the experience of having to undergo an "admonestation" or censure before the body of the reformed faithful. (See Estèbe, "Vers une autre religion," pp. 73–74.)

88. Larroque, *Essai sur la vie, etc.*, refused to use any of the material in Raemond's Book VIII which, he said, was filled with puerile stories and gossip.

(Larroque, p. 124, n.1.) In fact, the eighth book is rich in details concerning the discipline of the Calvinist church in France, and fascinating details on the way Calvinists worshipped. One of the best sections in the material on France is found in chapters 14–17–all devoted to the phenomenon of psalm-singing, and how it affected the French public.

Chapter 8. History and Politics

1. George Huppert, *The Idea of Perfect History* (Urbana, University of Illinois Press 1970), p. 7, calls attention to this fact.
2. Raemond, *L'Histoire, etc.*, p. 568 called Budé "ce grand homme pere des lettres." See David O. McNeil, *Guillaume Budé and Humanism in the Reign of Francis I* (Geneva: Librairie Droz, 1975).
3. On Scaliger, see Anthony Grafton, *Joseph Scaliger, A Study in the History of Classical Scholarship* (Oxford: Clarendon Press, 1983). He finds that sixteenth-century philology was governed by rhetoric and polemical tactics of which Scaliger was not exceptional in his use (pp. 228–29).
4. On Le Roy, see Werner L. Gundersheimer, *The Life and Works of Louis Le Roy* (Geneva: Librairie Droz, 1966), pp. 93–121.
5. A brief but deft account of De Thou is found in Claude-Gilbert Dubois, *La Conception de l'histoire en France au XVIe siècle* (Paris: A. G. Nizet, 1977), pp. 172–85, where he is shown as a patriotic idealist who largely achieved his objective, i.e., the writing of comparative history with minimal author involvement and an adherence to documentary evidence.
6. Pasquier's *Recherches* were the works of the author's lifetime, and termed "the greatest monument to sixteenth century French historical scholarship" by Donald R. Kelley, *Foundations of Historical Scholarship* (New York: Columbia University Press, 1970) pp. 271–300. The author finds him to have been committed to the "values of quantitative erudition" and sensitive to the uniqueness of French culture, as distinct from Roman.
7. On Bodin, see J. H. Franklin, *Jean Bodin and the Sixteenth-Century Revolution in the Methodology of Law and History* (New York, Cambridge University Press 1963), and H. Denzer, ed., *Bodin* (Munich: Beck 1973).
8. For Pithou, see Donald R. Kelley, *Foundations of Modern Historical Scholarship*, pp. 249–70. Pithou's interest in Gallican custom, combined with his passion for philology and law, made him "one of the founding fathers of medieval studies" (p. 264).
9. Kelley, *Foundations*, pp. 106–12, and *François Hotman A Revolutionary's Ordeal* (Princeton N.J.: Princeton University Press, 1973). An historical relativist, Hotman, like Pithou and Pasquier, turned away from "legal humanism" with its Roman sources toward medieval and Gallican sources of French history.
10. For La Popelinière, see Huppert, *Perfect History*, chap. 8, who says this historian wished to "elevate history to a philosophy" (p. 144).
11. Raemond observed in the dedication (to Malvyn) of *De Corona Militis* (Tertullian), which followed the 1594 edition of *Erreur Populaire*, that "Estienne de la Boetie, jadis riche honneur de nostre Parlement . . . disoit tres bien:

>Que de tourner d'une langue estrangere
>La peine est grande et la gloire est légère.

NOTES

12. The phrase "revival of scientific and erudite historiography" is drawn from the chapter heading (chap. 1) of E. B. Fryde's *Humanism and Renaissance Historiography* (London: The Hambledon Press, 1983), a book that treats exclusively of the new historiography in the Italian peninsula.
13. Donald R. Kelley, *Foundations*, p. 34.
14. Ibid., p. 38.
15. For Hebrew, Raemond relied on Abraham Levi, a resident of Bordeaux and on Fronton du Duc, a notable Jesuit linguist who was additionally a resource person for problems involving Greek.
16. Perhaps Raemond would have gone more deeply into the politics of Henry IV's reign had he lived longer. He had planned to write a ninth book on Henry's reign.
17. Raemond, *L'Anti-Papesse*, p. 437.
18. Franklin, *Jean Bodin*, p. 23.
19. Ibid.
20. Raemond, *L'Anti-Christ*, p. 280.
21. Ibid.
22. Raemond, *L'Histoire, etc.*, pp. 939–40.
23. Raemond, *L'Anti-Papesse*, p. 392.
24. Ibid.
25. Ibid.
26. Ibid., p. 393.
27. The romantic idealism shown here bears a striking resemblance to that which bloomed in France immediately after the Congress of Vienna. One is tempted to add that Raemond was a spiritual forebear of François René, vicomte de Chateaubriand.
28. Villars was Bishop of Raemond's native town, Agen.
29. Raemond, *L'Histoire, etc.*, pp. 945–46.
30. Kelley, *Foundations*, p. 266.
31. Dubois, *La Conception de l'histoire*, p. 174.
32. See Samuel Kinser, *The Works of Jacques-Auguste de Thou* (The Hague: Martinus Nyjhoff, 1966), pp. 312–13, who points out that not until later in the seventeenth century, and as a direct result of the Index ban, was De Thou considered quotable by conservative Catholics such as Bossuet, who called him a "very great author" (Kinser, p. 1).
33. Jacques-Auguste De Thou, *Histoire universelle depuis 1543 jusqu'en 1607* (translated from the Latin), (London, 1734), I, p. 333. Compare with this quotation from Raemond: "We have proved to our cost that Religion and the State are so glued together, that their division produces what one of our legists said of a ship: if you split it, you lose it. For in as much as Religion and the State must hang together in thick and thin, it is religion primarily that must strengthen and sustain it." (*L'Histoire, etc.*, p. 840).
34. By way of illustration, consider his argument concerning the respective rights and privileges of two established religions, Catholic and Calvinist (p. 61), and his willingness—at times—to concede mutual blame for civil war atrocities (p. 52). It is important to remember that Raemond's vitriol was not entirely directed against what he regarded as errors of belief or ritual. Much of it was the product of his fears, natural enough for a magistrate, of social instability that he connected—not without reason—to religious diversity.
35. According to Émile G. Léonard, *Histoire générale du Protestantisme*, p. 325, the yearning for Christian unity was a characteristic of the first third of the

seventeenth century. He points out that Henry IV had appointed a committee composed of Protestants such as d'Aubigné, the Protestant minister Daniel Chamier, and Turquet de Mayerne (Henry IV's physician and Bèze's godson) to consider ways and means of reuniting the two parties. This unity remained an ideal that, in the decade after Raemond's death (1601), continued to operate within French society increasingly to Catholic advantage. See also Jacques Pannier, *L'Eglise réformée de Paris sous Henri IV* (Geneva: Slatkine-Megariotis Reprints, 1977 [1st ed: 1911]) pp. 498ff., and Daniel Ligou, *Le Protestantisme en France de 1598–1715* (Paris, Société d'Enseignement Supérieur 1968), who notes: "Le sentiment que la désunion entre les Églises n'était pas quelque chose d'absolument décisif subsistait encore assez fortement au début du XVIIe siècle" (p. 50).

36. Nannerl O. Keohane, *Philosophy and the State in France* (Princeton, Princeton University Press, 1980), p. 83.

37. Raemond, *L'Anti-Christ*, p. 11. The passage was intended by Raemond to explain why Christ permitted his church to be afflicted by trials on earth prior to his second coming—because activity would keep it from lazy inattentiveness (the church militant). However, the line concerning still waters was a quote from an unnamed poet, and is an apotheosis to that kind of human activity that so many Renaissance men displayed in their own lives.

38. Ibid. (unpaginated Epistle preceding *L'Anti-Christ*).

39. Larroque, *Essai*, p. 19, n.1. Larroque makes it plain that the decision was made at court.

40. In the "Epistle to M. de Bellegarde" of the 1597 edition of *L'Anti-Christ* (Lyon) Raemond decried the "cruel catastrophy" of the regicide of Henry III, and in the strongest terms condemned the act that had sought, he claimed, the death of the French state, as well as of its monarch (p. 106).

41. Kelley, *Foundations*, p. 247.

42. Ibid.

43. John Calvin, *Institutes*, IV, p. 772. See also E. William Monter, *Calvin's Geneva* (New York, John Wiley and Sons 1967), p. 144, who observes, "In the sixteenth century, the intimate association of the ecclesiastical and the secular government of a community was generally assumed to be both natural and desirable."

44. See Paul Moussiegt, *Hotman et du Plessis-Mornay*, *théories politiques au XVIe siècle* (Geneva: Slatkine Reprints, 1970, 1st ed., 1899), p. 50, who found that both Hotman and Duplessis-Mornay assumed a popular will in the early Frankish centuries that was not wholly there.

45. Raemond, *L'Histoire, etc.*, p. 952, regretted that former historians of the church had not bothered to record details of early heretic practices. Clearly he would have preferred that they had made a sociological record of "les vus, moeurs, humeurs, & opinions de tous les vieux, & premiers Heretiques." His own history was influenced by the goals of other writers of universal histories.

46. The term "universal history" was first used in François Baudoin's *De Institutione Historiae Universae et Ejus Cum Jurisprudentia Conjunctione* (1561). Bodin and La Poplinière and others took up the problem, which they defined variously, agreeing generally that history should make connections between sacred, civil, military, and legal experience and take into account the specific circumstances (chronology, place, and events) that produced it.

47. Huppert, *Perfect History*, p. 93.

48. Calvin's birthplace, Noyon, in Compiègne, may seem somewhat farther to the north than the term south might imply. Noyon is situated between the

forty-ninth and fiftieth parallels, while Eisleben, Luther's birthplace, is located between the fifty-first and fifty-second parallels. Luther lived approximately one hundred fifty miles farther north than Calvin.

49. Raemond, *L'Histoire, etc.*, p. 886. It is interesting to compare such stereotypical thinking with a pronouncement made by the learned, but superstitiously erudite, Jerome Cardan (d. 1576) to the effect that prophets cannot be born near the poles, and have generally come from Palestine, a temporate climate with favorable stars. Lynn Thorndike, *A History of Magic and Experimental Science* (New York, Macmillan 1941), V, p. 575.

50. Ibid., VI, p. 98. Thorndike insists that genitures were thought capable of revealing by inductive methods that kind of astrological law which would render astrology scientific.

51. Raemond, *L'Histoire, etc.*, pp. 30–31. Thorndike (*op. cit.*, VI, p. 156) notes that although Popes Paul III, Pius IV, and Gregory XIII, the predecessor of Sixtus V, were personally favorable to astrological prediction, Sixtus V published a bull against it (5, January 1586) that forbade divination and the possession of books on the subject. This bull asserted that only God knows the future, which is a sentiment echoed by Raemond (*L'Histoire, etc.*, pp. 30–31), when he concluded his astrological discussion of Luther by saying that he recognized his own limitations and would abide by the judgment of his church.

52. Huppert, *Perfect History*, p. 135ff., says this book and two others, by the same author, "summed up the historical thought of an entire generation."

53. Raemond, *L'Histoire, etc.*, p. 993.

54. Catholic indignation at De Thou's frankness was still alive in the nineteenth century. A. J. Rance Bourrey, *J.-A. De Thou son histoire universelle et ses démêlés avec Rome* (Geneva, Slatkine Reprints, 1970; 1st. ed., 1881) took the position that the author deserved to be placed on the *Index* for his lack of loyalty to Rome.

55. Agrippa d'Aubigné, "Préface" to *Histoire universelle* (Paris, Librairie Renouard 1886), I, p. 2.

56. Ibid.

57. James Westphal Thompson, *A History of Historical Writing*, I, p. 564.

58. Huppert, *Perfect History*, p. 144.

59. His *Histoire, etc.*, abounds with brilliant and precocious insights, such as his recognition of indigenous reform movements in Bohemia before Hus, a notion that has received considerable attention by revisionists like Ernst Benz and others who emphasize the medieval origins of the Reform; his association of Zwingli and the sacramentarian positions; his perception of the holiness aspect of Anabaptist groups; his appreciation of the contribution that Francis I and the Turk, each in their own way, made to the survival of Protestant reform in Germany; an account of the formulation of the Augsburg Confession that accurately reflected the division of Lutherans and between Lutherans, Catholics, and Zwinglians; a deft account of the wars of the Schmalkald League; an awareness of the conservative aspects of Luther's formula for celebrating the Eucharist; a surprisingly sympathetic account of the doctrinal conservatism of the Lutheran reform in contrast to the Calvinist, etc.

60. Among his errors: an assessment of European relations before the Reformation as harmonious; his bland comment that the event was essentially a quarrel between Augustinian and Dominican ("Jacobin") monks; his charge that Calvin favored Arianism; that Mennonites were aggressive, not passive; that Thomas Müntzer was motivated primarily by leveling ideas rather than by chiliasm, a

point of view that anticipated Marxist interpretations and that has been corrected by Eric Gritsch, *Reformer Without a Church, The Life and Thought of Thomas Muentzer* (Philadelphia, Fortress Press 1967); that Luther was anti-intellectual; that Emperor Ferdinand's reign was uneventful, when the six years of his reign (1558–1564) were devoted to trying to settle religious differences in Germany; the prosecution of war against the Turk; monetary reform; the consolidation of the Aulic council, etc.

61. Cardinals Baronius, Bellarmine, Hosius; Nicholas Sanders (Sanderus), the English Jesuit professor at the University of Louvain; Alanus Copus, his compatriot; Albertus Pighius, Calvin's critic; Melchior Cano, the Spanish Dominican; and Frederick Staphylus number among these.

62. Polman, *op. cit.*, p. 317.

63. Thompson, *op. cit.*, I, p. 561.

64. This treatise was entitled *Traicté des vrayes essencielles et visibles marques de la vraye église catholique*, which appeared first in Latin in 1578. The French edition used here is the 1592 (Geneva) edition.

65. Ibid. Letter to the king (unpaged).

66. Ibid.

67. The subject of democracy versus elitism in the writings of Calvin and his followers with respect to civil and to ecclesiastical government is a matter of scholarly debate. See *Calvin and Calvinism Sources of Democracy*, Robert M. Kingdon and Robert D. Linder, eds. (Lexington, Mass., D. C. Heath and Company 1970), and in particular Kingdon, "Calvin's Followers Feared Democracy," pp. 45–49.

68. This is not to say that the *Histoire ecclesiastique*, which Bèze did not write, but to which he contributed his memoirs for 1561–1563, had no merit. The nineteenth-century critic, Pierre-André Sayous (*Études littéraires sur les écrivains Français de la Réformation* (Geneva, Slatkine Reprints 1970); 1st ed., 1881), I, pp. 337ff., noted that the work was a valuable expression of Calvinist mentality, even if it was part polemic. Much the same opinion is given by Dickens and Tonkin, *op. cit.*, p. 87.

69. The conservatism in Hotman's work is apparent in his opposition to change; the radicalism of his position was his portrayal of the popular will in the early Frankish constitution. Hotman's conclusions about that "ancient" constitution have been variously interpreted, as has the constitution itself. See Donald R. Kelley, *Foundations*, p. 209, who finds that Hotman did for the "ancient constitution" of France what Calvin did for the "primitive church," and observes that for Hotman "history had become a quest for lost innocence." A contrasting view is found in J. G. A. Pocock, *The Ancient Constitution and the Feudal Law* (Cambridge, Cambridge University Press 1957), who finds Hotman innocent of exaggerating the purity and antiquity of custom (p. 28). It is doubtful if either Hotman, Bèze, or Raemond were this innocent.

70. Dickens and Tonkin, *op. cit.*, p. 76, agree that Hotman's *Franco-Gallia* was both "informed," "useful to the radical Protestant parties," and "misinterpreted history from early Frankish times to prove that the Estates had always been recognized as expressing the people's sovereignty."

71. E. Harris Harbison, *Christianity and History* (Princeton, Princeton University Press 1964), pp. 270–88.

72. H. J. Martin, "Ce qu'on lisait à Paris au XVIe siècle," *Bibliothèque d'humanisme et de Renaissance*, XXI, 1959, p. 229.

73. These two were *Erreur Populaire* and *L'Anti-Christ*. Alexander Cooke, an

Englishman, wrote a rebuttal of the *Erreur*: *A Dialogue Betweene a Protestant and a Papist, Manifestly Proving that a Woman Called Joane was Pope of Rome against the Surmises and Objections Made to the Contrarie, by Robert Bellarmine, and Caesar Baronius Cardinals: Florimondus Raemondus, N. D. and Other Popish Writers, Impudently Denying the Same* (London, 1625). *L'Anti-Christ* was believed to have been written by a friend of Raemond's. (See chap. 8.)

Chapter 9. Postscript

1. Larroque, *Essai*, vol. 4, n.1, acknowledged his indebtedness to the Countess Marie de Raymond for a number of family documents. The countess was descended from Florimond's brother Jean. She died in Agen on the 24 April 1886. A portrait of the lady hangs in the municipal archives of Agen. She was an avid collector of manuscripts, a friend and patron of Larroque, and a collaborator of several scholars of local history.
2. Émile Doumergue, *Jean Calvin, La Jeunesse*, Appendix II, pp. 522–26, "Florimond de Raemond." In this section, the author recognizes Raemond's credulity but also his worthwhile knowledge about the reformed, his interesting commentary, and his original writing style.
3. We recall the difficulties experienced by the Catholic party in and around Bordeaux to find an adequate replacement for Raemond after his unexpected demise.
4. On universal history, see George Huppert, *The Idea of Perfect History*, p. 145.
5. Pierre l'Estoile, *Mémoires-Journaux* (Paris, 1889), IX, pp. 13–14.
6. Raemond, *L'Anti-Christ*, p. 354: "Je scay bien que je seray la butte de ceux, qu s'en prenans au chef de vostre Église, esparneront pas un des moindres, qui cobattens soubs vostre enseigne."
7. Leclerc, *Lettre Critique*, p. 331. Louis Richeome has been described as a sweet-tempered priest of considerable talent. He was founder of a college at Dijon, provincial of his order at Lyon and Rome as well as of Bordeaux, and a prolific polemicist. Richeome's biographer, Henri Brémond, *A Literary History of Religious Thought in France*, K. L. Montgomery, trans. (New York, Macmillan 1928), I, does not mention Raemond in his chapter on this man.
8. Le Double was also a *conseiller* in the Bordeaux *Parlement* and wrote a very long Latin poem praising Raemond's *L'Anti-Christ*.
9. Leclerc, *Lettre Critique*, pp. 359–60.
10. Ibid., p. 365.
11. David Blondel, *Familier esclaircissement*, pp. 39 and 79. My edition of Blondel's book is dated 1649 and is the second printing (Amsterdam). On these two pages the author states simply that the *Erreur* was "publié sous le nom du Sr. de Rémond."
12. Labbe's book was entitled *Coenotaphium Joanna Papissa Eversum* (1657). Pierre Labbe was a Jesuit priest and a distinguished savant (1607–1670).
13. Labbe apparently did not have access to the earlier editions of Blondel's work. See note 11 above.
14. These were the works of Samuel Desmarets (d. 1673), who wrote to assert the existence of a popess (*Joanna Papissa Restituta, Sive Animadversiones ... ad Davidis Blondelli*, etc. 1658); Vicentius Placcius (d. 1699) of Hamburg, whose *Theatrum Anonymorum & Pseudonymorum* was published only in 1708; and

Johann Albert Fabricius (d. 1736), whose *Decas Decadum, Sive Plagiariorum et Pseudonymorum Centuria* (1689) repeated these allegations.

15. Gilbert Burnet (1643–1715) was the author of the *History of the Reformation in England* (1679–1715) and numerous other works. He was elevated to the see of Salisbury in 1689, the bishopric being a reward for his loyalty to William and Mary. In 1686, while in exile in Holland, he published *Reflections on Mr. Varillas's History of the Revolutions That Have Happened in Europe in Matters of Religion, etc.*, a work soon translated into French. In 1687 he defended this work in yet another publication, and this defense was reprinted in 1689. In that year appeared Fabricius's *Decas Decadum Sive Plagiariorum et Pseudonymorum Centuria*, in which the allegations concerning Richeome and Raemond were repeated.

16. Bayle, *Dictionnaire Historique*, XII, art. "Rémond," remark C.

17. Ibid., p. 504. "Je laisse aux lecteurs à juger s'il y a là un fondement assez solide pour établir comme un fait certain que tous les écrits de controverse qui ont paru sous le nom de Florimond de Rémond avaient été composés par Richeome."

18. Bayle had printed a passage in this article from Matthieu's history containing the phrase "comme je crois" in connection with the (to him) doubtful authorship of *L'Anti-Christ*. Burnet, at the end of the century, had expanded the doubts and changed the "je crois" to "on croit," which made the charge appear very well grounded.

19. Bayle, *op. cit.*, XI, art. "Papesse," p. 373.

20. *Méthode pour étudier l'histoire*, last published, 1772.

21. Bayle, *op. cit.*, XII, art. "Rémond," remark D, p. 501. "Une fontaine publique pour quantité d'autres écrivains."

22. The worst offender, according to Bayle, (*op. cit.* Article "Ochin", remark Z, XI, p. 207) was Abraham Bzouski (Bzovius), a continuator of Baronius's *Annals*, who copied "mot à mot" some six pages of Raemond's "History of Heresy" pertaining to Ochino and Vermigli.

23. The Protestant scholar and pastor Pierre Jurieu said of Soulier that Bishop Sarlat only agreed to make him a curate if he could learn enough Latin to celebrate mass.

24. Henri Hauser, *Les Sources de l'Histoire de France* (Paris: Librairie Alphonse Picard et Fils, 1912,) IV, p. 321.

25. See Elizabeth Israels Perry, *From Theology to History: French Religious Controversy and the Revocation of the Edict of Nantes* (The Hague, Martinus Nijhoff 1973), p. 67, who points out that such criticism of Maimbourg derived in part from the polemical needs of Protestants.

26. Ibid., p. 79, n.7.

27. Richelieu's work was entitled *Traité qui contient la méthode pour convertir ceux qui se sont séparés de l'église* (1651).

28. See Jean-Robert Armogathe, "Les Vies de Calvin aux XVIe et XVIIe siècles, "in Phillipe Joutard, *Historiographie de la réforme* (Paris: Delachaux & Niestle S. A., 1977), pp. 48–49.

29. Ibid.

30. Alfred Rébelliau, *Bossuet* (Paris: Librairie Hachette, 1909), pp. 168, 280n.

31. Larmessin was one of the better portrait engravers of the seventeenth century. The one that appears in Bullart's *Académie des Sciences et des Arts contenant les Éloges Historiques des hommes illustres* was almost certainly drawn from the portrait by C. de Mallery, of which it is a reversed copy. Despite Larroque's disapproval (*Essai*, p. 2. n.3), it is a faithful and striking imitation of the original. The earliest known portrait of Raemond was an engraving by Thomas Leu, which appeared in the 1601 Latin edition of the popess myth, *Fabula Joannae*.

32. After the 1682 publication of Bullart's *Académie, etc.*, only five more printings of Raemond's books appeared. A Dutch translation of the *L'Histoire, etc.*, in 1690; a Latin edition of the same work in 1691; a Dutch translation of the *Erreur Populaire*, which accompanied the Dutch version of the history; another Latin edition of the history (1717); and a German translation of the history in 1746, making a total of thirty-seven printings of all Raemond's works since 1587. Of these, fifteen were of the *Erreur populaire*; four of *L'Anti-Christ*; seventeen *L'Histoire, etc.*; and one of Monluc's *Commentaires*.

33. There were more than stylistic changes in the transition from Renaissance-Baroque historiography to that of the eighteenth century. As Eric Cochrane observed (see "The Transition from Renaissance to Baroque: The Case of Italian Historiography," in *History and Theory*, XIX, no. 1, 1980, p. 21), the latter especially must be studied in the "context of contemporary social structures," and "in connection with the various aspects of post-Tridentine or post-Counter Reformation religious life." In this study we have labored to provide such contexts, but the stylistic aspects of Raemond's works must be considered in any discussion of his *nachleben* or literary longevity. Enthusiasm such as Raemond displayed for his faith and against all other sects would have offended against the taste of the Enlightenment.

34. Bayle, *Nouvelles lettres de l'Auteur de la critique générale de l'histoire du Calvinisme de Mr. Maimbourg* (1685) said of that author's histories that they were like "romans à clef" in which ostensibly historical personalities stand for people still living, often those targeted by the writer as objects for ridicule.

35. Rébelliau, *Bossuet*, pp. 374−75, n.3.

36. Jacques Lenfant, Letter "A son excellence Monsieur (Ezekiel) de Spanheim, Ministre d'État, etc." in Frederic Spanheim, *Histoire de la Papesse Jeanne* (Cologne, 1695), Translated from the Latin edition of 1691. Ezekiel was the ambassador to France from the Spanish Netherlands. His brother, Frederic, was a professor of theology at the University of Leyden.

37. Couture, *op. cit.*, p. 507.

38. "Talent inférieure, encore très estimable" Ibid., p. 505.

39. Another two twentieth-century authors who spent considerable effort writing about Raemond, Alan Boase, and Raymond Darricau, are not considered because their writing is either too brief (Boase), or insufficiently analytical (Darricau).

40. *La Conception de l'histoire en France au XVIe siècle* (Paris, 1977).

41. Ibid., p. 44.

42. Ibid., pp. 53 and 533.

43. Jacques Pannier, *L'Église réformée de Paris sous Henri IV* (Geneva: Slatkine−Megariotis Reprints, 1977), (1st ed., 1911), pp. 250−51.

44. Dubois, *op. cit.*, p. 533.

45. Ibid., p. 517.

46. Ibid., p. 527.

47. Ibid., p. 524.

48. In England, for example, between 1660 and 1688, the Anglican church was in the forefront of the movement to prevent any broadening of religious toleration whether to Roman Catholics or to other Protestant sects. Christopher Hill, *Antichrist in Seventeenth Century England* (p. 246) notes that the Toleration Act of 1688 served a political purpose. In just this way did Raemond tolerate Protestants in his day—for political reasons.

49. Martin Busch, *Florimond de Raemond et L'Anabaptisme*, p. 237.

50. Bayle, *Dictionnaire Historique*, XII, art. "Rémond," remark D, p. 506.

Bibliography

Printed Sources: Pre-1800 Authors

Aubigné, Agrippa d'. *Confession de Sancy*. Edited by Eugène Réaume and François de Caussade. Vol. II. Paris: A Lemerre, 1877.

———. "Préface" to *Histoire Universelle*. Paris: Librairie Renouard, 1886.

Baronius, Caesar. *Annales Ecclesiastici*. XIV. Augustin Theiner, ed. Barri-Ducis, et L. Guerin, 1868.

Bayle, Pierre. *Nouvelles lettres de l'auteur de la critique générale de l'histoire du Calvinisme de Mr. Maimbourg*. Ville-Franche: Pierre le Blanc, 1685.

———. *Dictionnaire Historique et Critique*. (1st ed., 1697). Paris: Desoer Libraire, 1820.

Bellarmine, Cardinal Robert Francis. "De Potestate Spirituali" (Bk. IV of *De Summo Pontifice*, Justinus Fèvre, ed., *Opera Omnia*. II. Frankfurt: Minerva, 1965.

———. "Ubi de Antechristo: Controversiarum De Membris Ecclesiae," Justinus Fèvre, ed., *Opera Omnia*. II. Frankfurt: Minerva, 1965.

Benoist, Élie. *Histoire de l'édit de Nantes, jusques à l'édit de révocation*. Delft: Adrien Beman, 1690.

Bèze, Theodore de. "Letter to the King." In *Traicté des vrayes essencielles et visibles marques de la vraye église Catholique*. La Rochelle: H. Haultin, 1592.

Blondel, David. *Familier esclaircissement de la question si une femme a esté assise au siège papal de Rome*. Amsterdam: Jean Blaev, 1649.

Brach, Pierre de. *Oeuvres Poétiques*. Edited by Reinhold Dezeimeris. Geneva: Slatkine Reprints, 1969. (Reimpression of the Paris ed. of 1861–1862.)

Bullart, Isaac. *Académie des Sciences et des Arts contenant les éloges historiques des hommes illustres*. Brussels: 1682.

Bullinger, Heinrich. *A Hundred Sermons upon the Apocalipse of Jesu Christ*. London: John Daye, 1573. (Sermon LXI)

Calvin, John. *Institutes of the Christian Religion*. Translated by John Allen, and edited by Benjamin B. Warfield. Philadelphia: Presbyterian Board of Christian Education, 1936.

———. *Institution of the Christian Religion*. Edited by Ford Lewis Battles. Atlanta, Ga.: John Knox Press, 1975.

———. "Reply to Sadolet." In *Theological Treatises*, translated and edited by J. K. S. Reid. London: SCM Press, 1954.

———. "The True Method of Giving Peace." In *Theological Treatises*, translated and edited by J. K. S. Reid. London: SCM Press, 1954.

———. "Articles Agreed upon by the Faculty of Sacred Theology of Paris in

Reference to Matters of Faith at Present Controverted: with the Antidote." In *Theological Treatises*, translated and edited by J. K. S. Reid. London: SCM Press, 1954.

———. "Vera Christianae Pacificationis et Ecclesiae Reformandae Ratio." In *Joannis Calvini Opera Quae Supersunt Omnia*. VII. Brunswick: C. A. Schwetschke and Sons, 1868.

———. *Commentaries on the Book of the Prophet Daniel*. Translated by Thomas Meyers. Grand Rapids, Mich.: Wm. B. Eerdmans Publishing Co., 1949.

Chrysostom, (St.) John. "Epistolam Secundam ad Thessalonicenses," in J. P. Migne's *Patrologiae Cursus Completus*. ser. Graeca, 62. Brepols: Turnhout, 1980.

Clement VIII (Pope). "Dilecto Filio Florimundo Raemundo, etc." Letter of 11 Mar 1599 in Raemond's *L'Histoire*. Rouen: 1647.

Cooke, Alexander. *A Dialogue Betweene a Protestant and a Papist, Manifestly Proving That a Woman Called Joane Was Pope of Rome Against the Surmises and Objections Made To the Contrarie, by Robert Bellarmine, and Caesar Baronius Cardinals: Florimondus Raemondus, n.d., and Other Popish Writers, Impudently Denying Same*. London: John Haviland, 1625.

De Thou, Jacques-Auguste. *Histoire universelle depuis 1543 jusqu'en 1607*. Edited by Pierre Désfontaines. Paris: 1733. (1st complete ed., 1620, in Latin.)

Gerhard, Johann. *Locorum Theologicorum*. V. Jena: Tobias Steinmann, 1620.

Gaufreteau, Jean de. *Chronique Bordeloise*. Bordeaux: Charles Lefebvre, 1877.

Hus, John. *Documenta Mag. Joannis Hus Vitam, Doctrinam, Causam Constantiensi Consilio Actam et Controversias de Religione in Bohemia (1403–1418)*. Edited by Frantisek Palacky. Osnabrück: Biblio-Verlag, 1966.

James I (King of England). "A Fruitfull Meditation . . . of the vii–x Verses of the Second Chapter of the Revelation." In *The Works of the Most High and Mightie Prince, James, etc*. London: Robert Barker and John Bill, 1616.

Leclerc, Laurent-Josse (abbé). *Lettre critique sur le dictionnaire de Bayle*. The Hague: 1732.

Lefèvre d'Étaples, Jacques. *The Prefatory Epistles of Jacques Lefèvre d'Étaples and Related Texts*. Edited by Eugene F. Rice. New York: Columbia University Press, 1972.

L'Estoile, Pierre de. *Mémoires-Journaux*. IX. (1607–1609). Edited by Alphonse Lemerre. Paris: 1889.

Luther, Martin. "Condemnatio doctrinalis librorum Martini Lutheri per quosdam Magistros Nostros Lovanienses et Colonienses facta. Responsio Lutheriana ad eandem damnationem, 1520." In *Luthers Werke: kritische Gesammtausgabe*. Vol. 6, Weimar: H. Böhlau, and Graz: Akademische Druck & Verlaganstalt, 1966. (1st. edition, 1888), pp. 170–195.

———. "To the Christian Nobility of the German Nation Concerning the Reform of the Christian Estate, 1520." In *Luther's Works*. Vol. 44, Helmut T. Lehmann, general editor. *The Christian in Society*. I, edited by James Atkinson; translated by Charles M. Jacobs; revised by James Atkinson. Philadelphia: Fortress Press, 1966, pp. 115–217.

———. "Against Hanswurst." In *Luther's Works*. Vol. 41, *Church and Ministry* III, edited and translated by Eric W. Gritsch. Philadelphia: Fortress Press, 1966, pp. 179–256.

———. "Against the Roman Papacy, an Institution of the Devil." In *Luther's Works*. Vol. 41, *Church and Ministry* III, edited and translated by Eric W. Gritsch. Philadelphia: Fortress Press, 1966, pp. 257–376.

———. "The Babylonian Captivity of the Church, 1520." In *Luther's Works*. Vol. 36, *Word and Sacrament*. II, edited by Abdel Ross Wentz; translated by A. T. W. Steinhäuser; revised by Frederick C. Ahrens and Abdel Ross Wentz. Philadelphia: Muhlenberg Press, 1959, pp. 3–126.

———. "Concerning the Answer of the Goat in Leipzig." In *Luther's Works*. Vol. 39, *Church and Ministry* I, edited by Eric W. Gritsch; translated by Eric W. and Ruth C. Gritsch. Philadelphia: Fortress Press, 1970, pp. 117–35.

———. "The Estate of Marriage." In *Luther's Works*. Vol. 45, *The Christian in Society II*, edited and translated by Walther I. Brandt. Philadelphia: Muhlenberg Press, 1962, pp. 11–49.

———. "Freedom of a Christian." In *Luther's Works, Career of the Reformer I*. Vol. 31, edited by Harold J. Grimm. Philadelphia: Muhlenberg Press, 1951, pp. 333–77.

———. "On the Papacy in Rome." In *Luther's Works, Church and Ministry* I, Vol. 39, edited by Eric W. Gritsch.; translated by Eric W. and Ruth C. Gritsch. Philadelphia: Fortress Press, 1970, pp. 49–104.

———. *The Table Talk*, edited by Wm. Hazlitt. London: George Bell and Sons, 1902.

Monluc, Blaise de. *Commentaires et lettres de Blaise de Monluc*, edited by Alphonse de Ruble. Paris: Mme. V. Renouard, 1864–1872.

———. *Commentaires*, edited by Paul Courteault, with *Preface* by Jean Giono. Paris: A. J. Picard and Cie; and Editions Gallimard, 1964.

Montaigne, Michel de. "Apology for Raymond Sebond," in The Complete *Essays of Montaigne*. Edited and translated by Donald M. Frame. Stanford, Calif.: Stanford University Press, 1979. (First published in 1957 in *The Complete Works of Montaigne*.)

———. "Of the Arms of the Parthians." In *The Complete Essays of Montaigne*, edited and translated by Donald M. Frame. Stanford, Calif.: Stanford University Press, 1979. (First published in 1957 in *The Complete Works of Montaigne*.)

———. "Of Custom." In *The Complete Essays of Montaigne*, edited and translated by Donald M. Frame. Stanford, Calif.: Stanford University Press, 1979. (First published in 1957 in *The Complete Works of Montaigne*.)

———. "Of Moderation." In *The Complete Essays of Montaigne*, edited and translated by Donald M. Frame. Stanford, Calif.: Stanford University Press, 1979. (First published in 1957 in *The Complete Works of Montaigne*.

———. "Of Prayers." In *The Complete Essays of Montaigne*, edited and translated by Donald M. Frame. Stanford, Calif.: Stanford University Press, 1979. (First published in 1957 in *The Complete Works of Montaigne*.)

Mornay, Philippe Duplessis. *Mémoires et correspondances* VII and IX. Geneva: Slatkine Reprints, 1969. (First edition, 1834–1825.)

Oudin, François (père). "Fronton du Duc." In Jean-Pierre Nicéron, *Mémoires pour servir à l'histoire des hommes illustres de la république des lettres*. Paris: Briasson, 1737. Vol. XXXVIII.

Panvinio, Onofrio. *Annotationi*. (Appended to *Battista Platina Cremonese Delle Vite De'Pontefici*.) Venice: II Barezzi, 1650.

Pasquier, Etienne. *Oeuvres*. Amsterdam: 1723. II.

Pius II (Pope). *Der Briefwechsel des Eneas Silvius Piccolomini*, edited by Rodolf Wolkan. Vienna: A. Hölder, 1918.

Platina (Bartolomeo de' Sacchi). *Hystoria de Vitis Pontificum Periucunda*. Venice: Philippo Pincio, 1504.

Quick, John. *Synodicon in Gallia Reformata: Or, The Acts, Decisions, Decrees, and Canons of Those Famous National Councils of the Reformed Churches in France*. Vol. I. London: T. Parkhurst & J. Robinson, 1692.

Raemond, Florimond de. "De Monsieur de Raymond." In Pierre de Brach's *Oeuvres poétiques*. Edited by Reinhold Dezeimeris. II. Geneva: Slatkine Reprints, 1969.

———. "A Madamoiselle Diane De Foix, sonnet." In Pierre de Brach's *Oeuvres poétiques*. Edited by Reinhold Dezeimeris. II. Geneva: Slatkine Reprints, 1969.

———. "Au Sieur De Brach, sonnet." In Pierre de Brach's *Oeuvres poétiques*. Edited by Reinhold Dezeimeris. II. Geneva: Slatkine Reprints, 1969.

———. "Lettre de Florimond de Raemond à M. de Candale, captal de Buch, evêque d'Aire." Transcribed by M. le Marquis de Castelnau d'Essenault (Archives Historiques du Département de la Gironde). 24. Bordeaux: Imprimerie Gounouilhou, 1835.

———. *Erreur Populaire de la Papesse Jane*. (Anon. ed.) Bordeaux: S. Millanges, 1587.

———. "A la noblesse de Gascongne." In Blaise de Monluc. *Commentaires et Lettres*. (De Ruble) Paris: Mme. V. Renouard, 1864–1872.

———. "Avis au lecteur." In Blaise de Monluc, *Commentaires et Lettres*. (De Ruble). Paris: Mme. V. Renouard, 1864–1872.

———. "Lettre de Florimond de Raemond à Monseigneur Le Duc d'Espernon, Paer et Colonel de France." In Blaise de Monluc, *Commentaires et Lettres*. (De Ruble). Paris: Mme. V. Renouard, 1864–1872.

———. *De la couronne du soldat*. Translated from the Latin of Q. S. Tertullian, by Florimond de Raemond, Conseiller du Roy en la Cour de Parlement de Bourdeaux. A Bourdeaux: S. Millanges, 1594.

———. "Lettre de Florimond de Raemond à Malvyn" (1597). Municipal Archives of Bordeaux, ms. Delpit, fos. 210 v°–212212 1⁰, copy. Reproduced in Paul Courteault, *Geoffroy de Malvyn, magistrat et Humaniste Bordelais*. Appendix. Paris: Librairie Honoré Champion, 1907.

———. "Lettre de Florimond de Raemond à M. Duplessis" (1597). In Philippe Duplessis-Mornay, *Mémoires et correspondance*, no. CXVI. VII. Geneva: Slatkine Reprints, 1969.

———. "Lettre de Florimond de Raemond à M. Duplessis" (1597). In Philippe Duplessis-Mornay, *Mémoires et correspondance*, no. CXVII. VII. Geneva: Slatkine Reprints, 1969.

———. *L'Anti-Christ et l'anti-papesse*. 2d ed. Paris: Chez Abel l'Angelier, 1599.

———. "A Monsieur De Belle-Garde, grand escuyer de France" (precedes the above ed. of *L'Anti-Christ*).

———. "Lettre de Florimond de Raemond à M. Duplessis" (1599). In Philippe Duplessis-Mornay, *Mémoires et correspondance*, no. CXVII. IX. Geneva: Slatkine Reprints, 1969.

———. "A reverendissime Messire Nicolas de Villars, Conseiller du Roy en ses conseils d'estat & privé, evesque & Comte d'Agen." Dedication to the eighth Book of *L'Histoire, etc.* Rouen: Pierre Maille, 1647.

———. "Voeu de l'Autour." Proceeds Book I of *L'Histoire, etc.* Rouen: Pierre Maille, 1647.

———. *L'Histoire de la naissance, progrez et decadence de l'heresie de ce siècle.* (1st ed., 1605) Rouen: Pierre Maille, 1647.

Raemond, François de. "A monseigneur l'illustrissime & reverendissime Cardinal Baronius." Dedication of Book V of *L'Histoire, etc.*

———. "A monseigneur l'illustrissime et reverendissime Cardinal de Sourdis." Dedication of Book III of *L'Histoire, etc.*

Schedel, Hartman. *Chronica Universalis.* (*Nuremberg Chronicle*). Nuremberg: Anton Koberger, 1493.

Spanheim, Frederic. *Histoire de la Papesse Jeanne.* Translated by Jacques Lenfant. Cologne: 1691.

Tertullian, Q. V. *Liber de Praescriptionibus Adversus Haereticos.* In *Patrologiae Cursus Completus Omnium SS. Patrem, Doctorum Scriptorumque Ecclesiasticorum.* Edited by J. P. Migne. I. Turnhout, Belgium: Brepols, Reprint of the edition of 1844.

Zinzerling, Justus. *Voyage dans la vieille France.* Translated by Thalès Bernard. Paris: Dentu, Vanier, etc., 1859.

Printed Sources: Post-1800 Authors

Albistur, Maité, and Daniel, Armogathe. *Histoire du feminisme Français du moyen age à nos jours.* Paris: Editions des Femmes, 1977.

Algermissen, Konrad. *Christian Denominations.* Translated by J. W. Grundner. St. Louis: B. Herder Book Co., 1946.

Andrieu, Jules. *Bibliographie générale de l'Agenais.* Paris: A. Picard, 1887.

Armogathe, Jean-Robert. "Les vies de Calvin aux XVIe et XVIIe siècles." *Historiographie de la réforme.* Edited by Philippe Joutard. Paris: Delachaux & Niestle S.A., 1977.

Bady, René. *L'Homme et son institution de Montaigne à Berulle 1580–1625.* Paris: Société d'Édition "Les Belles Lettres."

Bainton, Roland. *Women of the Reformation in Germany and Italy.* Minneapolis: Augsburg Publishing House, 1971.

———. *Women of the Reformation in France and England.* Minneapolis: Augsburg Publishing House, 1973.

———. *Women of the Reformation from Spain to Scandinavia.* Minneapolis: Augsburg Publishing House, 1977.

Balsama, George D. *The Decomposition and Rebirth of Post-Reformation France.* Dubuque, I: Kendall/Hunt Publishing Company, 1974.

Barke, Herbert. *Bales "Kynge Johan" und sein Verhaltnis zur zeitgenössischen Geschictschreibung.* Würzburg: K. Triltsch, 1937.

Baraclough, Geoffrey. *The Medieval Papacy.* New York: Harcourt, Brace, and World, Inc., 1968.

Bäumer, Remigius. *Martin Luther und der Papst*. Münster: Aschendorff, 1979.

Baumgartner, Frederic J. *Radical Reactionaries: The Political Thought of the French Catholic League*. Geneva: Librairie Droz, 1975.

Bedouelle, Guy. *Lefèvre D'Étaples et l'intelligence des écritures*. Geneva: Librairie Droz. 1976.

Benz, Ernst. *Wittenberg und Byzanz, Begegnung und Auseinandersetzung der Reformation und der Ostlich Orthodoxen Kirche*. Munich: Wilhelm Fink Verlag, 1971.

Benzing, Josef. *Die Buckdrucker des 16. und 17. Jahrhunderts Im Deutschen Sprachgebiet*. Wiesbaden: Otto Harrassowitz, 1963.

Berriat-Saint-Prix, Jacques. *Jacob Cujas and Seine Zeitgenossen*, a translation by Ernst Spangenberg of Berriat-Saint-Prix's *Histoire du droit romain, suivi de l'histoire de Cujas*, 1821. Leipzig: J. F. Hartknoch, 1822.

Bethman, Ludwig. "Sigiberti Gemblacensis chronographia." In *Mon. Germ. Hist. Script.*, edited by Heinrich Pertz. Hanover: Impensis Bibliopolii Aulici Hahniani, 1844, VI, pp. 268–474.

Bizer, Ernst. *Studien Zur Geschichte Des Abendmahlsstreits Im 16. Jahrhundert*. Darmstadt: Wissenschaftliche Buchgesellschaft, 1962.

Boase, Alan. *The Fortunes of Montaigne*. London: Methuen & Co., Ltd., 1935.

Boase, Alan, and François Puchon. *La vie et l'oeuvre de Jean de Sponde*. Geneva: Éditions Pierre Cailler, 1949.

Bousset, Wilhelm. *Der Antichrist in der Überlieferung des Judentums des Neuen Testaments und der Alten Kirche. Ein Beitrag zur Auslegung der Apokalypse*. Gottingen: Vandenhoeck and Ruprecht, 1895.

Bouwsma, William J. *Concordia Mundi: The Career and Thought of Guillaume Postel (1510–1581)*. Cambridge, Mass.: Harvard University Press, 1957.

———. *John Calvin: A Sixteenth Century Portrait*. New York: Oxford University Press, 1988.

Brémond, Henri. *A Literary History of Religious Thought in France. I. Devout Humanism*. Translated by K. L. Montgomery, New York: Macmillan, 1928.

Briggs, Robin. *Early Modern France 1560–1715*. Oxford: Oxford University Press, 1977.

Broderick, James. *The Life and Work of Blessed Robert Francis Cardinal Bellarmine. S.I. 1542–1621*. (2 vols.) New York: P. J. Kenedy & Sons, 1928.

Brown, Frieda S. *Religious and Political Conservatism in the Essays of Montaigne*. Geneva: Librairie Droz, 1963.

Bungener, Félix. *Calvin sa vie son oeuvre et ses ècrits*. Paris: J. Cherbuliez, 1862.

Burckhardt, Andreas. *Johannes Basilius Herold Kaiser und Reich im protestantischen Schrifftum des Asler Buchdrucks um die Mitte des 16 Jahrhunderts*. Basel: Verlag von Helbing & Lichtenhahn, 1967.

Busch, Martin. "*Florimond de Raemond (vers 1540–1601) et l'Anabaptisme*. (2 vols.) (Unpublished doctoral dissertation). Strasbourg: Université des Sciences Humaines de Strasbourg. Faculte de Théologie Protestante, 1980–1981.

Busson, Henri. *Le rationalisme dans la littérature Française de la Renaissance*. Paris: Librairie Philosophique J. Vrin, 1957.

———. *Littérature et théologie: Montaigne, Bossuet, La Fontaine, Prévost*. Paris: Presses Universitaires de France, 1962.

Cameron, Keith. *Agrippa D'Aubigné*. Boston: Twayne Publishers, 1977.

Campenhausen, Hans von. *Ecclesiastical Authority and Spiritual Power in the Church of the First Three Centuries.* Translated by J. A. Baker. Stanford: Stanford University Press, 1969.

Charron, Jean. *The "Wisdom" of Pierre Charron, an Original and Orthodox Code of Morality.* Chapel Hill, N.C.: University of North Carolina Press, 1961.

Christensen, Carl. C. *Art and the Reformation in Germany.* Athens: Ohio University Press, 1979.

Couderc, J.-B. *Le Venérable Cardinal Bellarmin.* 2 vols. Paris: V. Retaux et fils, 1893.

Courteault, Paul. *Geoffroy de Malvyn Magistrat et Humaniste Bordelais 1545(?)−1617.* Paris: Bibliothèque Littéraire de la Renaissance. (III). Paris: Honoré Champion, 1907.

Couthial, Pierre. "The Golden Age of Calvinism in France, 1533−1633." In *John Calvin His Influence in the Western World.* Edited by W. Stanford Reid. Grand Rapids, Mich.: Zondervan Publishing House, 1982.

Cristiani, Léon. *L'Église à l'époque du Concile de Trente.* Paris: Bloud & Gay, 1948.

D'Aubigné, Merle J. H. *History of the Great Reformation.* New York: Robert Carter, 1843.

Dauzat, Albert. *Dictionnaire étymologique des noms de famille et prénoms de France.* Paris: Librairie Larousse, 1951.

Davis, Natalie. *Society and Culture in Early Modern France.* Stanford, Stanford University Press, 1977.

De La Tour, Pierre Imbart. *Les Origines de la réforme.* Paris: Librairie Hachette et Cie., II, 1909.

Denzer, Horst, ed. *Bodin.* Munich: Beck, 1973.

Desgraves, Louis. *Répertoire bibliothèque des livres imprimés en France au XVIIIe siècle.* Baden-Baden: Éditions Valentin Koerner, 1978.

───. *Répertoire des ouvrages de controverse entre Catholiques et Protestants en France (1598−1685).* Geneva: Librairies Droz, S.A., 1984.

───. "Johannes Sleidan and Reformation History." In *Reformation Conformity and Dissent.* Edited by R. Buick Knox. London: Epworth Press, 1977.

Dickens A. G. *The German Nation and Martin Luther.* London: E. Arnold, 1974.

───. and John Tonkin, with Kenneth Powell. *The Reformation in Historical Thought.* Cambridge, Mass.: Harvard University Press, 1985.

Dodgson, C., "Tertullian." In *A Library of Fathers of the Holy Catholic Church* (Oxford: Parker, 1842), X.

Döllinger, Johann Jos. Ign. v. *Die Papst-Fabeln des Mittelalters.* (1st ed., 1863). Frankfurt-am-Main: Minerva, 1962.

Dompnier, Bernard. "L'Histoire religieuse chez les controversistes réformés du début du XVIIe siècle." In *Historiographie de la Réforme.* Edited by Philippe Joutarde. Paris: Delachaux & Niestle S.A., 1977.

D'Onofrio, Cesare. *Mille Anni di Leggènda: Una Donna Sul Trono di Pietro.* Rome: Romana Società Editrice, 1978.

Doumergue, Émile. *Jean Calvin les hommes et les choses de son temps.* I. *La Jeunesse de Calvin.* Lausanne: Georges Bridel & Cie., Éditeurs, 1899.

Dreano, Maturin. *La Pensée religieuse de Montaigne.* Paris: Gabriel Beauchesne et ses fils, 1936.

———. *La Religion de Montaigne*. Paris: Librairie A.-G. Nizet, 1969.

Dress, Walter. "Popes." In *The Encyclopedia of the Lutheran Church*. Minneapolis: Augsburg Publishing House, 1965.

Dubois, Claude-Gilbert. *La Conception de l'histoire en France au XVIe Siècle*. Paris: A.-G. Nizet, 1977.

Edwards, Mark U. *Luther's Last Battles*. Ithaca, N.Y.: Cornell University Press, 1983.

Eisenstein, Elizabeth. "The Advent of Printing and the Protestant Revolt." In *Transition and Revolution*. Edited by Robert M. Kingdon. Minneapolis: Burgess Publishing Company, 1974.

Emmerson, Richard Kenneth. *Antichrist in the Middle Ages*. Seattle: University of Washington Press, 1981.

Fairfield, Leslie P. *John Bale, Mythmaker for the English Reformation*. West Lafayette, Ind.: Purdue University Press, 1976.

Febvre, Lucien. "Une Question mal posée les origines de la Réforme Française et le problème général des causes de la Réforme" (1929). Reprinted in *Au Coeur Religieux du XVI Siècle*. Paris: Sevpen, 1957.

Felice, Paul de. *Lambert Daneau*. Geneva: Slatkine Reprints, 1971. (1st ed., 1882.)

Forstman, H. Jackson. *Word and Spirit Calvin's Doctrine of Biblical Authority*. Stanford, Calif.: Stanford University Press, 1962.

Frame, Donald. *Montaigne, A. Biography*. New York: Harcourt, Brace, & World, Inc., 1965.

Franklin, Julian H. *Jean Bodin and the Sixteenth-Century Revolution in the Methodology of Law and History*. New York: Cambridge University Press, 1963.

Franzen, August. *Kleine Kirchengeschichte*. Freiburg: Herderbucherei, 1965.

Fryde, E. B. *Humanism and Renaissance Historiography*. London: The Hambledon Press, 1983.

Fuellenback, John. *Ecclesiastical Office and the Primacy of Rome*. Washington, D.C.: Catholic University of America Press, 1980.

Ganoczy, Alexandre. *Calvin théologien de l'église et du ministère*. Paris: Les Éditions du Cerf. 1964.

———. *Le Jeune Calvin genèse et évolution de sa vocation réformatrice*. Wiesbaden: Franz Steiner Verlag GMBH, 1966.

Garrisson-Estèbe, Janine. *Protestants du Midi 1559–1598*. Toulouse: Privat, 1980.

———. "Vers une autre religion et une autre église (1536–1598)." In *Histoire des Protestantes en France*. Edited by Robert Mandrou, et al. Toulouse: Édouard Privat, 1977.

Gombrich, E. H. *The Story of Art*. New York: Phaidon Publishers Inc., 1957.

Grafton, Anthony. *Joseph Scaliger, A Study in the History of Classical Scholarship*. Oxford: Clarendon Press, 1983.

Gritsch, Eric. *Reformer Without a Church. The Life and Thought of Thomas Muentzer, 188?–1525*. Philadelphia: Fortress Press, 1967.

Gundersheimer, Werner L. *The Life and Works of Louis Le Roy*. Geneva: Librairie Droz, 1966.

Harbison, E. Harris. *Christianity and History*. Princeton, N.J.: Princeton University Press, 1964.

Harris, Jesse W. *John Bale, A Study in the Minor Literature of the Reformation*. Urbana: 1940.
Haskins, Charles Homer. *The Rise of Universities*. New York: Henry Holt and Company, 1923.
Hasler, August Bernhard. *How the Pope Became Infallible*. Translated by Peter Heinegg. New York.: Doubleday & Company, 1981.
Hauser, Arnold. *The Social History of Art*. II. New York: Vintage Books, 1959.
Hauser, Henri. *Les Sources de l'histoire de France*. IV. Paris: Librairie Alphonse Picard et Fils, 1912.
Hay, Denis. *The Italian Renaissance*. Cambridge: Cambridge University Press, 1970.
Headley, John M. *Luther's View of Church History*. New Haven: Yale University Press, 1963.
Hendrix, Scott H. *Luther and the Papacy*. Philadelphia: Fortress Press, 1981.
Höpfl, Harro. *The Christian Polity of John Calvin*. Cambridge: Cambridge University Press, 1982.
Horkheimer, Max. "Montaigne und die Funktion der Skepsis," *Kritische Theorie*, II. *Eine Dokumentation*, Alfred Schmidt, ed. Frankfurt a.M.: S. Fischer Verlag, 1968, pp. 201–59.
Huppert, George. *The Idea of Perfect History*. Urbana, Ill.: University of Illinois Press, 1970.
Irwin, Joyce. "Society and the Sexes," in *Reformation Europe: A Guide to Research*. Edited by Steven Ozment, St. Louis: Center for Reformation Research, 1982.
Iserloh, Erwin, Joseph Glazik and Hubert Jedin, *Reformation and Counter Reformation*. Translated by Anselm Biggs and Peter W. Becker, (Vol. V of *History of the Church*, edited by Hubert Jedin,) New York: The Seabury Press, 1980.
Janssen, Herman. *Montaigne fidéiste*. Nijmegen-Utrecht: N. V. Dekker & van de Vegt en J. W. van Leeuwen, 1930.
Jedin, Hubert. *Kardinal Caesar Baronius Der Anfang Der Katholischen Kirchensgeschicts-Schreibung Im 16. Jahrhundert*. Munster: Aschendorff, 1978.
Jensen, De Lamar. *Reformation Europe Age of Reform and Revolution*. Lexington, Mass.: D. C. Heath and Company, 1981.
Jouannet, F. *Statistique du Département de la gironde*. II. Paris: P. Dupon et Cie., 1843.
Jugé, Clément. *Jacques Peletier, du Mans (1517–1582) essai sur sa vie, son oeuvre, son influence*. Paris: A. Lemerre, 1907.
Kelley, Donald R. *Foundations of Modern Historical Scholarship Language, Law, and History in the French Renaissance*. New York: Columbia University Press, 1970.
———. *François Hotman A Revolutionary's Ordeal*. Princeton, N. J.: Princeton University Press, 1973.
———. *The Beginning of Ideology Consciousness and Society in the French Reformation*. Cambridge: Cambridge University Press, 1981.
Keohane, Nannerl O. *Philosophy and the State in France*. Princeton, N. J.: Princeton University Press, 1980.

King, Margaret Leah. "Book Lined Cells: Women and Humanism in the Early Italian Renaissance." In *Beyond Their Sex, Learned Women of the European Past*. Edited by Patricia H. Labalme, New York: New York University Press, 1980.

Kingdon, Robert M. *Calvin and Calvinism Sources of Democracy*? with Robert D. Linder, Eds. Lexington, Mass.: D. C. Heath and Company, 1970.

Kinser, Samuel. *The Works of Jacques-Auguste De Thou*. The Hague: Martinus Nijhoff, 1966.

Knecht, R. J., *Francis I*. Cambridge: Cambridge University Press, 1982.

Kuntz, Marion L. *Guillaume Postel Prophet of the Restitution of all Things His Life and Thought*. The Hague: Martinus Nijhoff, 1981.

Laplanche, François. *L'Écriture, Le Sacré et L'Histoire: Érudits et politiques Protestants devant La Bible en France au XVIIIe siècle*. Amsterdam: APA-Holland University Press, 1986.

Larroque, Philippe Tamizey de. *Essai sur la vie et les ouvrages de Florimond de Raymond*. Paris: August Aubry, 1867.

Latourette, Kenneth Scott. *A History of Christianity*. New York: Harper and Row, 1975.

Lebrun, François. *La Vie conjugale sous l'ancien régime*. Paris: Armand Colin, 1975.

Lefranc, Abel. *La Jeunesse de Calvin*. Paris: Librairie Fishbacher, 1888.

Léonard, Émile G. *Histoire générale du Protestantisme*. 2 vols. Paris: Presses Universitaires de France, 1961.

Levi, Anthony. *French Moralists: The Theory of the Passions 1585–1649*. Oxford: Clarendon Press, 1964.

Lienhard, Marc. *Martin Luther un temps, une vie, un message*. Paris: Le Centurion, 1983.

Ligou, Daniel. *Le Protestantisme en France de 1598 à 1715*. Paris: Société d'Édition d'Enseignement Supérieur, 1968.

Loewen, Harry. *Luther and the Radicals*. Waterloo, Ont.: Wilfrid Laurier University, 1974.

Lortz, Joseph. *The Reformation A Problem for Today*. Westminster, Md.: The Newman Press, 1964.

———. *The Reformation in Germany*. London: Darton, Longman, & Todd, 1968. (First edition, 1939).

McDonnell, Kilian. *John Calvin, the Church, and the Eucharist*. Princeton, N. J.: Princeton University Press, 1967.

McLaughlin, R. Emmet. *Caspar Schwenckfeld Reluctant Radical*. New Haven, Conn.: Yale University Press, 1986.

McNeil, David O. *Guillaume Budé and Humanism in the Reign of Francis I* Geneva: Librairie Droz, 1975.

McNeill, John T. *The History and Character of Calvinism*. New York: Oxford University Press, 1954.

Maier, Paul Luther. *Caspar Schwenckfeld on the Person and Work of Christ*. Assen: Royal Van Gorcum Ltd., 1959.

Mandrou, Robert, et al. *Histoire des Protestants en France*. Toulouse: Édouard Privat, 1977.

Mandrou, Robert. *Magistrats et sorciers en France au XVIIe siècle*. Paris: Librairie Plon, 1968.

———. *Introduction to Modern France 1500−1640*. R. E. Hallmark, Trans. New York: Holmes & Meier, 1976.

——— "Pourquoi Se Réformer?" in *Histoire des Protestants en France*. Toulouse: Édouard Privat, 1977.

Manns, Peter. "Luther und die Heiligen," In *Reformation Ecclesiae. Beiträge zu kirchlichen Reformbemühungen von der alten Kirche bis zur Neuzeit. Festgabe für Erwin Iserloh*. Edited by Remegius Bäumer. Paderborn: Schöningh, 1980.

Maron, Gottfried. *Das Katholische Lutherbild Der Gegenwart*. Göttingen: Vandenhoeck & Ruprecht, 1982.

Martimort, Aimé-Georges. *Le Gallicanisme*. Paris: Presses Universaires de France, 1973.

Martin, Victor. *Le Gallicanisme et la réforme Catholique essai historique sur l'introduction en France des décrets du Concile de Trente (1563−1615)*. 1st ed., 1919. Geneva: Slatkine-Megariotis Reprints, 1975.

Massner, Joachim. *Kirchliche Überlieferung und Autorität im Flacius-kreis; Studien zu den Magdeburger Zenturien*. Berlin: Lutherisches Verlagshaus, 1964.

Mau, Rudolf. "Luthers Stellung zu den Türken," In *Leben und Werk Martin Luthers von 1526 bis 1546*. Edited by Helmar Junghans, Göttingen: Vandenhoeck & Ruprecht, 1983.

Méthivier, Hubert. *L'Ancien régime en France XVIe−XVIIIe siècles*. Paris: Presses Universitaires de France, 1981.

Migne, J. P. *Patrologia Latina*. CXLII. Paris: Garnier, 1879−1880.

Milner, Benjamin Charles. *Calvin's Doctrine of the Church*. Leiden: E. J. Brill, 1970.

Monter, William. *Calvin's Geneva*. New York: John Wiley and Sons, 1967.

Moore, W. G. *La Réforme Allemande et la littérature Française*. Strasbourg: Publications de la Faculté des Lettres de l'Université de Strasbourg.

Morris, Joan. *The Lady Was a Bishop*. New York: Macmillan, 1973.

Morrison, Karl F. *Tradition and Authority in the Western Church 300−1140*. Princeton, N. J.: Princeton University Press, 1969.

Mours, Samuel. *Le Protestantisme en France au XVIe siècle*. Paris: Librairie Protestante, 1959.

Mousnier, Roland. *L'Assassinat d'Henri IV 14 Mai 1610 le problème du Tyrannicide et l'affermissement de la monarchie absolue*. Paris: Éditions Gallimard, 1964.

Moussiegt, Paul. *Hotman et du Plessis-Mornay, théories politiques au XVIe siècle*. Geneva: Slatkine Reprints, 1970. (1st ed., 1899.)

Moyne, Thérèse. "L'Imagerie de controverse Catholique dans les livres illustrés à Lyon, etc." In *Historiographie de la Réforme*. Edited by Philippe Joutard, Paris: Delachaux & Niestle, S.A., 1977.

Naz, R., ed. *Dictionnaire de Droit Canonique*. Paris: Letouzey et Ané, 1942.

Neuser, W. H., ed. *Calvinus Theologus, Die Referate des Congrès Europeen de Recherches Calviniennes* (European Congress on Calvin Research). 16−19 Sept. 1974, in Amsterdam. Neukirchen-Vluyn: Neukirchener Verlag, 1976.

O'Gilvy, M. *Nobiliaire de Guienne et de Gascogne*. II. 1st ed., 1958. Paris: Éditions du Palais Royal, 1973.

Oyer, John. "The Influence of Jacob Strauss on the Anabaptists," in *The Origins and Characteristics of Anabaptism*. Edited by 1st ed., 1911. Marc Lienhard, The Hague: Nijhoff, 1977.

Pannier, Jacques. *L'Église réformée de Paris sous Henri IV*. 1st ed., 1911. Geneva: Slatkine-Megariotis Reprints, 1977.

———. *Recherches sur l'évolution de Calvin jusqu'à sa conversion*. Strasbourg: Istra, 1924.

Parker, T. H. L. *John Calvin: A Biography*. London: J. M. Dent & Sons Ltd., 1975.

Pater, Calvin A. *Karlstadt as the Father of the Baptist Movements: The Emergence of Lay Protestantism*. Toronto: University of Toronto Press, 1984.

Pauck, Wilhelm. *The Heritage of the Reformation*. Glencoe, Ill.: Free Press, 1961, (1st. edition, 1950).

Pelikan, Jaroslav. *Obedient Rebels*. New York: Harper & Row, Publishers, 1964.

Pennington, Kenneth. *Pope and Bishops*. Philadelphia: University of Pennsylvania Press, 1984.

Perry, Elizabeth Israels. *From Theology to History: French Religious Controversy and the Revocation of the Edict of Nantes*. The Hague: Martinus Nijhoff, 1973.

Pesch, Otto. *Die Theologie der Rechtfertigung bei Martin Luther und Thomas von Aquin, Versuch eines systematisch-theologischen Dialogs, in Walberger Studien*, Theol. Reihe, IV. Mainz: Matthias-Grünewald-Verlag, 1967.

Pesch, Rudolf. "The Position and Significance of Peter in the Church of the *New Testament*, A Survey of Current Research," In *Papal Ministry in the Church*. Edited by Hans Kung, New York: Herder and Herder, 1971.

Pocock, J. G. A. *The Ancient Constitution and the Feudal Law*. Cambridge: Cambridge University Press, 1957.

Polman, Pontien. *L'Élément historique dans la controverse religieuse du XVIe siècle*. Gemblou: J. Duculot, Éditeur, 1932.

Popkin, Richard H. *The History of Scepticism from Erasmus to Descartes*. Assen: Van Gorcum & Comp. N.V., 1960.

Potter, G. R. *Zwingli*. London: Cambridge University Press, 1976.

Potthast, August. *Bibliotheca Historica Medii Aevi*. Berlin: W. Weber, 1896.

Preus, Robert D. *The Theology of Post-Reformation Lutheranism*. Saint Louis: Concordia Pub. House, 1970.

Pullapilly, Cyriac K. *Caesar Baronius Counter-Reformation Historian*. Notre Dame, Ind.: University of Notre Dame Press, 1975.

Rabb, Theodore K. "Conclusion: St. Bartholomew and Historical Perspective," In *The Massacre of St. Bartholomew: Reappraisals and Documents*. Edited by Alfred Soman. The Hague: Martinus Nijhoff, 1974.

Rance-Bourrey, A. J. *J.-A. De Thou, son histoire universelle et ses démêlés avec Rome*. 1st ed., 1881. Geneva: Slatkine Reprints, 1970.

Rébelliau, Alfred. *Bossuet*. Paris: Librairie Hachette, 1909.

Reid, W. Stanford, ed. *John Calvin His Influence in the Western World*. Grand Rapids, Mich.: Zondervan Pub. House, 1982.

Renaudet, Augustin. *Pré-Réforme et Humanisme à Paris Pendant les Premières Guerres D'Italie (1494–1517)*. 2nd ed., revised and corrected; 1st ed., 1916. Paris: Librairie D'Argences, 1953.

Reusch, Franz Heinrich, and Joh. Jus. Ign. V. Döllinger, translators, *Die Selbstbiographie des Cardinals Bellarmin*. Bonn: P. Neuser, 1887.

Reyburn, Hugh Y. *John Calvin, His Life, Letters, and Work*. London: Hodder and Stoughton, 1914.

Rice, Eugene F. *The Renaissance Idea of Wisdom*. Cambridge, Mass.: Harvard University Press, 1958.

Richards, Jeffrey. *The Popes and the Papacy in the Early Middle Ages*. Boston: Routledge & Kegan Paul, 1979.

Rider, Frederick. *The Dialectic of Selfhood in Montaigne*. Stanford, Calif.: Stanford University Press, 1973.

Rilliet, Jean. *Calvin*. Paris: Arthème Fayard, 1963.

Roelker, Nancy Lyman. "Family, Faith, and Fortuna: The Chatillon Brothers in the French Reformation." (Chapter 9 of *Leaders of the Reformation*. Edited by Richard L. DeMolen, London: Susquehanna University Press, 1984.

Rowell, Geoffrey. *The Liturgy of Christian Burial*. London: Alcuin Club S.P.C.K., 1977.

Sabrié, Jean B. *De l'humanisme au Rationalisme: Pierre Charron, l'Homme, L'oeuvre, l'Influence*. Paris: Alcan, 1913.

Sayous, Pierre-André. *Études littéraires sur les écrivains Français de la Réformation*. I. 1st ed., 1881. Geneva: Slatkine Reprints, 1970.

Schmidt, Charles. *Gérard Roussel prédicateur de la Reine Marguerite de Navarre*. Geneva: A. Cherbuliez et Cie., 1845.

Sclafert, Clément. *L'Âme religieuse de Montaigne*. Paris: Nouvelles Éditions Latines, 1951.

Scribner, R. W. *For the Sake of Simple Folk*. Cambridge: Cambridge University Press, 1981.

Sider, Ronald J. *Andreas Bodenstein Von Karlstadt: The Development of His Thought 1517−1525*. Leiden: E. J. Brill, 1974.

Soman, Alfred, ed. *The Massacre of St. Bartholomew: Reappraisals and Documents*. The Hague: Martinus Nijhoff, 1974.

Sommervogel, Carlos. *Bibliothèque de la compagnie de Jésus*, III. Paris: Alphonse Picard, 1892.

Sperk, Klaus. *Mittelalterliche Tradition und Reformatorische Polemik in den Spielen John Bales*. Heidelberg: Winter, 1973.

Spinka, Matthew. *Advocates of Reform from Wyclif to Erasmus*. London: SCM Press, 1953.

———. *John Hus's Concept of the Church*. Princeton, N. J.: Princeton University Press, 1966.

Steinmann, Martin. *Johannes Oporinus, Ein Basler Buchdrucker um die Mitte des 16. Jahrhunderts*. Basel: Verlag von Helbing & Lichtenhahn, 1967.

Telle, Émile. *L'Oeuvre de Marguerite d'Angoulême reine de Navarre et la querelle des femmes*. 1st ed., 1937. Geneva: Slatkine Reprints, 1960.

Thibaut-Payen, Jacqueline. *Les Morts, l'église et l'état recherches d'histoire administrative sur la sépulture et les cimitières dans le ressort du Parlement de Paris aux XVIIe et XVIIIe siècles*. Paris: Éditions Lanore, 1977.

Thomas, Jules. *Le Concordat de 1516 ses origines son histoire aux XVIe siècle*, 3 vols. Paris: A. Picard, 1910.

Thompson, James Westphal. *A History of Historical Writing.* I. New York: Macmillan, 1942.

Thorndike, Lynn. *A History of Magic and Experimental Science.* New York: Macmillan, 1941.

Tierney, Brian. *Origins of Papal Infallibility 1150–1350, A Study on the Concepts of Infallibility, Sovereignty and Tradition in the Middle Ages.* Leiden: E. J. Brill, 1972.

Trevor-Roper, Hugh. *The Rise of Christian Europe.* New York: Harcourt, Brace, and World, Inc., 1965.

Troeltsch, Ernst. *The Social Teaching of the Christian Churches.* II. Translated by Olive Wyon, London: George Allen & Unwin, Ltd., 1931.

Ullmann, Walter. *The Growth of Papal Government in the Middle Ages.* London: Methuen & Co., Ltd., 1955.

Urech, Édouard. *Guillaume Farel.* La Chaux de Fonds: Éditions Saint-Clair, 1965.

Vaillancourt, Jean-Guy. *Papal Power: A Study of Vatican Control over Lay Catholic Elites.* Berkeley: University of California Press, 1980.

Verheus, Simon L. *Zeugnis and Gericht, Kirchengeschichtliche Betrachtungen bei Sebastian Franck und Matthias Flacius.* Nieukoop: B. De Graaf, 1971.

Vienot, John. *Histoire de la réforme Française des origines à l'édit de Nantes.* Paris: Librairie Fischbacher, 1926.

Vindry, Fleury. *Les Parlémentaires Français au XVIe siècle.* II. Paris: Librairie Honoré Champion, 1910.

Vovelle, Michel. *Mourir autrefois attitudes collectives devant la mort aux XVIIe et XVIIIe siècles.* Paris: Éditions Gallimard/Juilliard, 1974.

Vryonis, Speros. *Byzantium and Europe.* New York: Harcourt, Brace and World, Inc., 1967.

Waddington, Charles. *Ramus sa vie, ses écrits, et ses opinions.* Paris: Charles Meyrais et Cie., 1855.

Waitz, G. "Mariani Scotti Chronicon." *Mon. Ger. Hist. Script.*, edited by Georgius Heinrich Pertz (Hanover: Impensis Bibliopolii Avlici Hahniani, 1844) V, pp. 481–562.

Walker, Williston. *A History of the Christian Church.* New York: Charles Scribner's Sons, 1959. (1st ed., 1918).

———. *John Calvin, The Organiser of Reformed Protestantism 1509–1564.* (1st ed., 1906) New York: Schocken Books, 1969.

Wallace, Ronald S. *Calvin's Doctrine of the Christian Life.* Edinburgh: Oliver and Boyd, 1959.

———. *Calvin's Doctrine of the Word and Sacrament.* Edinburgh: Oliver and Boyd, 1953.

Walton, Robert C. *Zwingli's Theocracy.* Toronto: University of Toronto Press, 1967.

Warnicke, Retha M. *Women in the English Renaissance & Reformation.* Westport, Conn.: Greenwood Press, 1983.

Weiland, Ludwig. "Martini Oppaviensis Chronicon Pontificum et Imperatorum." In *Mon. Germ. Hist. Script.*, edited by Georgius Heinrich Pertz. Hanover: Weidmannsche Verlagsbuchhandlung, 1872. XXII, 377–97.

Wendel, François. *Calvin, The Origins and Development of His Religious Thought.* Translated by Philip Mairet, London: Collins, 1963.

Wenger, John Christian. *Even Unto Death: The Heroic Witness of the Sixteenth-Century Anabaptists.* Richmond, Va.: John Knox Press, 1961.

Wicks, Jared, ed. *Catholic Scholars Dialogue with Luther.* Chicago: Loyola University Press, 1970.

Wiesner, Merry E. *Women in Sixteenth-Century Europe: A Bibliography.* St. Louis: Center for Reformation Research, 1983.

Willaert, Leopold. *La Restauration Catholique.* Namur: Sécretariat des Publications, 1960.

Williams, George Huntston. *The Radical Reformation.* Philadelphia: The Westminster Press, 1962.

Wilson, Adrian. *The Making of the Nuremberg Chronicle.* Amsterdam:, Nico Israel, 1976.

Wood, Clement. *The Woman Who Was Pope.* New York: W. Faro, 1931.

Wyntjes, Sherrin M. "Women in the Reformation Era." In *Becoming Visible: Women in European History*, edited by R. Bridenthal and C. Koonz. Boston: Houghton Mifflin, 1977.

Yoder, John H. "Introduction." In *The Origins and Characteristics of Anabaptism.* Edited by Marc Lienhard, The Hague: Nijhoff, 1977.

Periodicals

Allain, E. "Un Document inédit sur Florimond de Raymond." *Revue Catholique de Bordeaux*, 1892, 701.

Augier, L. M. Untitled article. *L'Aquitaine Semaine Religieuse de l'Archdiocèse de Bordeaux.* 29 April 1892. Pp. 269–70.

Baron, Hans. "The Querelle of the Ancients and Moderns," *Journal of the History of Ideas* XX (1959): 3–22.

Boase, Alan. "Montaigne annoté par Florimond de Raemond." *Revue du seizième siècle* XV (1928): 237–78.

———. "Montaigne et la Sorcellerie." *Humanisme et Renaissance* II (1935): 417–21.

Bonnat, R. "F. de Raymond à Bordeaux." *Revue Agenais* LII (1925): 129–32.

Bonnet, Pierre. "Une Nouvelle série d'annotations de Florimond de Raemond aux *Essais* de Montaigne." *Bulletin de la société des amis de Montaigne*, no. 10, (Apr.–Je., 1959); 10–23.

Clasen, Claus-Peter. "The Sociology of Swabian Anabaptism." *Church History* 32 (1963), 150–180.

Clinchamp, J. De. "Notices biographiques et littéraires. J. Peletier." *Bulletin du Bibliophile* (1847), 283–308; 439–468.

Cochrane, Eric. "The Transition from Renaissance to Baroque: The Case of Italian Historiography." *History and Theory* XIX, no. 1 (1980): 21–38.

Couture, Léonce. "Florimond de Raymond." *Revue de Gascogne* IX (1868), in 3 parts: 102–10, 361–71, 497–512.

Darricau, Raymond. "La Vie et l'oeuvre d'un parlementaire Aquitain Florimond de Raemond (1540–1601)." *Revue Française d'histoire du livre* (1971); 109–28.

Grimm, Harold. "Social Forces in the German Reformation." *Church History* 31 (1962): 3–13.

Labadie, Ernest. "Additions et rectifications à la bibliographie de quelques écrivains Agenais." *Revue de l'Agenais* (1906): 3–38.

Larroque, Philippe Tamizey de. "L'Emprisonnement de F. de Raymond." *Revue de Gascogne* XXXVI (1895): 127–28.

———. "Le Fils ainé de F. de Raymond," *Revue de Gascogne* XXXVI (1895); 222–24.

Martin, H. J. "Ce qu'on lisait à Paris au XVIe siècle." *Bibliothèque D'Humanisme et de Renaissance* XXI (1959); 222–30.

Martin, William. "Waiting For the End." *The Atlantic Monthly* 249, no. 6 (June 1982); 31–37.

Momméja, J. "La Dévise de F. de Raymond." *Revue de l'Agenais* (1908); 561–64.

Roelker, Nancy Lyman. "The Appeal of Calvinism to French Noblewomen in the Sixteenth Century." *The Journal of Interdisciplinary History*, II, no. 4 (1972); 391–413.

———. "The Role of Noblewomen in the French Reformation." *Archiv für Reformationsgeschichte* 63, (1972); 168–95.

Sider, Ronald J. "Karlstadt and Luther's Doctorate." In *Journal of Theological Studies* 22 (1971), 168–69.

Staats, Reinhart. "Luther's Geburtsjahr und das Geburtsjahr der Evangelischen Kirche 1519." In *Bibliotek und Wissenschaft* 18 (1984), 61ff.

Scriptural References

Daniel 7:25, 8:8–12, 8:11
Deut. 33:22
Ezek. 38:1–9, 38:16
Gen. 49:17
Gal. 2:8
Jer. 8:16
I John 2:18, 2:22, 17:18
Luke 23:31–32
Mark 16:16
Matt. 24:4–5, 24:24
Phil. 3:18
Rev. 13:17–18
I Thess. 2:14–16
II Thess. 2:3–4

Archives

ARCHIVES MUNICIPALES DE BORDEAUX

MS Delpit, f°s 210 V^o–212 1^0, copie
Fonds Payen
MS 24867
MS 597

DÉPARTEMENTALES DE LA GIRONDE

Édits Royaux, B. 38; and nos. CLXXXVI, CXXIII
B.N., LD4 1921–1922, and Vols. XX, XXIV, XXV
Série H, registre no. 355
Série B (Archives Judiciaires) 1925
Vol. 24, 1835 (Archives historiques au département de la Gironde, vol. 24, no. XXXIII, 1587)

Anonymous Work

Plaintes des églises réformées au roi sur plusieurs injustices qui leur sont faites, etc. 1597.

Index

Abelard, Peter, 98
Absolutism, 127–29, 137, 149, 170 n.64
Agen, 19, 53
Ailly, Pierre d', 98
Albert of Brandenburg, 171 n.74
Albigensians, 80
Anabaptists, 23, 59, 99, 100, 150
Antichrist, 9, 10, 13, 38, 54–55, 79–92, 95, 141, 143, 147, 149
Anti-Christ, L', 34, 36, 37–39, 48, 52, 54–55, 131, 148–49
Anti-Papesse, L', 55. See also *Erreur Populaire de la Papesse Jane*; Pope Joan
Angoulême, 11, 115–16
Antiochus IV, 80
Apocalypse, 88
Apostolic succession, 10
Arande, Michel d', 106–7
Arians (Arianism), 84, 98, 211 n.60
Aristotle, 100, 128, 186 n.15
Armenian heretics, 98
Astrology, 97
Auberi, Nicole, 24–25, 164 n.13
Aubigné, Théodore Agrippa d', 37, 138
Augsburg Confession, 39
Augsburg, Diet of, 8
Augustine, St., 98, 103, 199 n.62
Authoritarianism, 148, 152. See also Absolutism

Bale, John, 38, 55, 91, 183 n.3, 187 n.19
Baptism, 11, 99, 100, 121, 186 n.16. See also Pedobaptism
Baronius, Caesar (Cardinal), 40–41, 63, 72, 74, 84, 95, 127, 212 n.61
Baroque, 146
Bayle, Pierre, 77, 141–44, 146–47, 150–51
Bellarmine, Robert (Cardinal and St.) 75, 81, 83, 86–87, 212 n.61

Belle-Garde, M. de, 131
Benoist, Élie, 58, 170 n.57
Bernard, St., 98
Bèze, Théodore de, 12, 20, 22, 35–36, 54, 89, 91, 106, 110–12, 120, 131, 136–38
Biel, Gabriel, 98
Blondel, David, 78, 142, 147
Boccaccio, Giovanni, 68–69
Bodin, Jean, 90, 127
Bohemia, 127
Bolsec, Jerome, 110
Boniface III, 80
Bordeaux, *Parlement* of, 9, 20, 25, 40, 48–49, 53, 57–58, 62, 64, 178 n.62
Bordeaux, University of, 21
Bossuet, Jacques-Bénigne (Bishop), 145–46
Brach, Pierre de, 27, 29, 32, 64
Briçonnet, Guillaume (Bishop), 107–8
British Isles, 127
Briçonnet, Guillaume, 24, 106, 124
Bucer, Martin, 106
Buchanan, George, 21
Buchman, Theodor (Bibliander), 86–87
Budé, Guillaume, 24, 106, 124
Bullart, Isaac, 146
Bullinger, Heinrich, 91, 95, 119
Burials, 57, 59, 60, 123
Burnet, Gilbert, (Bishop), 25, 142, 147, 150
Busch, Martin, 150, 197 n.44

Cabala, 38, 126
Cajetan (né Giacomo de Vio. Dominican Master General and Cardinal), 99
Calvin, John, 11, 39, 55, 59, 63, 70, 81, 84–87, 90, 95, 105–8, 123, 132–33, 145–46
Calvinism (Calvinists), 11, 22, 36–37, 59–61, 98, 105, 110, 121

233

234　　　　　　　　　　INDEX

Calvinist Consistories, 12, 62, 83, 122, 126
Cano, Melchior, 212 n.61
Carlstadt, Andreas Bodenstein von, 75, 101, 104
Carvajal, Juan de, 68
Catholic League, 49, 53, 56–57, 131
Catholic tradition, 95, 105, 119
Celibacy, 75–76, 102–3, 121
Centuriators, 75, 82, 183 n.30. See *Magdeburg Centuries*
Chaillou, Anthony, 116
Chalcedon, Council of, 39, 82
Charles V (Emperor), 44, 88–89
Charles IX, 25, 44
Charron, Pierre, 39–40
Chrysostom, John (St.), 80
Chytraeus, David, 87
Clement VII (Pope), 72
Clement VIII (Pope) 173 n.4, 175 n.41
Colladon, Nicholas, 91, 110–12
Communion. See Eucharist
Conciliarists, 36, 68
Concordat of 1516, 45
Constance, Council of, 68, 75
Constantinople, Patriarch of, 39
Constantius II (Pope), 84
Copus, Alan, 212 n.61
Controversy. See Polemic
Counter Reformation, 30, 48, 50, 70, 77, 94
Courteault, Paul, 53–54
Couture, Léonce, 147, 150
Crespin, Jean, 20, 84
Crusade, 128
Crucifix (cross), 89–90, 118, 190 n.53
Cujas, Jacques, 42

Dan, House of, 85
Daneau, Lambert, 87, 91–92, 149, 187 n.19
Daniel, Book of, 79–80, 86
Dantecourt, Jean Baptiste, 144
Divorce, 102–3, 121
Donatist heretics, 98
Dorat, Jean, 91
Doumergue, Émile, 140
Drelincourt, Charles, 145
Du Bartas, Guillaume de Salluste, 23, 27, 43
Du Bois, Claude-Gilbert, 148–50

Du Bourg, Anne, 20, 22
Du Duc, Fronton, 40
Du Four, Arnold, 131
Du Fresnoy, Langlois, 143
Du Moulin, Pierre, 148
Du Mouchy, Antoine (Demochares), 109
Du Perron, Jacques Davy (Cardinal), 35, 37, 109
Du Plessis-Mornay, Philippe, 33, 37–42, 91, 126, 131, 148
Dupréau, Gabriel (Prateolus), 109
Du Tillet, Louis, 115–16, 205 n.53

Eck, Johannes, 98–99
Elective principle of government, 127–28
Enlightenment, 146, 215 n.33
Enoch and Elias (Elijah), 85–86
Erasmus, 34, 71, 89, 100, 106
Erreur Populaire de la Papesse Jane, 36, 48–50, 55, 66, 72, 77, 136, 142. See also *Anti-Papesse, L'*; Pope Joan
Estienne press, 71
Eucharist, 11, 101, 116, 118–21, 211 n.59

Fabricius, Johann Albert, 142
Farel, Guillaume, 106–7, 109
Felix II (Pope), 84
Feminism. See Misogyny; Women
Ferdinand I (Emperor), 212 n.60
Feuillants, 31, 64
Fideism, 34, 94
Family life, 121
Fisher, John (Bishop and St.), 98
Flacius Illyricus, Matthias, 38. See also Centuriators
Foresti, Giacomo Filippo, 69
Francis I, 21, 45, 76, 106, 128
Franciscans, 80
Frederick II, 80
French vernacular, 9–11, 48, 55, 81
Funerals. See Burials

Gallican(ism), 42, 44, 49, 83, 144
Gallican liberties, 13, 43–44, 46, 75
Galphridus of Oxfordshire, 71
Gaufreteau, Jean de, 28
Gens de robe (robins), 54
Gerhard, Johann, 68

Geneva, 118–19, 121, 131, 143, 150
Germans, 75, 87
Gillis, Marie de (Mother of Florimond), 19
Gog and Magog, 79, 85, 87–88
Gournay, Marie de, 185 n.63
Goulart, Simon, 84
Gregory I (Pope), 82
Gregory IX (Pope), 80
Guise, House of, 56
Guyenne, College of, 20

Hadrian II (Pope), 74
Henry II, 171 n.73
Henry III, 44, 128
Henry IV, 20, 35, 37, 43, 47, 49, 51–52, 56, 128, 130–31, 136, 141, 144, 148. *See also* Navarre, Henry of
Heresy (and heretics), 19–25, 61, 94, 96, 98, 104, 123, 127
Herold, John, 71
Hesshusen, Tileman (Hesshusius), 110
Heterodoxy, 124, 130
Hildaric, 75–76
Hippocrates, 133
History of Heresy (Histoire de la naissance, progrez et décadence de l'heresie de ce siècle), 36, 44, 49, 55, 59, 62–63, 93, 99, 109, 110, 123, 129, 134, 142, 144, 147–48
History: writing of, 9–11, 39, 50–51, 78, 92–95, 109, 124–39, 140. *See also* Raemond, Florimond: as a historian
History, universal, 12, 133–34, 142, 149, 151
Hosius, Stanislas (Cardinal), 212 n.61
Hotman, François, 12, 125, 131, 137, 138
Hübmaier, Balthasar, 100
Huguenots, 22, 25–27, 37–41, 45, 51, 53, 56, 59, 62, 122–23, 148
Humanism (humanist), 95, 114
Hungary, 127
Hus, Jan, 68, 81, 84, 91, 98
Hussites, 70, 80

Images, 118, 194 n.17
Index, 41, 129, 134, 175 n.41

Infallibility, 83–84, 95, 119, 136, 176 n.48
Innocent XI (Pope), 144
Irenaeus (Bishop and St.), 38, 91

James VI (of Scotland and James I of England), 87–88
Jesuits, 33, 40–45, 63
Jews, 59, 79–80, 85–86
Joachim of Fiore, 80
John the Baptist (St.): festival of, 28, 118
John VIII (Pope), 74–75
John XXII (Pope), 84
Joyeuse, François de, 64, 175 n.41
Junonius, 98

Labbe, Pierre (père), 142, 147
La Boétie, Estienne de, 25, 125
Lancre, Catharine de Rosteguy de (first wife of Florimond), 28
Lancre, Pierre de, 28, 158 n.58
La Popelinière, Henri Lancelot Voisin de, 125, 132, 134
Larmessin, Nicolas de, 146
Larroque, Philippe Tamizey de, 10, 12–13, 25–26, 140, 147
Latomus, Jacob, 83
Launoy, Jean de, 146–47
Leclerc, Laurent-Josse (abbé), 141–43, 147
Le Double, Pierre, 141
Lefèvre d'Étaples, Jacques, 69, 98, 106–8
Leipzig disputation, 99
Lenfant, Jacques, 146
Leo X (Pope), 45–46
Lepanto, Battle of, 89
Le Roy, Louis, 125, 132–33
Leu, Thomas, 214 n.31
Liberius (Pope), 84
Lindanus, William, 109
Lipse, Juste (Lipsius), 175 n.41, 181 n.95
Lord's Supper. *See* Eucharist
Louis XIII, 49
Louis XIV, 49
Luther, Martin, 11, 45, 70, 72, 75, 79–88, 90–91, 95, 97–105, 112, 133, 145, 212 n.60

INDEX

Lutheranism, 11, 44, 97–105, 107, 112, 117
Lutherans, 59, 87, 110, 121

Magdeburg Centuries, 64, 94, 169 n.56
Mailly, Jean de, 67
Maimbourg, Louis, 144–46
Mallery, Charles de, 214 n.31
Malvyn, Geoffroy de, 130
Marburg Colloquy, 114
Marcellinus (Pope), 83
Marguerite de Navarre, 76, 96, 106–7, 144
Marot, Clément, 144
Marianus Scotus, 67, 72
Marriage, 11, 102–4, 121–22
Martyrs, 130
Mass, 118–19. *See also* Eucharist
Masson, Papire, 145
Matthieu, Pierre, 141
Meaux, 11, 96, 106–8, 112
Melanchthon, Philip, 87, 194 n.12
Mentalités, 9, 59, 94, 97, 151
Meslon, André de, 28
Misogyny, 29, 69, 75–77, 107. *See also* Women
Mohammed, 87
Monluc, Blaise de, 43, 50–54
Montaigne, Michel de, 25, 32–35, 38, 43, 73, 91, 125, 130
Müntzer, Thomas, 100, 197 n.44, 211 n.60
Muslims, 59, 87, 96. *See also* Turk

Nantes, Edict of, 43, 46, 48, 58, 61–62, 97, 123, 129
Nantes, Revocation of Edict of, 12, 46, 144, 149
Navarre, Henry of, 28, 56. *See also* Henry IV
Nero, 80
Nicholas I (Pope), 74–75
Nicholas II (Pope), 83
Nicholas, Bishop of Taborites, 68
Nicodemites, 115, 117
Noaille, François & Gilles de, 194 n.12

Ochino, Bernardino, 143
Olivétan (Pierre Robert), 108, 111–12
Olivi, Peter, 83
Oporinus (Johann Herbster), 72

Original sin, 103–4

Palma-Cayet, Pierre-Victor, 109, 118, 205 n.54
Panvinio, Onofrio (Panvinius), 67, 70–71
Papal infallibility. *See* Infallibility
Papal primacy (authority) 10, 34, 39, 81–83
Pasquier, Etienne, 12, 33, 42–47, 68, 73–74, 126, 145
Paul, St., 79–80, 89
Paul II (Pope), 69
Pedobaptism, 99
Peletier, Jacques du Mans, 27
Peter, St., 39, 66, 81–82
Peucer, Caspar, 90
Philology, 124–26
Phocas (Emperor), 39, 80–81
Photius, 74–75
Pico della Mirandola, Giovanni, 90, 166 n.30
Piccolomini, Aeneas Sylvius (Pope Pius II), 68
Pigge, Albert (Pighius), 212 n.61
Pithou, Pierre, 71, 125
Plaintes, 56–58, 61–62
Platina (Bartolomeo de' Sacchi), 69, 73
Plato, 128, 133
Poissy, Colloquy of, 89, 97
Poitiers, 116–17
Poitiers, University of, 24
Poitou, 11, 117. *See also* Poitiers
Polemic, 9–10, 12, 35, 48–49, 66, 91, 93, 100, 118, 120, 123, 130, 132, 137, 139, 141, 144, 148, 150–52
Politiques, 10, 13, 33, 44, 49
Polonus (Martin of Troppau), 72
Pope Joan, 9–10, 13, 49, 66–78, 95, 125, 141, 143, 146–47, 213 n.14. See also *Anti-Papesse, L'*; *Erreur Populaire de la Papesse Jane*
Postel, Guillaume, 164 n.13, 194 n.12
Pragmatic Sanction, 45
Presles, College of, 21–22, 42
Printing and publishing, 71–72
Probatio sexus, 69, 73
Protestant Reformation. *See* Reformation
Psalmody, 194 n.12

Pyrrhonism, 34. *See also* Scepticism

Radicals. *See* Religious radicals
Raemond, Florimond: and absolutism, 128–29, 131–32; art and architecture, 29–31; archaeology, 30; authorship questioned, 141–43, 150; birth, 19; children, 29, 64, 142; on common people, 23, 96, 122; La Combe-Suquet, 19, 31; *conseiller* buys Montaigne's seat, 25; on cruelty, 52, 174 n.29; death, 64, 180 n.92; democracy and, 36; edition of Monluc's *Commentaires*, 50; edition of Sponde's *La Response au traicté, . . . des Marques de l'Église.*, 36; education, 20–24; favorite ecclesiastical writers, 212 n.61; fideism of, 95; *franc bourgeois* (of Bordeaux), 31; and heresy, 19–25, 61, 94, 96, 98, 127; as a historian, 10, 49–57, 63, 66, 71–72, 74, 78, 93–95, 99–100, 108–17, 123, 125–29, 132–39, 151–52; intolerance of, 123, 149; kidnapping of, 25–27; magistracy, 9, 11, 25–26, 48–49, 55–61, 122, 135; marriage(s), 28–29; and Montaigne, 32–35; motto, 25; poetry of, 26–27, 29; as polemicist, 9–12, 23, 25, 35, 48–50, 54, 57, 63–64, 75, 77, 81–93, 95, 99–100, 112, 114, 132, 136, 138–39, 150–52; on religious diversity, 13, 35, 59, 61, 94, 123, 129–30, 150; on religious tradition, 34–35; scepticism of, 34, 91, 95; theology and, 172 n.2, 127; translations of Tertullian, 173–74 n.11; vineyards, 31–32; and witchcraft, 164 n.15, 176 n.48; and women, 29, 77, 107; works contemplated, 176 n.48
Raemond, Florimond, Jr. (son), 29
Raemond, François (son), 29, 64, 142
Raemond, Jean-Charles (son), 64
Raemond, Robert (father), 19
Raemond, Robert (brother), 130
Ramus, Peter, 21, 42
Raymond, Marie de (Countess), 213 n.1

Reformation, Catholic. *See* Counter Reformation
Reformation, Protestant, 45, 62, 70, 75–77, 89, 93, 96, 98, 104–5, 107, 118–19, 127, 145
Reginaldus, 109–10
Reason (rationalism), 12, 34, 91–92, 149
Religious diversity, 61, 123, 129, 133, 150. *See also* Heresy (and heretics); Toleration (of religious difference)
Religious radicals, 99–105, 164 n.13, 211 n.60. *See also* Anabaptists
Religious ritual, 11, 26, 59–60, 89–90, 93–96, 99–102, 118–21. *See also* Baptism; Burials; Eucharist
Religious unity (uniformity), 12, 46, 49, 94, 131, 148
Renaudet, Augustin, 108
Reuchlin, Johannes, 90
Richeome, Louis, 40, 141–42
Rivet, André, 142, 145
Rouen, *Parlement* of, 58
Roussel, Gérard, 106–7, 144
R. T. (minister of Béarn), 50
Ruble, Alphonse de, 52–53

Sacramentarians, 100–101, 211 n.59. *See also* Anabaptists; Religious radicals; Spiritualism
Sadoleto, Jacopo, 111, 113–14
Sainctes, Claude de, 109
St. Bartholomew Day Massacre, 194 n.12
Sanders, Nicholas (Sanderus), 81, 212 n.61
Scaliger, Julius Caesar, 21
Scaliger, Joseph Justus, 124–25
Scepticism, 34, 91, 95. *See also* Pyrrhonism
Schedel, Hartman, 68
Schwenckfeld, Caspar, 101
Sevigné, Marie de Rabutin-Chantal, 146
Sex and sexuality, 103–4, 122, 132
Sforza, Lodovico, 88
Sigebert of Gembloux, 71
"666," 38, 90–91, 97, 133, 192 n.83
Scandinavia, 127
Simon Magus, 98

Sleidan, Johann (né Philippson), 95, 99, 110
Soulier, Pierre, 144
Sourdis, François (Cardinal), 32, 64
Spanheim, Ezekiel de, 215 n.36
Spanheim, Frederic, 146, 215 n.36
Spiritualism, 100–102, 104–5
Sponde, Jean de, 33, 35–38, 55
Strasbourg, 106
Suffridis Petri of Louvain, 72
Suleiman I, 88
Surius, Lawrence, 109

Taborites, 68
Tertullian, 55, 81, 125, 133, 147, 173–74 n.11
Thomas Illyricus (frère), 144 n.12
Trois Imposteurs, Les, 21
Toleration (of religious difference), 13, 35, 59, 130, 139
Totalitarianism, 13, 149–50. *See also* Absolutism
Toulouse, *Parlement* of, 58
Toulouse, University of, 23–24, 117
Transylvania, 127
Trent (Tridentine), 43, 46, 83
Turk, 79–80, 86–89, 171 n.73

Ultramontane, 43, 61

Urban IV (Pope), 67
Urban VIII (Pope), 73
Uzès, Robert d', 69

Valla, Lorenzo, 125, 186 n.11, 187 n.17
Varillas, Antoine, 142–43
Vaudois (heretics), 98, 108
Vermigli, Peter Martyr, 143
Vignier, Nicolas, 86, 92, 142, 190 n.51
Villars, Nicolas de, 129
Vindocin, Jerome, 20, 22
Vinet, Élie, 21
Virginity, 103, 121
Vitruvius, 133

Wars of religion, 50–52, 56, 94, 130–31, 139, 149
Westphal, Joachim, 110–11, 112–14
William of Occam, 98
Witchcraft, 158 n.58, 164 n.15, 176 n.48
Wolmar, 11, 111–15
Women, 29, 69, 76–77, 96, 107, 145, 185 n.63. *See also* Misogyny
Wycliffe, John, 80, 98, 101

Zephyrinus (Pope), 83
Zurich, 119
Zwingli and Zwinglianism, 86, 99, 100–102, 104, 112, 211 n.59